26942

264 BIL

WITHDRAWN

18 JUN 2022

THE COLLEGE OF RIPON
AND YORK ST. JOHN
RIPON CAMPUS

‾INGTON   R.‾

/

COLLEGE OF EDUCATION, RIPON

LIBRARY

38961.

D1351477

THE LITURGICAL MOVEMENT
AND METHODISM

THE
LITURGICAL MOVEMENT
AND
METHODISM

RAYMOND J. BILLINGTON

LONDON
EPWORTH PRESS

© Raymond J. Billington 1969
First published in 1969
by Epworth Press
SBN 7162 0054 6

PRINTED AND BOUND IN ENGLAND BY
HAZELL WATSON AND VINEY LTD
AYLESBURY, BUCKS

This book is dedicated with love to my longsuffering parents, who must sometimes have wondered whether it was all worth it.

ACKNOWLEDGEMENTS

THE author and publishers are grateful for permission to quote from the following: Faber and Faber, *Liturgy and Society* by A. G. Hebert. Faith Press, *This Day Belongs to God* by Roger Schutz and *The Taizé Daily Office*. The *Guardian*, 'In Which to Preach' by G. Cope. Lutterworth Press, *passim*. Macmillan and Co. Ltd., *Selections From Early Church Writings* ed. H. M. Gwatkin. Mowbray, *Liturgy Coming to Life* by J. A. T. Robinson. Nisbet, *Worship* by E. Underhill. Sheed and Ward Ltd, *Life and Liturgy* by Louis Bouyer and *Liturgy and Doctrine* by Charles Davis. S.P.C.K., *Eucharistic Faith and Practice* by Y. Brilioth. S.C.M. Press, *The Liturgical Movement and the Local Church* by A. R. Shands; *The Faith of My Parish* by T. Allen; *Liturgical Renewal* by J-D. Benoit; *On Being the Church in the World* by J. A. T. Robinson. *Studia Liturgica*. Oxford University Press, *An Outline of Christian Worship* by W. D. Maxwell; *Principles of Christian Worship* by R. Abba; *Social Implications of the Liturgical Renewal* by A. Lichtenberger; *The Liturgical Renewal of the Church* ed. M. H. Shepherd. University of Chicago Press, *The Liturgical Renaissance of the Roman Catholic Church* by E. Koenker.

CONTENTS

AUTHOR'S NOTE

FOR any minister in the modern age, an essential guide is contained in Paul's words, 'I have become all things to all men'. To some people this approach may well indicate a lack of integrity; but I fail to see how anyone can possibly communicate with more than a narrow range of people if he puts himself into a permanent strait-jacket.

I state this by way of apology to those readers who are more familiar with my 'non-church' than with my liturgical views. While I admit that there is a strong element of schizophrenia apparent in my thinking, the situation is logical enough to me (which may well be a symptom of the malady!). For most of my working life I am in communication with people to whom religious language is incomprehensible, so that to use it would constitute a barrier between us. With these people, my attempt is always to express the meaning, in human, practical terms, of the concepts and dogmas symbolized by the religious words.

However, in a situation and among people where such language and such concepts are not unfamiliar, there seems no reason to avoid them. For this reason I find it impossible to go along with those Church reformers who would transform the liturgy out of all recognition for the sake of modernization (usually described with the blessed word 'relevance'): this does not bring in 'outsiders' and often only deters—and sometimes embarrasses—life-long worshippers.

It is this last group whom I have had in mind while writing this book. The vast majority of my time is in fact now spent outside the immediate context of Church life, and even in the small space of three years (the time between writing and publication of the book) my own emphasis has inevitably swung more and more to that of 'non-religious' concepts and activity. Yet I hope that some in the Church, who have found what they need there, and do not desire to move further afield, will receive help from a world-wide movement which has certainly revitalized Church life in many parts of the world.

Whatever may lie in the future for me personally, my indebtedness to the Church will remain. It is therefore with a sense of gratitude that I offer this book to the Methodist people. Whatever I am, they have helped to make it.

This book was written as a thesis for the degree of M.A. in the faculty of theology at Birmingham University. I wish to express my thanks to the Professor of Theology, Dr J. G. Davies, for his help and suggestions in planning the work.

I should like also to thank my friend George Lockett for preparing the indices. Long listed among the saints, he has thus listed himself among the martyrs.

Woolwich, April 1968   R.J.B.

INTRODUCTION

'NO MAN is an island'—and the Christian denominations do not constitute an archipelago. There may well have been a time when each branch of the Church saw itself as self-sufficient; but that time is no longer with us. We live in an age when contact with other peoples, nations, races is becoming increasingly a part of everyday life. Generally speaking, the Church has realized this. Members of a particular denomination are aware of, and ready to learn from, what is taking place in other denominations. In consequence, the distinctions between them are becoming less clear-cut; and the realization is taking firmer hold on Christians that they cannot experience the plenitude of God's gifts in isolation from one another.

Unfortunately, Methodists are not the best of listeners or keenest of learners. More than in any other of the major denominations in Britain, they continue to maintain the wishful thought that God has been especially generous with them when sharing out His gifts. The idea survives, even if it is not always explicitly stated, that other denominations need what they possess more than they need other denominations.

One direct result of this attitude is the general indifference to, if not ignorance of, such movements in the world Church as the Liturgical Movement. There has been less study of this, less consideration of what it may imply for the worshipping and witnessing life of Methodism than in any other major denomination (under which epithet I include the Roman Catholics, Anglicans, and the great Free Churches: the Presbyterians, Baptists, Congregationalists, and Methodists. Salvationists and others may object to this limiting, but for the purposes of this study this group will suffice). For all her vaunted freedom, Methodism has in fact become firmly entrenched in her groove. Some of her ministers and laymen are aware of what is happening in the world Church; but most of them (like Raymond George) are in specialized work outside the circuit norm. It is rare to find a circuit minister who is both alive to what is happening in other denominations and courageous enough to experiment in his own.

The ironical factor in all this is that Methodism can derive no real satisfaction from the present situation. She may still look complacent, but her smile is becoming increasingly forced; facts and figures cannot be discounted. The facts are that in almost every sphere where any assessment can be made, Methodism is on the wane. Church membership figures show a continuous decline—and the decline is becoming steeper year by year. In the connexional year 1964–5 the decrease was over eight thousand, representing over one per cent of the total; and this decline was not limited to rural or 'down-town' areas but was fairly evenly distributed over all parts of the country, including the hitherto sacrosanct suburbia. Even more significant was the number of candidates for the ministry: sixty-nine—about half the number normally anticipated. This incredibly low figure may be partly attributable to the sense of uncertainty arising from the Anglican-Methodist conversations; but it is becoming increasingly clear that for all the work of the Methodist Youth Department, young men, even the most dedicated of them, are showing greater reluctance to offer themselves for full-time service in their Church. Many state quite openly that they feel they can be of greater service in 'secular' employment. The Christian ministry no longer presents itself to their minds as the acme of devotion to their Master.

The conviction behind this study is that the time is long overdue for Methodism to rid herself of her insularity and take a close look at what God is doing in and through His people in other branches of His Church. It requires a sense of reality to be aware of the present situation, and the humility to accept that others may have much to teach them. In some ways this may already be too late. In his book *A Future for the Free Churches?*, Christopher Driver, a Congregationalist layman, asks whether these Churches can survive in their present form.[1] In an ably-expounded final chapter he concludes that they cannot; and one finds it difficult to disagree with him.

1. S.C.M. 1962.

Already there are indications that large numbers of Free Churchmen realize this, and are taking joint action accordingly. The Presbyterian-Congregationalist conversations are one sign of this; the Anglican-Methodist Report another.

Nevertheless, even if these conversations do eventually result in action, the indications are that it will be almost a generation before they drastically change local Church life. Long before that it seems inevitable that the great indifference of the mass of the people will have forced other changes, however reluctantly accepted, on the Churches. If this is so, one of the basic requirements will be for these Churches to adapt themselves to the new situation; and this process is likely to involve so complete and thorough a change that many contemporary writers feel it is not pretentious to describe it as a 'new Reformation'.[2] Increasingly, as a result, there is discussion of what the Church is and what it was created to do; and of how it can best pattern itself to achieve this in our time.

In this process, each branch will need all the guidance it can get. It is difficult to avoid the conclusion that the insights afforded to those Churches most affected by the Liturgical Movement are particularly certain guides for all Christians, and not least for Methodists. In this study, therefore, we shall try to discover what these insights are. We shall begin by looking briefly at the main trends in the Church's worship through the centuries. This will not be in any way definitive, but will simply set the scene. Then we shall consider the Liturgical Movement: its history, and the names and experiments associated with it; and, in greater detail, the issues it has brought into relief: the meaning of the Church as the Body of Christ, the function of worship as an expression of this, the Eucharist as the supreme expression of corporate worship, and the essential link between worship and witness. We shall look briefly at how the building can serve the liturgy, and the symbols of worship genuinely help a congregation; and we shall see how the movement is bringing people back to the basic doctrines of the faith.

Then we shall turn to Methodism, and consider first her

2. Cf. *The New Reformation?* by J. A. T. Robinson, S.C.M., 1965.

own heritage. This will involve a fairly close study of Wesley's own liturgical practice at different points in his life; there will follow a quick summary of developments and trends in Methodism down to the present day. Then, in what will be the major part of the study, we shall seek to apply the insights of the Liturgical Movement to the Methodism of today. In this section we shall deal in some detail with the various objections which Methodists would raise. We shall try to avoid shirking any of these, or hesitating to follow to the conclusions to which the different principles seem to be pointing. In many cases it will be found that the Movement is reiterating points and emphases that Wesley himself brought out two hundred years ago. Finally, we shall look at the future in an attempt to foresee the likely pattern of the 'Coming Great Church'.

Clearly, this study will be of most interest to Methodists. But in so far as the future of Methodism is inextricably linked with that of the other denominations, not excluding the Roman Catholics, the conclusions reached may well be of some interest to other denominations too. If the thesis presented here is correct, that Methodists must listen to what people of other traditions have to say, there may be some truth in the converse.

CHAPTER ONE

TRENDS IN WORSHIP THROUGH THE CENTURIES

A. NEW TESTAMENT WORSHIP

WHERE early Church worship is concerned it is foolish to be dogmatic. We are given hints here and there in the New Testament, suggesting various customs and practices. From these emerges a general picture; but the situation was clearly still fluid, so that to make absolute statements rather than tentative suggestions is to claim greater authority than is possible.

From references in the New Testament, four practices emerge:

(i) *The Agape, or Love Feast.* The main passage in which this is discussed is 1 Corinthians 11:17–34, where Paul condemns his readers for the abuses they have allowed to creep into their religious meals together. (The fact that Paul here writes his classic description of the institution of the Eucharist by Jesus may indicate that the two were held in close relation in the early Church, but there is no evidence that this was so.) Pliny's letter to Trajan in A.D. 112 first describes a form of Christian worship, which may or may not have been the Eucharist, then adds: 'After this was done, their custom was to depart, and meet together again to take food, but ordinary and hapless food . . .',[1] which suggests that the Eucharist and Agape, if they were ever held consecutively, were soon separated. From the time of St. Cyprian, the Agape seems to have become 'more and more a charity supper';[2] by the end of the patristic age it had fallen into disuse, to be revived only occasionally and spasmodically at times of evangelical fervour (the Wesleyan revival included it).

1. Cf. Ignatius, Letter to the Smyrnaeans (8) Tertullian, Apology (39).
2. *Oxford Dictionary of the Christian Church*, Oxford, p. 23.

(ii) *Glossolalia, or Speaking with Tongues.* This appears to have been a common phenomenon in New Testament times. Acts 2:4 states that 'they were all filled with the Holy Spirit and began to speak in other tongues, as the Spirit gave them utterance.' In 1 Corinthians 14 Paul outlines the principle to bear in mind when meeting this phenomenon: its effect on the speaker and its value for the listeners. He is clearly suspicious of it, but recognizes that it is one form of outlet for people in a highly emotional spiritual state. It seems to have died away by the end of the first century, though it has constantly reappeared during times of religious revival.

These two types of worship have been alluded to because they occurred; but it is only the next two which are relevant to this study.

(iii) *Worship in Synagogues and Temples.* The first disciples were Jews, who had therefore been trained to worship and pray regularly in their Synagogue. Synagogue worship centred on the reading and expounding of the Scriptures (of which the Law was naturally deemed the most important), together with hymns—mostly psalms—and prayers, most of which were recited by all the congregation and had assumed a fixed form by the time of Christ. This was not an absolute rule, however; individual members were encouraged to enrich the worship with their own prayers, and T. W. Manson suggests: 'Perhaps the Lord's Prayer may be regarded in this light as a prayer made by Jesus for the use of the community of His followers.'[3]

The Temple did not play so big a part in the lives of the Jews, except for those who lived in the capital, Jerusalem, where it was situated. To quote Manson again: 'The centralization of the Sacrificial ritual in Jerusalem was one of the first big steps in teaching Israel to do without it.'[4] However, while the disciples remained in Jerusalem they continued to make full use of the opportunities presented by the Temple. Acts 3:1 records how 'Peter and John were going up to the temple at the hour of prayer, the ninth hour'[5]—that is, at

3. *Christian Worship*, ed. N. Micklem, Oxford, 1936, p. 39.
4. Op. cit., p. 34, 'The Jewish Background'.
5. The quotation, like all other Biblical quotations throughout, is from the R.S.V.

3 p.m., in connexion with the afternoon sacrifice. Acts 5:42 describes how the disciples taught and preached in the Temple, and 10, verses 3, 9 and 30 show how they later tried to maintain the Temple 'hours' for prayer.[6]

Despite this, it was the worship of the Synagogue with which the early Christians were most familiar, and one need not feel surprised that it strongly influenced the earliest types of Christian worship (despite the fact that, strangely enough, in those passages in the early chapters of Acts where the Synagogue is mentioned it is in connexion with opposition to Christianity—6:9; 9:2). Like the Synagogue worship, that of the Christians centred on the Word; the difference was that now prophecy, not the Law, had pre-eminence. To the Scriptures of the 'Old Testament' were gradually added the various 'New Testament' books, together, of course, with others which were eventually to be rejected from the Canon. We have an example in Colossians 4:16 of how these new books became known: 'And when this letter has been read among you, have it read also at the church of the Laodiceans'.[7] The psalms were still sung, but to these were added Christian hymns: '. . . be filled with the Spirit, addressing one another in psalms and hymns and spiritual songs, singing and making melody to the Lord with all your heart'.[8] These hymns probably included those provided in the Prologue to St. Luke's Gospel; and it is being increasingly recognized that the Book of Revelation probably contains many parts of early Christian liturgies, whether hymns or prayers. In chapters 4 and 5, for instance, there appear what must have been four hymns of praise, three of them beginning with, 'Worthy art thou . . .'.[9] Here we have in most primitive form an early expression of one aspect of genuine Christian worship—the *acknowledgement* (not assessment) of the worth-ship of God. It would be interesting to discover more about the origin of this phrase. 1 Timothy 3:16 is also probably at least part of an early hymn: 'He was manifested in the flesh, vindicated in the

6. Cf. Acts 2:46; 5: 20ff; and, with reference to Paul, 22:17.
7. Cf. 1 Timothy 4: 13; 1 Thessalonians 5: 27.
8. Ephesians 5:19; cf. Colossians 3:16; 1 Corinthians 14:2.
9. Revelation 4:8b, 11; 5:9, 13.

3

Spirit, seen by angels, preached among the nations, believed on in the world, taken up in glory.'

The prayers of the Synagogue were altered to make them suitable to be addressed to Christ, and the God He made known. Acts 2:42 and 1 Timothy 2:1f. mention prayers in general; it is probable that extracts from early prayers are to be found at different points of the New Testament. Furthermore, because the Christians emerged from a tradition (Synagogue worship) where formal prayers and responses were normal and usual, and because there was a natural desire (suggested, for instance, by Paul's disapproval of some of the individualistic practices in Corinth) for common practices in worship, it is probable that the prayers referred to in Acts 2:42 were of a formal and liturgical character. The Lord's Prayer was probably so used in earliest times. It is also probable that Aramaic words such as 'Abba' (Romans 8:15, Galatians 4:6), 'Amen' (1 Corinthians 14:16) and 'Maranatha' (1 Corinthians 16:22) were used. J. M. Ross, a Presbyterian writing in *Faith and Unity*,[10] has compiled from the New Testament a series of versicles and responses which may well have been the sort of prayers which were in general use in the early Church:

V. Behold, I come quickly.
R. Amen: come, Lord Jesus (Revelation 22:20).
V. The Lord is risen.
R. The Lord is risen indeed, and hath appeared unto Simon (Luke 24:34).
V. If any man love not the Lord, let him be anathema.
R. Maranatha (1 Corinthians 16:22).

The services also included a sermon or exposition of the Scriptures[11] of which sections of the Gospels were probably parts. The fact that Timothy 'made the good confession in the presence of many witnesses'[12] suggests the existence of an early confession of faith which had to be spoken by converts before baptism, and also by the congregation in their worship generally. 1 Corinthians 15:1–4 may well be part, or the whole

10. *Faith and Unity*, May 1963, p. 49.
11. Cf. 1 Corinthians 14:26; Acts 20:17.   12. 1 Timothy 6:12.

of a primitive creed. In addition to these elements of worship, alms were collected for the poor.[13]

(iv) *The Eucharist.* To the Synagogue-style worship based on the Word the early Christians added a form of worship which, more than anything else, made them aware of Christ's continuing presence with them: the worship of the Upper Room. On this theme in particular it is foolhardy to be dogmatic, at any rate concerning New Testament practice. It is too easy to take evidence from later customs and transfer the ideas gleaned back into primitive practice. It is easy to assume, for instance, that from the start this service was based on the Last Supper that Jesus had with His disciples in the Upper Room, and that 1 Corinthians 11:23–26 represents the most primitive tradition. But Oscar Cullman argues most forcefully that there was an earlier tradition whereby the Eucharist was linked with the appearances of the *Risen* Christ, and the memory which the disciples had of meals then shared with Him.[14] He suggests (p. 9) that the earliest definition of the Eucharist in Acts 2:42 as 'breaking of bread' makes no mention of the wine in the Pauline passage: it is a description of a simple meal. He refers to the Acts of Thomas and the Acts of Peter to show that in some areas, down to the third century, not wine but water was taken with the bread. He refers to the sign of the fish as, among other things, a eucharistic symbol for some of the early Christians, and links it with John 21 where we are told that Jesus ate bread and fish with His disciples. As a crucial additional argument he quotes from Peter's sermon in Acts 10:40f: 'God raised him on the third day and made him manifest; not to all the people but to us who were chosen by God as witnesses, who ate and drank with him after he rose from the dead.' Cullmann concludes that 'it was considered to be a characteristic feature of the appearances that they took place during a meal.'[15] He also notes the joy which accompanies the breaking of bread according to Acts 2:46. He suggests that the word 'hagal-

13. 2 Corinthians 9:10–13; cf. 1 Corinthians 16:1; Romans 15:26.
14. 'The Meaning of the Lord's Supper in Primitive Christianity'; in *Essays on the Lord's Supper*, ed. J. J. Davies and Raymond George, Lutterworth, 1958.
15. Op. cit., p. 11.

liasis' seems 'incompatible with a recalling of the Last Supper and with the words that Jesus uttered on that occasion.' He concludes:

'It therefore appears likely that the idea of the Resurrection of Christ was associated, in the minds of the disciples, with the recollection of one or more meals taken with their Master during the period from Easter to Pentecost. And when later these same disciples met to eat together, the recollection of the other meals during which the Risen One appeared to them for the first time must naturally have been very vivid to them. We can now understand why the Christian community in the Apostolic Age celebrated its meals "with joy". *The certainty of the Resurrection* was the essential religious motive of the primitive Lord's Supper. . . . When they assembled "to break bread", they knew that the Risen One would reveal His presence in a manner less visible but no less real than previously.'[16]

Cullmann goes on to suggest that Paul's contribution was not to deny this experience but to link it with the Last Supper in the Upper Room. This was partly because there is an essential link, in God's process of redemption, between the death and Resurrection of Christ. But even more important than this were the words Jesus uttered on that occasion: 'This is my body; this is my blood of the covenant'—in the Marcan account. Cullmann agrees with Lietzmann[17] that these words do not derive from later liturgical practice, and that there is no reason to doubt their authenticity on the lips of Jesus. He states:

'Jesus uttered them in order to affirm that, *by His death*, a new covenant was concluded between God and the Messianic community. This Messianic community, of which the Old Testament speaks, is the community of Christ's disciples. The covenant between God and this new community would not be established except through the death of Jesus. That is what Jesus Himself had foreseen, and it is the meaning which He gave to His own death . . . And it is this idea that is to be found at the basis of the parabolic saying about the bread and the wine.'[18]

16. Op. cit., p. 9.
17. Op. cit., p. 18. Lietzmann's views are to be found in *Messe und Herrenmahl. Eine Studie zur Geschichte der Liturgie*, 1926.
18. Op. cit., pp. 18f.

The fact that later the Pauline concept came so much to the fore that the more primitive concept fell into the background is no fault of the Apostle's. Cullmann argues that a unification of the two concepts is both possible and desirable; and we shall see that in some manifestations of the Liturgical Movement this is happening.

It is worth noting how close is the link between Paul's narrative and what took place in the Upper Room (which is one reason why the title 'The worship of the Upper Room' is apt). Gregory Dix, in *The Shape of the Liturgy*, followed by a host of others[19] has noted that the four actions of our Lord at the Last Supper assumed great significance: He took (bread and wine); He blessed (or gave thanks); He brake; He gave. So the worshippers took the offerings of bread and wine, to be received by the presiding elder, and these offerings symbolized the redemption and sanctification of the material through the Incarnation of the Eternal; the prayer of blessing or thanksgiving became the central part of the Eucharist (hence the name), the thanksgiving being for the whole process of God's redemption as expressed in the life, death, and Resurrection of the Lord Jesus, with the consequent sanctification of the worshippers' time, talents, and possessions. The bread was broken, and the wine poured out as a symbol both of the death of Christ for His followers and of their lives broken for Him; and all shared in the gift handed to them, the one loaf and the common cup symbolizing their unity in His Body.

Another important point of disagreement about the Last Supper relates to the nature of the meal Jesus shared with his disciples in the Upper Room. Was this the Passover or a Kiddush? This latter consisted of a religious discussion, held weekly on the eve of the sabbath and before the great religious festivals, attended by devout male Jews—often a Rabbi and his disciples. After the discussion came a simple meal of bread and wine mixed with water, when a cup was passed from one to the other and prayer offered. A strong advocate for this as the meal Jesus shared with the disciples is William Maxwell.[20]

19. Including *Liturgy Coming to Life* by J. A. T. Robinson, Mowbray, 1960. Seee specially pp. 67–75.
20. W. D. Maxwell, *An Outline of Christian Worship*, O.U.P., 1936, pp. 5–7.

He argues that it could not have been the Passover, because Jesus' trial and Crucifixion would then have been, according to Jewish law, illegal. Moreover, the whole tone of the meal reflected the Kiddush. This was always observed by a group of male friends, whereas the Passover was a family affair. There is no mention in the Last Supper narrative of various elements essential for a Passover: a paschal lamb; unleavened bread (ordinary bread was used at a Kiddush); individual cups (only one in the Kiddush and at the Last Supper); the reading of the story of the exodus from Egypt. Furthermore, the fact that the Eucharist came to be celebrated weekly like the Kiddush rather than annually like the Passover suggests to Maxwell that the disciples understood that their regular weekly meetings with their Master were to continue as before.

This last point can be quickly countered with the thought that if, as Cullmann suggests, the most primitive motive for the Eucharist was not the Last Supper but the Resurrection of Jesus, it would be quite natural to meet weekly on Sunday, the day of Resurrection.

The other arguments have been countered in great detail by Jeremias.[21] It is difficult to summarize his arguments briefly but some attempt must be made. He suggests that the word used for bread in Mark 14:22 ('artos') can be taken to mean unleavened as well as leavened bread (as it is in 2:26). The lack of references to the Paschal lamb and other details of the Passover he attributes to the Evangelists' desire to keep the narrative to a minimum and exclude all superfluous detail. He denies that the common cup was not used at the Passover, quoting *objections* to this practice as late as the second century A.D. Concerning the (alleged) illegality of the events surrounding the trial and crucifixion of Jesus, he takes each episode in turn. For eight of these—Gethsemane, the bearing of arms by the Temple guard, the tearing of the robe, the participation of Jews in the Roman court, Simon of Cyrene arriving on the 15th Nisan, the execution, taking down the body, and the preparation of spices, he finds justification in the Torah: (the only conjectural note concerns Simon of Cyrene, who may not even have been a Jew). For the buying

21. J. Jeremias, *The Eucharistic Words of Jesus*, S.C.M., Chapter One.

of a shroud he quotes the argument that the rule about the necessities of life could have allowed it (with Deuteronomy 21:23 as an added inducement). The meeting of the Sanhedrin is the most difficult point, but Jeremias suggests that with such passages as Deuteronomy 17:8, 12f; or 13:7,13 in mind— passages which emphasize the need to impress a law-breaker with the enormity of his deed, and more particularly deter the greatest possible number from repeating it—the trial and punishment would be as public as possible; it might well have been argued that a trial during the most important festival of the year would create the strongest possible deterrent to any likely followers of Jesus.

The main objection to supposing that the Last Supper was a Passover is of course the divergence between John and the Synoptics. But Jeremias suggests that John may have changed the story to give heightened dramatic effect to the account of the Crucifixion; that 13:1 is no more than a general statement that Jesus knew *beforehand* of his impending death; and that various details in the Johannine account—such as the reason adduced for Judas's exit in 13:27: that he was going to buy provisions for the feast, implying that he had little time left before the law would prevent his doing this—indicate that John is not denying the Synoptic view.

In support of this viewpoint, Jeremias argues that the time of the meal—night—is in full accord with a Passover but not a Kiddush; that ten to twelve people was the usual number for a Passover meal (a lamb would serve that number); that the references in Mark 14:22 and Matthew 26:26 to breaking bread during the meal, rather than at the start as usual, fits the Passover, as also does the use of wine, particularly red wine. That Judas was delegated to give to the poor (John 13:29f) reflects a regular aspect of the Passover; the hymn sung (Mark 14:26; Matthew 26:30) was probably the second half of the Paschal Hallel at the end of the meal. The fact that the disciples went with Jesus to the Mount of Olives rather than to Bethany fits the rules of the Passover that nobody should leave Jerusalem during the feast. (To accommodate the great numbers who arrived, the city was extended to include Bethphage but not Bethany.) Finally, Jesus' words interpreting the bread and wine were in full harmony with the Paschal ritual, part of which was to interpret the elements of the meal. To clarify this section, and put the distribution of bread and wine at the Last Supper in its context, it may be valuable to outline the Passover ritual.[22]

A. PRELIMINARY COURSE

Word of blessing by paterfamilias over first cup.
Preliminary dish—green and bitter herbs, sauce of fruit purée.
Meal proper served but not eaten; second cup mixed, put in place, not drunk.

B. PASCHAL LITURGY

Paschal Haggadha read by paterfamilias in Aramaic.
First part of Paschal Hallel in Hebrew.
Second cup drunk.

C. MAIN MEAL

Grace by paterfamilias over unleavened bread.
Meal: lamb, unleavened bread, bitter herbs with fruit purée and wine.
Prayer over third cup.

D. CLOSE

Second part of Hallel.
Praise over fourth cup.

If we are to attempt to fit the words of Jesus into this ritual, it would seem that his words over the bread must be identified with the grace at the start of the main meal, and over the wine with the grace over the fourth cup at the end of the meal; in other words, statements which have been telescoped by the Evangelists originally took place separately, before and after the main meal.

Jeremias's arguments clearly carry the greater weight, which means that the Marcan account is right and the Johannine wrong. It is worth bearing in mind, however, that the main significance of the Last Supper lay in the fact that the death of the host was imminent, whether it was a Passover meal or not, though if it was the symbolism is heightened. As Manson says: 'The deepest meaning of the supper itself is independent of its connexion with the Passover, and must be

22. Outlined by Jeremias, op. cit.

sought in the purpose and method of the whole ministry of Jesus.'[23]

There are other problems about the Eucharist which need not be discussed at length here. Massey H. Shepherd poses one in an article in 'Studia Liturgica':

'Can one distinguish here the Eucharistic sacrament from the *Agape* meal, as so many liturgiologists try to do? Is it possible to say that one part of the meal was more sacred or more common than another? And—to the literally minded—the evangelist poses a mocking problem: How did so many converts meet together in such small quarters for a common meal? On the other hand, if they were scattered in numerous house-church groups, how did they maintain that unity of being "together" and of having "all things common"?'[24]

The fact that this can be written by an expert in the field confirms one's wariness in making absolutist statements. Fortunately, the thesis under consideration does not stand or fall according to the point of view adopted on these issues. We shall later consider the theology of the Eucharist, particularly as expounded under the influence of the Liturgical Movement. Meanwhile, the importance of the two main types of worship found in the New Testament which survived, in however modified a form, through the centuries, is summarized by William Maxwell:

'Thus Christian worship, as a distinctive indigenous thing, arose from the fusion, in the crucible of Christian experience, of the Synagogue and Upper Room. Thus fused, each completing and quickening the other, they became the norm of Christian worship. Christian worship found other forms of expression, but these belong to the circumference, not to the centre. The typical worship of the Church is to be found to this day in the union of the worship of the Synagogue and the sacramental experience of the Upper Room; and the union dates from New Testament times.'[25]

Perhaps Maxwell overstates the case for a fusion in New Testament times, but there is no doubt that these two forms of worship were seen as pre-eminent by the early Christians. We shall now look more briefly at the post-apostolic develop-

23. Manson, op. cit., p. 49.
24. *Studia Liturgica*, Vol. 1, No. 2, June, 1962, pp. 85f.
25. Maxwell, op. cit., p. 5.

ments, with the particular object of seeing to how great an extent these two have been kept in harmony, or totally integrated.

B. LATER DEVELOPMENTS

Our main concern in this brief résumé is to examine the extent to which the Church through the centuries has been able to maintain a balance between the two main primitive types of worship: that centred on the Word and that on the Sacrament—preaching and Eucharist.

There is little tangible evidence in the sub-Apostolic age, found in the letter of Clement (A.D. 96), Pliny's Letter to Trajan (112) and the Didache (130–40). It had been generally assumed that ch. xxxiv of Clement's letter made reference to the Sanctus as having a place in worship, but this has now been rendered questionable by Van Unnik.[26] Pliny's reference is extremely vague: '. . . it was their habit on a fixed day to assemble before daylight and sing by turns a hymn to Christ as a god; and that they bound themselves with an oath . . .'. The word used for 'oath' is 'sacramentum', which may or may not be significant. Pliny then proceeds to describe the meal we quoted when mentioning the Agape, which may have been an early method of holding communion, though on the surface it seems not. The Didache does not belong to the main stream of development, which is in itself an interesting insight into the emerging situation: though there were tendencies, in the main centres, to reach uniformity in worship, there was as yet no universal procedure. About this we can feel only grateful, for it means that the Church has as part of its liturgical heritage the famous and beautiful prayer from the Didache: 'As this broken bread was scattered upon the mountains and being gathered together became one, so may Thy Church be gathered together from the ends of the earth into Thy kingdom . . .'

From these extracts we may reach two tentative conclusions: (1) The tendency to make fixed forms of prayer which seems to have occurred from New Testament times was continued and probably intensified, although these forms varied from

26. W. C. Van Unnick, '1 Clement 34 and the "Sanctus" ', *Vigiliae Christianae* V, 1951, pp. 204–248.

place to place. (2) There continued a weekly celebration of the Eucharist.

By the time of Justin Martyr, midway through the second century, it is clear that the worship of the Synagogue and the Upper Room were so blended as to become two complementary parts of one act of worship. Justin writes:

'On the day called the Feast of the Sun, all who live in towns or in the country assemble in one place, and the memoirs of the Apostles or the writings of the Prophets are read as time permits. Then, when the reader has ended, the President instructs and encourages the people to practise the truths contained in the scripture lections. Thereafter, we all stand up and offer prayers together; and, as I mentioned before, when we have concluded this prayer, bread and wine and water are brought. Then the President likewise offers up prayers and thanksgiving according to his ability, and the people cry aloud saying Amen. Each one then receives a portion and share of the elements over which thanks have been given; and which are also carried and ministered by the deacons to those absent.'[27]

Thus prayer, reading, and instruction were united with, and reached their climax in, the distribution of bread and wine; both the Biblical and sacramental elements of worship were apparently reckoned incomplete alone. Irenaeus and Tertullian, later in the century, make briefer references to the Eucharist. It is clear that by then this service was the major obligation for all Christians. There were only three excuses which could be offered for missing the weekly celebration: when under discipline or, temporarily or permanently, excommunicated; when sick—and if possible the sacrament would be taken to these; and when in prison for the faith—and whenever possible, often at great risk, the sacrament was taken to Christians in this state.

The oldest complete liturgy which is extant is contained in the *Apostolic Tradition* of Hippolytus (225). Beginning with the Sursum Corda, it continues with this 'giving of thanks':

'We give thee thanks, O God, through thy beloved son Jesus Christ, whom thou didst send to us in the last times to be a saviour and redeemer and the messenger of thy will; who is thy inseparable

27. Justin, Apol. lxv–lxvii; cf. Tertullian, de Corona 3; Irenaeus, Adv. haer. IV xxviii 4–6.

13

Word, through whom thou madest all things, and in whom thou wast well pleased. Thou didst send him from Heaven into the Virgin's womb; he was conceived and was incarnate, and was shown to be thy Son, born of the Holy Spirit and the Virgin; who, fulfilling thy will and preparing for thee a holy people, stretched out his hands in suffering, that he might free from suffering them that believed on thee.

'Who when he was being betrayed to his voluntary suffering, that he might destroy death, break the chains of the devil, tread Hell underfoot, bring forth the righteous (therefrom) and set a bound (to it), and that he might manifest his Resurrection, took bread . . . etc.'

After the Words of Institution, the Tradition concludes with the prayer which includes the Epiclesis:

'Wherefore we, being mindful of his death and resurrection, do offer unto thee this bread and this cup, giving thanks unto thee for that thou hast deemed us worthy to stand before thee and minister as thy priest. And we beseech thee that thou wouldst send thy Holy Spirit upon the oblation of thy holy Church; and that thou wouldst grant it to all the saints who partake, making them one, for fulfilment of the Holy Spirit and for the confirmation of their faith in truth; that we may praise and glorify thee through thy Son Jesus Christ, through whom be glory and honour to thee, to the Father and to the Son with the Holy Spirit in thy Holy Church, both now and for ever. Amen.'

Commenting on this liturgy, Massey Shepherd writes:

'. . . As also in the later liturgies, (it) clearly exhibits a direct descent from the Jewish Benedictions recited at meals. . . . Not only the form, but the basic content of the prayer are simply Christian translations of the three fundamental themes of these Jewish table blessings: the creation and provident activity of God, the redemption of his people and formation of the covenant-community, and the fulfilment of his promise for the final establishment of his kingdom. The theme of creation and providence was maintained in the Christian formularies as a direct affirmation of the beauty, goodness, and beneficent order of the world that God had made, in conscious opposition to the Gnostic heresy. The redemption theme obviously celebrated the work of Christ instead of the Jewish re-calling of the deliverance from Egypt. And the specific recounting of the institution at the Last Supper provided the Christian state-ment of the inauguration of the new covenant. The petition for the descent of the Holy Spirit marked the peculiarly Christian viewpoint regarding the "last times", since the gift and presence of the Spirit was the manifest sign of the dawn of the eschatological event, the earnest of the promised Age to Come.'[28]

Thus we have confirmation that the practice of the early Church was maintained and expanded during subsequent centuries.

It appears, therefore, that for a number of centuries the two elements of Christian worship, the Word and the Sacrament, were viewed as complementary and so expressed in the liturgy. This was probably true until the fourth century, at any rate until the conversion of Constantine. There followed a thousand years in which this harmony was, generally speaking, lost. In the East this was caused largely by the advent of the notion of mystery as the supreme aspect of the liturgy, leading to the action of the Eucharist's being hidden by a screen from the worshippers (though at least an emphasis on weekly communicating was retained). In the West it was harmed by an increasing emphasis on the magic of the rite, the idea of a propitiatory sacrifice, and the doctrine of transubstantiation (though it is impossible to be certain to what extent this was accepted before the writings of Paschasius Radbertus in the ninth century).

It is not our purpose to study this development in detail; our concern is with the fact that, through the Dark and Middle Ages, the Word, whether in the Scriptures or in expositions by preachers, became subservient to the Sacrament. It must be admitted that the two are not natural partners: there is an inherent tension between them, so that people tend to be instinctively inclined towards one or the other. Few leaders of the Church have managed to achieve the balance which seems to be expressed in Justin's description (we shall see that Wesley was a rare exception); and it will be part of our thesis that one of the great contributions of the Liturgical Movement to the ongoing life of the Church is to press for a recovery of this harmony.

It is interesting to ask what the reasons were for the declining emphasis on preaching, but again there can be no definitive answer. Both Eastern and Western Churches eventually

28. Massey Shepherd, op. cit., p. 91.

arrived at the viewpoint that the liturgy was a means of instruction *per se*. This is fine, provided the liturgy is itself completely intelligible throughout. But even then, without a definite part of the service in which the preacher can relate the great truths of the Gospel and doctrines expressed in the liturgy to the immediate situation, there is the danger that the congregation will divorce their worship from their life in the world.

One may speculate that after Constantine's conversion life became so much easier for Christians that some of the 'hard' sayings of the Gospel lost their relevance or became unpalatable. Certainly a prominent theme in early sermons—fortitude amidst persecution—no longer applied to their situation. Perhaps, too, the fact that many of the Church's leaders were engaged in profound metaphysical discussions led the less intellectually equipped clergy to feel that these were matters for experts, and best left alone. The influence of the Mystery Religions must not be overlooked: there must have been strong inducements to syncretize.

C. THE REFORMATION AND AFTER

Luther

It is not as a liturgiologist that Luther is chiefly remembered; nevertheless, he inaugurated various interesting and instructive experiments, even if the liturgical works he himself produced were ultra-conservative.

The chief criticism of the Mass which he makes (and was making as early as 1516 in his sermons on the Ten Commandments) is that the Mass was primarily a spectacle to be observed by the congregation, not a service in which they were to take part. The service should be fundamentally an expression of the fellowship of the congregation with their Lord. So he fiercely opposed the approach of the Church as he knew it. The congregation's duty was to attend, whether they understood what took place or not; their very attendance was an act of merit. They would then be privileged to see the sacrifice of Christ, taking place objectively in the Mass, and epitomized in the Canon. The magical quality which was thereby read into the Mass seemed to Luther to be the basis for so much of the abuse which had crept in, and quite alien to the spirit and teaching of the New Testament. In *The Babylonish Captivity of the Church*, he wrote:

'The third captivity of this sacrament is that most sacrilegious abuse by which it has come about that at this day there is nothing in the Church more generally received or more widely held than that the Mass is a good work and a sacrifice. This abuse has brought an endless flood of other abuses, until faith in the sacrament has been utterly extinguished and a divine sacrament has been turned into an article of trade, the subject of bargaining and business deals.'

Luther's 'Formula Missae' of 1523 was, as we have said, conservative in its reforms. It was not the first of its kind. Work had already been done by Krumbach, Veler, Zell, Strauss, Diepolt, and Rhegius. In 1522 Kantz had produced his 'Evangelische Messe'; while contemporaneously with Luther Müntzer was producing his own (less radical) Mass (1523–6), the Strasbourg Orders of 1524–6 were produced, along with the Nuremberg Masses of 1524–6, the Zürich Communion Service of 1525, the Basel Communion Service 1525–6, and others. Luther's aim was to make the Mass more suited for congregations without throwing everything overboard and starting afresh, as in Switzerland. His basic principle was that only those parts of the Mass should go which were directly contrary to New Testament teaching. In effect, this meant retaining almost everything in the Roman Mass, with the exception of the Canon of the Mass, because, as we have seen, this intensified the idea of the Mass as a spectacle. Over-elaborate music and medieval ceremony also were excluded. The Latin language was retained throughout, with the exception of the sermon, the lessons, and the (optional) hymns.

Luther did not share with Calvin and the Strasbourg reformers their desire to introduce a didactic note to the worship, either in the prayers or by way of (often long-winded) exhortations. Only in the sermon could he see any justification for this element. However, because he laid great emphasis on the sermon (and was so brilliant a preacher himself) there was no danger of his congregations remaining long in ignorance about their faith or the meaning of the Sacrament.

The 'Formula Missae' seemed far too conservative to Carlstadt and other enthusiasts ('Schwärmer'); they represented that element in religious revival which had manifested itself at Corinth (reflected in 1 Corinthians 14) and was certainly to be found in the Methodist Revival. They saw the service as primarily aimed at stirring up the feelings of the worshippers, and they did not mind how revolutionary their practices might be. The abolition of vestments, the destruction of images, and putting the bread on communicants' hands were some of the ways in which they expressed their mood. These may not appear too drastic to us, but Luther found any kind of extremism almost as abhorrent as papistry (as his attitude during the Peasants' Revolt shows) and would have none of these.

In his 'German Mass' of 1526 he went a little further in reform, though liturgically this was not an improvement. (Luther himself always preferred his 'Formula Missae'.) Again his main aim was to bring the congregation even more into active participation in the worship. His only positive contribution to this was the introduction of new German hymns, such as 'Ein' Feste Burg'—mostly written by himself. One does not deny the importance of these congregationally, but one has seen too often in the Methodist scene today how their use, or over-use, can be made an excuse for not introducing genuine congregational participation into the basic liturgy. An outline of the 'German Mass' will show how drastically Luther treated the liturgy of the Upper Room.

LITURGY OF THE WORD

Introit or German Hymn
Kyrie eleison
Salutation and collect
Epistle
German Hymn
Gospel
Apostles' Creed (during which the elements were prepared)
Sermon

LITURGY OF THE UPPER ROOM

Paraphrase of the Lord's Prayer

Exhortation

Recitation of Words of Institution, accompanied by Fraction

Communion, during which hymns were sung

Post-communion collect

Aaronic Blessing

Whatever its liturgical deficiencies, this service certainly encouraged congregations to take a positive part in their worship. But because of Luther's lack of liturgical expertise (and also because he was not the great dictator he is sometimes thought to have been) the door was open to widespread experiments throughout Germany and beyond. Some of these followed him closely—particularly in Wittenberg, Prussia, Central and North German villages, and in Sweden. The services produced in this last area are liturgically sounder than Luther's 'German Mass'—beginning with Olavius Petri's Mass (first used in 1524) which was revised five times, followed by the Mass of Laurentius Petri in 1572 (he has been described as 'the Cranmer of Sweden', Olavius as its Luther); a more radical service was prepared in 1576, the Mass of John III (the so-called 'Red Book'); this was used until 1593, after which there was a return to Laurentius until 1600 when the Communion Office of Charles IX was produced. The fact that the Swedish Archbishop Brilioth has been a pioneer of the Liturgical Movement outside the Roman Church is an indication of the depth of liturgical thought in that country.

More conservative than Luther, apart from those of Müntzer mentioned above, were the liturgies of Brandenburg (Latin Masses 1540), Austria, 1571, Erfurt and parts of Bavaria. To this day it is a frequent practice in Bavaria for the wafer to be taken on the tongue in Lutheran services. The Brandenburg-Nuremberg school had as its liturgiologists: Ottheinrich, Buchholzer, and von Jagow. The liturgy of 1533 here was one of the influences motivating the Reformation of Cologne, which had some part in shaping the Edward

VI Prayer Book of 1549. In Württemberg and South Germany the orders followed closely the preaching services of the Middle Ages, and were similar to Zwingli's reforms, in that they contained little genuine liturgy and the whole service was conducted from the pulpit. Their influence can be seen in the liturgies of Schwäbisch-Hall (1543), Baden (1556), Pfalz (1556), and Worms (1560). Hesse and South West Germany produced liturgies with individual characteristics distinguishing them from all others.

It is fascinating to consider these different schools in Germany, particularly when comparing them with the uniformity expressed through the Book of Common Prayer. The important points which emerge for our present purposes, however are (1) it was accepted as axiomatic that a united Church did not demand uniformity in worship; and (2) the acceptance of the fact that this includes even the question of the frequency of communion. Luther himself began by desiring it daily, then settled for it weekly; but this was by no means the rule throughout the Lutheran Church, and today it is held, on an average, monthly. Admittedly there was a greater stress on orthodoxy and uniformity after the Thirty Years War; but this mood did not last for ever. It led to the reaction of Pietism, and in turn to the Aufklärung (Rationalism)— incidentally the opposite way round to their appearance in this country. Neither of these helped the liturgy: Pietism destroyed its form, Rationalism its content. It was not until the nineteenth century, largely through the writings and experiments of Loehe, that there was any recovery in liturgical insights and practices. Loehe's new form of the Mass and other Church services led to the collections by Sehling and Richter of the Liturgies of the Church, and prepared the way for various forms of liturgical experiment which are being expressed in the Lutheran Church today.

(b) Zwingli

Having dealt at some length with Luther, we can now turn to his contemporaries to see where and in what particulars they differed from him in their views of worship. Zwingli was more radical than Luther, introduced more of a didactic note into his liturgies, and came out openly in favour of quarterly communion. In his first revision of the Mass, 'De Canone Missae Epicheiresis', he went further than Luther and prepared his own substitute for the Canon. More radical still was his first German rite in 1525 entitled, 'Action oder Bruch des Nachtmals', which became the norm for all later Zwinglian worship. In a preface he states openly that ceremonies and ritual are reduced to their barest form, excluding even the use of music (though this was later restored by popular demand). There is no prayer of consecration or of intercession. Maxwell comments:

'While both Luther and Zwingli stressed fellowship as an essential aspect of the Lord's Supper, their rites strangely failed to give expression to it. In neither rite is there a sense of communion with the whole Church on earth and in heaven; and in Zwingli's rite, after the antiphonal recitation of the psalms had broken down, there was no point where there was common action. In content, the Zwinglian rite must be regarded as the least adequate of all the Reformation liturgies.'[29]

(c) Strasbourg

Because Lutheran influence was dominant here until 1530, when Bucer, with his Zwinglian tendencies, became superintendent, it became a middle way between Luther and Zwingli. The first German Mass was celebrated in 1524, and closely resembles that of Luther. Under Bucer's influence, more drastic changes were gradually introduced, though they never reached the lengths of Zwingli's. There was an emphasis on the need for intelligibility to all, with the whole congregation joining in the service wherever possible. After 1537 this need appears to have been so heartfelt that successive revisions made the prayers and exhortations increasingly longer and more didactic. Moreover, many ancient prayers and responses, such as the Gloria in Excelsis, the Kyries, the Sursum Corda, the Sanctus, and the Benedictus Qui Venit were either replaced by metrical psalms or hymns, or cut out altogether. The rite of 1537–9 is the one on which Calvin based his Genevan liturgy.

29. Maxwell, op. cit., p. 87.

(d) Calvin

We used the word radical in connexion with some aspects of Luther's work. But in his liturgical practices he was a true reformer: he took what he had and altered it for his own purposes. It is Calvin who, in this field, merits the title radical: he rejected what had been handed to him, and, returning to the roots, began again, avoiding what he believed to have been the wrong direction taken in the tradition he had received. The basis of his liturgical practices, therefore, was the early Church as outlined in the New Testament, at least as far as he was allowed to act by the Genevan magistrates. Because Scripture was for him supreme, and because he could not in all honesty avoid the conclusion that the Acts of the Apostles speaks of a weekly celebration of Communion, he therefore sought it for himself and his followers. The magistrates frustrated this desire, opting for a quarterly celebration at Christmas, Easter, Whitsuntide and Harvesttide (some omitted Whitsuntide); and it is ironic that the Presbyterian Church of Scotland today generally follows the imposition of the magistrates, rather than the declared will of Calvin.

The Strasbourg liturgy of 1537 which Calvin took and used almost *in toto* in Geneva gives full recognition to the two parts of the service: the ministry of the Word and of the Upper Room. His didactic interest is shown in his addition of a long paraphrase of the Lord's Prayer; his Biblical interest in the addition of the Decalogue. His rite became the norm of worship for the Calvinist Churches of France,[30] Switzerland, South Germany, Holland, Denmark and elsewhere.

To what extent, then, did the Continental Reformers restore the dual balance of primitive worship? Clearly the preaching of the Gospel and exposition of the Word had a more central place in worship than it had had for a thousand years. Equally clearly (and understandably) the pendulum did not always keep the two parts of worship in balance. The swing towards emphasis on the Word was in most cases only achieved by a lessening of interest in the Eucharist. This is

---

30. Though there were, of course, local variations.

quite clear with Zwingli; clear, too, in Lutheranism as a whole, even though Luther expressed himself in favour of a weekly celebration. The influence of Bucer in Strasbourg inevitably made for the same effect; and while Calvin, more than any other, recognized the validity of Word and Sacrament as interrelated, the effect of his work was the same as with the others: the gain on the one hand was counterbalanced by a loss on the other. Although this is not obvious from a study of sixteenth-century worship, during the next three hundred years it became increasingly evident, until eventually the notes of mystery, of oblation, of thanksgiving, had almost entirely given way to the didactic element. The congregation were given every encouragement to understand what was taking place: but what took place made increasingly fewer demands on their mental faculties.

D. THE REFORMATION IN ENGLAND

(a) Cranmer and the Book of Common Prayer

The history of the Book of Common Prayer, interesting though it is, is not our concern here, and can therefore be briefly summarized. After several orders of worship between 1543 and 1548 had paved the way for reform, Cranmer produced in 1549 the 'First Prayer Book of Edward VI'. In this Cranmer was naturally influenced by the prayers of the Church in which he had been reared; in the order of worship and the theology he was even more influenced by the liturgies of the Lutheran Church, especially those of Kassel, Cologne, and Brandenburg-Nuremberg. In his treatment of the Canon Cranmer followed Zwingli rather than Luther: he replaced the Roman one with a new one. Unfortunately, the new Communion Service fell between two stools, pleasing neither the conservatives nor the radicals. The latter had the greater influence, for the revised service published three years later omitted much from the 1549 book which had seemed to them to reflect Roman practices and beliefs: vestments, prayers for the dead, the Epiclesis, the Peace, the Agnus Dei and the Benedictus Qui Venit. The words 'mass' and 'altar' were removed. Regarding some of these changes and other changes in the order of the service W. J. Grisbrooke writes rather bitterly:

'The prayer for the sanctification of the elements is replaced by a form clearly designed expressly not to bless them. The "prayer of humble access" is removed from its place preparatory to the communion, and . . . placed before the consecration, where it cannot be referred to the eucharistic elements; the Benedictus is removed from the Sanctus, presumably lest it should be held to imply any real coming of Christ in communion. . . . Even the Lord's Prayer is placed after the communion to make certain that none misinterpret the petition for daily bread.'[31]

The Elizabethan Prayer Book of 1558 brought back the 1549 Words of Administration, the Manual Acts, and the oblation of the people. After the Puritan interregnum a further revision was undertaken, but the result, authorized in 1662, hardly differed at all from the 1558 book. (The main difference was the authorization of the Authorized Version for the lexions, a book which could hardly have been used a century earlier.) Then in 1928 came the abortive attempt to have a new book authorized, restoring the Communion Service to something nearer the 1549 order.

The services of the Book of Common Prayer have the great virtue of being succinct in their language. There is no verbosity or floweriness in the prayers; they are clear and dignified. Moreover, Biblical ideas if not actual phraseology run through these prayers—which is one of the reasons why many Anglicans are reluctant to attempt any revision of the book.

The main virtue of the book, however, is the use for which it was intended. Cranmer prepared orders of Morning Prayer and Evensong, into which were compressed the seven 'hours' or Choir Offices observed, chiefly in monasteries, throughout the Middle Ages, for daily use. (The 'hours' from which they were drawn were in effect a formalization of the private devotions and family prayers of the early Church.)[32] Cranmer's intention was that the former service should act as a part of an Ante-Communion on Sundays, to be followed by

31. *Studia Liturgica*, Vol. 1, No. 3, September, 1962, pp. 159f: 'The 1662 Book of Common Prayer: its History and Character.'
32. Cf. the references in Acts on p. 3.

the Litany and the Communion proper. In general, Morning Prayer should act as the Ministry of the Word, to be followed by that of the Upper Room in the Communion Service proper. This never became popular: apart from the time involved (not, perhaps, so great a problem for sixteenth- as for twentieth-century man) the people were not used to such frequent Communion. Under Puritan influence this feeling was intensified, so that by the time of Wesley it was somewhat rare to find celebrations more than quarterly, and certainly not in country churches. The Oxford Movement of the nineteenth century aimed to restore the Eucharist to its primitive place as the central act of worship for the Church; the cleavage thus brought about in the Church was caused not so much by this aim as by the second generation Anglo-Catholics' adoption of Roman ceremonial which laid the 'ritualists' open to the charge of breaking the law. The Liturgical Movement in this country is, as we shall see, encouraging the most vital aspects of the Oxford Movement, evidence for which is afforded by the increasingly widespread practice of the Parish Communion. But the Church of England is still hampered by the tradition of the 8 a.m. Communion Service on a Sunday, with Morning Prayer as a separate service at eleven. The really ironical aspect of all this is that most of the Methodist (and other Free) churches which consider themselves to be liturgically advanced are adopting this pattern for themselves.

There are many criticisms which can be levelled at the Book of Common Prayer, many of which are presented by J. G. Davies.[33] Those which most concern us are his criticisms of the Eucharist as the service now stands. He points out that it has a 'truncated' Ministry of the Word. At the very least this part of the service needs the addition of an Old Testament lesson—which Cranmer did not include as he was allowing for it in the Ante-Communion Mattins. One feels that more time could be found for the sermon than is allowed for even in the Parish Communion. Moreover, there must be more congregational participation. The present order, Dr. Davies

33. *Studia Liturgica*, Vol. 1, No. 3, pp. 167ff: 'The 1662 Book of Common Prayer: its Virtues and Vices.'

reminds us, 'is mainly a monologue'. In an interesting footnote to his article, he states:

'If we take the communion service and include the third exhortation and the proper for the first Sunday in Advent, we find that the congregation has some 700 words to say and the celebrant 3,500. This number for the celebrant however does not include the words he uses for the notices, the banns or the sermon. Moreover the congregational part does not affect the character of the service; it still remains a monologue interrupted at four main points—the responses to the commandments, the creed, the confession and the Gloria.'[34]

We shall see that these two criticisms of the Prayer Book Communion Service express two of the major elements in the ideas of the Liturgical Movement.

(b) The Puritans

The Puritanism which concerns us is that which sprang from Calvin: the Presbyterians in particular, the Congregationalists, and, to a lesser extent (for they had idiosyncrasies not followed by the others) the Baptists. These all had several emphases, uppermost of which was the supreme authority of Scripture. They demanded express Scriptural warrant for all the details of public worship (hence their opposition to the Prayer Book which did not make such things as vestments, organs, the sign of the cross, and church ornaments illegal). From this followed their belief in the centrality of preaching. They felt (with, one feels, a certain amount of justice) that the Book of Common Prayer was not entirely explicit about the sermon. As opposed to its equivocal position there, Richard Baxter began his 'Reformed Liturgy' (1661) with an invocatory prayer having the petition: 'May thy word be spoken and heard by us as the word of God.'

The question arises, Did their emphasis on preaching blot out any sense of liturgical worship? In the classical period of Puritanism, the seventeenth century, there are signs that a sense of liturgy was not lacking, at least among the Presbyterians. The Westminster Directory of 1644, the one attempt at uniformity of Puritan worship made under parliamentary

34. Op. cit., p. 173.

authority, suggested that both written and extemporary prayer could be used in worship, and some of the Puritans followed this suggestion in their practice. Baxter's 'Reformed Liturgy', although it never really got off the ground, is just one example of a Puritan attempt to use liturgy, incidentally based even more strongly on Scripture than was the Prayer Book. The Puritans felt that there was Scriptural warrant for not using collects or litanies, consequently in the experiments in written prayers that were made these were always recast as long prayers spoken by the preacher with the congregation joining only in the Amen. The Puritans' hearts were never really in this type of prayer however; in fact most Independents and Baptists felt that any form of written prayer was alien to New Testament teaching and prevented the worship from being really controlled by the Holy Spirit. Isaac Watts, a Congregationalist, did write a *Guide to Prayer* in 1715 which strongly recommended careful preparation of prayers, both in language (which should be 'grave and decent, which is a medium between magnificence and meanness'),[35] form, and content. He even suggested that preachers should prepare the themes of their prayers for a year ahead—a personal variant of the Church Year! But this book was not influential, and most preachers fell into the practice of simply starting their services with a long extemporary prayer which included any number of elements—thanksgiving, intercession, confession, or petition. It is sad to reflect on how the stately, liturgical prayers of the Reformed tradition were replaced by these long, didactic, extemporary utterances, openly treated as preliminaries to the sermon. The wheel had indeed come full circle—and in some parts of England this type of worship is still quite widespread in the Free Churches. It is not so long ago that the writer heard a preacher in a Northern chapel suddenly declare in the middle of his sermon: 'And as I told you in the prayer . . .'.

As to the frequency of communion there were wide divergences. In some Independent churches it was a weekly event, but monthly became the norm. The Presbyterians settled for Calvin's enforced practice at Geneva, rather than for his

35. Quoted by A. G. Matthews in *Christian Worship*, ed. Micklem, p. 176.

avowed aim. Baptist practice closely followed that of the Independents. Had the form of worship suggested in the Westminster Directory been carefully observed, it would have been possible to say that although Puritan worship did not as a rule include the Sacrament, at least it was sacramental in form: the Liturgy of the Word should lead to prayers of thanksgiving and dedication, and to the offertory—all of these elements of the Liturgy of the Upper Room. This would have been preferable to the distinct cleavage between the two in Anglican practice. But as we have seen, this liturgical approach to worship was only a temporary stage for most of the Puritans.

The most lasting contribution they made consisted in the hymns which—after a struggle with the more conservative members who felt that only psalms should be sung—were written for, and sung in, Puritan worship. The history of Puritan worship, evolving eventually to that of the nonconformists in the eighteenth and nineteenth centuries, is a sharp reminder of the difficulty of keeping the Word and the Sacrament in harmony. But one cannot condemn out of hand a tradition which produced the supremely inspired hymns of Isaac Watts.

Wesley's approach to worship will have to be considered in greater detail than any period so far considered. But it appears preferable to treat Wesley, and the later developments in Methodism, when we concentrate our attention on present-day Methodism in relation to the Liturgical Movement. Before we do this, we must first look at the Movement, at its history and its insights.

CHAPTER TWO

THE LITURGICAL MOVEMENT

A. THE MEANING OF LITURGY

I N the previous chapter the word 'liturgy' was used on several occasions, and because no definition was offered there, it must be admitted that questions were being begged.

The traditional use of the word in English limits it to the prescribed public worship of the Church, and particularly, quite simply, to the Eucharist. This is emphatically the case in the Eastern Church, as the title of their Eucharist, 'The Divine Liturgy of St. John Chrysostom', indicates. It is because of this traditionally particularized use of the word that one has to be wary when using it in the presence of many Free Churchmen. To them it speaks of stereotyped orders of service, incense, elaborate symbolism, and the complete absence of simplicity.

The trouble is that this traditional use, which dies hard, does grave injustice to the real extent of the word's meaning. A. R. Shands puts it thus: 'Far from emphasizing the external formality of worship, "liturgy" expresses the fact that Christian worship is a present *experience*—the action of Christ in the midst of His people and the action of Christians in response.'[1] If this were fully understood, much of the hostility would be shown to be groundless; in fact the word would be recognized as one of the most basic and expressive in the whole of the Christian vocabulary.

It derives from the two Greek words 'laos' (meaning 'people') and 'ergon' (meaning 'work'). In classical Greek it described any kind of public duty on behalf of the State. Some act of diplomacy on behalf of the State in relation to another State would be described as performing a liturgy; so also would

---

1. A. R. Shands, *The Liturgical Movement and the Local Church*, S.C.M., 1959, p. 18.

be the presentation of a gift to the State—a piece of land, a building, or a ship. By the time of the Septuagint (c. 132 B.C.) it was used chiefly in the religious sense, particularly in reference to the services of the Temple. In the New Testament it occurs either as a noun or a verb some twelve times. In Hebrews 8:2 Jesus is described as a minister (leitourgos) in the sanctuary, and in v. 6 his ministry is contrasted with Moses': He was a liturgist in its fulfilment. Paul also applies the word to himself: '. . . because of the grace given me by God to be a minister (liturgist) of Christ Jesus to the Gentiles in the priestly service of the gospel of God'.[2] In Philippians 2:25 Paul uses the word in connexion with Epaphroditus—'a messenger and *minister* to my need'. In Acts 13:2 it refers to the worship of the early Christians; but in Romans 15:27 it is used to describe *service* in material blessings. These last two quotations are particularly important, for they bring out between them precisely that twofold aspect of liturgy which we shall see emerging through the influence of the Liturgical Movement. In Romans 13:6 the authorities of the State are actually described as God's liturgists in the duties they perform (here is an almost classical use of the word); and elsewhere in Hebrews it is used of either the office or function of priests in general.[3]

If, then, we are to recapture the basic concept of the word, liturgy must be seen fundamentally as *action*. The Eucharist, for example, is the *act* of giving thanks, and further action is embodied within it: externally or visibly in the four actions already enumerated—'took', 'blessed', 'broke', and 'gave'. The self-offering of the members in the Eucharist, in and through their common Lord, is another aspect of this action.

The word is of supreme importance because it arises from the New Testament view of the Church as the Body of Christ—all the members corporately acting on their Lord's behalf. Allied to this (in fact integrally related to it) is the sense of unity which the first Christians seem to have had between their action in their services together and their action beyond these: between their worship and their witness. These are the only two things for which the Church exists; but it is amazing (and at times a little frightening) how easily one or the other of these has been

2. Romans 15:16.   3. Cf. Hebrews 1:7; 10:11.

neglected by different branches of the Church. If the word liturgy, and a right understanding of it, had been kept at the centre of the Church's thinking this divorce would not have happened so easily. Its rediscovery can only be to the greater glory of God and the fulfilment of His will—in other words it will help to further the Kingdom of God. In its reminder that worship must express action between, on the one hand, God who in His mercy makes Himself known to His people, and on the other hand the congregation who, united in Christ, respond to God's initiative by offering themselves to Him, we have the key to the rediscovery of basic Christian worship. And in the application of this in the sphere of Christian witness we have the key to the doctrine of priesthood and the chosen people of God.

Thus, even the most deep-seated fears of the word can be dispelled. It does *not* stand for written orders to the exclusion of extemporary prayer (though as we shall see there are strong arguments favouring the former much of the time). Rather it stresses the activity of the Body of Christ: in worship by the corporate offering of itself to God in oblation and obedience (itself made possible only by God's action through Christ in the midst); and then in witness by the obedient rendering of itself to Him to be used as He wills in the world which He made and loves. To quote Shands again:[4] 'We are "liturgical" when we love the brethren because in this we are presenting ourselves to God. "Your brother is the altar on which you lay your sacrifice." '

B. HISTORY OF THE LITURGICAL MOVEMENT

It is no easy matter to attempt to classify a Movement so widespread and various as the Liturgical Movement. All that is possible in this section is to outline the main stages and areas of application, leaving for our next section the discussion of the different principles and insights which emerge. We can identify three stages of the Movement (some would say three movements, but they are inter-related). The first was in the nineteenth century and characterized by ritual and aesthetics, and

4. Shands, op. cit., p. 20.

the desire that the congregations should both have *better* worship and also appreciate it more. The second was roughly from the start of this century until the last war, which was generally the period of liturgical writing and the delineation of the basic principles of worship. The third (a stage less distinct from the second than this was from the first) was the post-war period, the period of liturgical experiment reaching 'down' to parish level. At each stage we shall consider first the Roman and second the non-Roman developments.

(a) First stage: The nineteenth century

It must be accepted that the main motive behind the thoughts expressed at this stage was not a desire for the betterment of the people, but a result of the Romantic Revival, with its love of the past, both medieval and classical. This Revival developed a love of history, and the Church readily assimilated this; the Latin and Greek Fathers and the medieval Church were among the historical elements in the Church rediscovered at this time. This mood found forceful expression in the life and work of Dom Guéranger (1805–75). He was greatly concerned about the spiritual indifference of the French people following the Revolution. He believed that the answer, or antidote, to this lay in the restoring of ancient liturgical traditions. He was a Benedictine monk, and he set about achieving his aim by transforming the Abbey of Solesmes into something akin to a medieval religious community. The most lasting of his reforms was the re-establishment of the Gregorian chants in the liturgy, which helped worshippers to understand the true nature of liturgical singing. He was, unfortunately, a fervent infallibilist (ultramontanist) and this caused him to deal violently with those elements in French ceremonial not uniform with the Roman ritual and calendar. His opus magnum was *L'Année Liturgique*, but his work lacked the critical qualities of the true scholar. Roman Catholics today disparage Guéranger's work, but Massey Shepherd defends him thus:[5]

'Dom Guéranger laid such foundations that without his pioneering the work of twentieth-century reformers would be impossible. One

5. Ed. Massey H. Shepherd: *The Liturgical Renewal of the Church*, O.U.P., New York, 1960, p. 25.

must remember that, however romantically conceived, however pressed into service for an ultramontanist programme, his concern to restore the Roman rite in the purity of its text, ceremony and chant was an essential starting point for any progressive work of reform.'

The developments at this stage outside the Roman Church were in some ways similar to, but independent of, the work of Guéranger. We have seen that the Oxford Movement in England had as one of its chief aims the restoration of the Eucharist as the chief Sunday worship of the Church of England and that an aim of the later Anglo-Catholics was to introduce medieval and Continental ceremonial into their worship. These elements must be acknowledged as having been a part of the early expression of the Liturgical Movement; but one cannot feel that they are important for the application of its insights to our Church situation today.

We have seen how, in Germany, the writings of William Loehe emerged in strong opposition to the aftermath of Pietism and its converse, Rationalism, and were the stepping-stone to many liturgical developments in Germany in the twentieth century.

(b) Second stage: The twentieth century to 1939

I. THE ROMAN CATHOLIC CHURCH

This stage originated in an encyclical of Pope Pius X (1903) in which he said: 'Active participation in the public and solemn prayer of the Church is the primary and indispensable source of a true Christian spirit.' Six years later at the Congress of Malines in Belgium this theme was taken up. Benoit describes vividly[6] how the desire of a certain Benedictine from Mont César to express the need for Church members to know and fully share in their liturgy was almost frustrated—but not quite. 'Thus it was', writes Benoit, '... that Dom Lambert Beaudouin delivered his epoch-making speech foreshadowing the liturgical movement.' This speech was, fortunately, along the lines of the papal encyclical. He stated that the liturgy is not something just to be observed by the congregation, but something in which all should actively participate, bringing before God 'the

6. J.-D. Benoit, *Liturgical Renewal*, S.C.M., 1958, pp. 69f.

THE LITURGICAL MOVEMENT AND METHODISM

whole man in the whole Christian community'.[7] This was in line with the move to encourage Church members to more frequent communion which had resulted from the encyclical. Among other things, Dom Beaudouin proposed the production of a vernacular Missal.

At Mont César he was able to continue with his teaching and writing, his most influential book being *La Pieté de L'Église* (1914). Under his leadership the clergy were called to undertake intensive study of the whole theme of liturgy; and a French translation of the Mass was made.

Possibly even more influential was the work done under Dom Ildefons Herwegen at the Benedictine Abbey of Maria Laach in Germany. This abbey produced two writers of genius: Romano Guardini, whose *Spirit of the Liturgy* ought to be compulsory reading for every ordinand, and Dom Odo Casel, who edited and undertook a major part of the writing of the series *Jahrbuch für Liturgiewissenschaft*. Casel's writings on the theme of liturgy and the meaning of sacramental theology have probably been more influential outside Roman Catholicism than anyone else's. Massey Shepherd says of him:[8]

'He has infused into the arid scholasticism of official Roman dogma the fertile Platonic mysticism of the early Fathers. He has brought to bear upon the liturgical rites of Western Catholicism much of the spirit of Eastern Christian worship, and struck deep roots for them in both the Biblical faith and the sacramental experience of the whole Graeco-Roman world, where Christianity brought into a new, creative unity the finest insights and aspirations of the Jew and the Greek.'

The next development took place in Austria. In 1919 an Augustinian monk, Pius Parsch, became parish priest of the church of St. Gertrud in Klosterneuberg. He tried to apply the ideas of the Liturgical Movement to the parish situation. His two series of pamphlets 'Lebe mit der Kirche' and 'Bibel und Liturgie' were effective aids in this, as also were his Bible Hours which he held with keen laymen, during which the relevance of the Bible to the Liturgy emerged.

The Movement spread into Holland, Spain, and Italy, and,

7. Shands, op. cit., p. 22, supplies this quotation.
8. Massey Shepherd, op. cit., p. 33.

in 1925, to America where it was again the Benedictines (chiefly at their Abbey of St. John in Collegeville, Minnesota) who were most active and who founded the liturgical magazine, *Orate Fratres* (now called *Worship*). In England, the Movement has been rather derivative, with Abbot Cabrol its chief exponent. It is interesting that he was once a Benedictine monk at Solesmes.

II. THE NON-ROMAN CHURCHES
(EXCLUDING THE EASTERN ORTHODOX)

1. *Lutheran*

Although not the first Lutheran to be influenced by the Movement, probably the most influential was Archbishop Brilioth of Sweden, whose *Eucharistic Faith and Practice* (1930) has made an impression even on the Roman Church—evidence of which is given in Louis Bouyer's *Life and Liturgy* which expands Brilioth's ideas on the five elements of the Eucharist (to be discussed when we consider the insights of the Movement). In Germany the leader of the 'Hochkirche' movement, Friedrich Heiler, a former Roman Catholic, brought out the link between the Liturgical and Ecumenical Movements. His best-known book in England is *The Spirit of Worship*, in which he shows his interest in and knowledge of the psychological approach to worship. More idiosyncratic are the writings of Rudolph Otto: but at least his plans for the renewing of worship show a commendable zeal to be relevant to the contemporary situation. In America, the Lutheran Liturgical Association, founded in 1898, did memorable work in bringing out the basic principles of liturgy; it is unfortunate that the Memoirs of this association are not available in this country. The most recent product of American Lutheranism is their *Service Book and Hymnal*, a splendid production. It contains a preface to the liturgy and to its music, the Communion Service set to music in two settings, along with the Proper Prefaces and Season Graduals, Mattins and Vespers set to music, Minor Propers, Suffrages, the Litany, the Psalms, the Canticles, Collects and Prayers, Bidding Prayers, Occasional Services, General Rubrics, 602 hymns, and Indexes which include a remarkable Liturgical Index with hymns chosen to relate to the Propers for the day, processional, introit, psalm paraphrase to follow the Old Testament lesson, Epistle, Gradual and Gospel. One wishes that such a book could be placed in the hands of every English worshipper!

2. *The Church of England*

The first stage in Anglicanism had been, as we have seen, the Ritualistic controversy of the nineteenth century. Apart from the rancour associated with this, the liturgical danger, as Louis Bouyer pointed out[9] was that of leading worshippers to the very attitude which the Roman liturgiologists were fighting: the veneration of the Blessed Sacrament. Massey Shepherd, with his usual breadth of spirit, defends this development on two grounds:

'It finally succeeded in breaking the rigid uniformity of Anglican worship that had bound it for over two centuries, and thus opened to Anglicans both a more just appreciation of the comprehensiveness of their own tradition, and a wider experience of the fulness of Christian worship. It helped to open the eyes of Anglicans to the needs of "all sorts and conditions of men", who were repelled by the arid, overly intellectualized and formalized use of the Prayer Book into which the Anglican churches had largely withdrawn after the separation of the dissenting bodies. Ritualism also fostered a new interest in the study of liturgiology.'[10]

The next stage in the Anglican Church was that of Prayer Book revision, which, though, as we have seen, abortive, yet made people more aware of the wide extent of their heritage— Catholic and Evangelical—and brought out the important principle of unity in essentials, diversity in non-essentials. The third stage, which is still continuing, has been marked by liturgical experiment at parish level. Its pioneers were Fr. Hebert, whose books *Liturgy and Society* and *The Parish Communion* have probably been, along with *The Shape of the Liturgy*—the major work of the other pioneer, Dom Gregory Dix—the most influential writings on this theme published in England.

9. L. Bouyer, *Life and Liturgy*, Sheed and Ward, 1956, p. 48.
10. Shepherd, op. cit., pp. 46f.

3. *The Nonconformists and the Reformed Churches*

Benoit states that in the French Reformed Church the father of the modern Liturgical Movement was Eugène Bersier, pastor of the Étoile Church in Paris. Not many followed his lead, and more recently impetus to the movement has been given by Wilfred Monod in France, Jules Amiguet in Switzerland, and, influencing both countries, Richard Paquier, who founded the 'Church and Liturgy' group.

In the Congregational Church a growing interest in liturgy was evinced by their symposium, *Christian Worship* (1936), and the publication in 1948 of their service-book, *A Book of Public Worship*. The same mood is seen in the Presbyterian Church with their *Book of Common Order* (1940) and the writings of William Maxwell.[11] Even in the Baptist Church there is a nascent interest in liturgy, expressed particularly in the books of Neville Clark and Ian Gilmore. The Salvation Army does not come under the scope of this study, but it is interesting to note that among the younger officers there is a quite widespread desire to introduce the Eucharist into their worship.

There is no writer in Methodism who has produced a book on worship comparable with those of Clark, Maxwell, or, in the Congregational Church, Abba. We shall see that J. E. Rattenbury pioneered the way to a new approach to Wesley; and in Raymond George we have a liturgiologist of the highest calibre.

(c) Third Stage: The last 25 years

Inevitably stages two and three overlap, and some of the work already described within the context of stage two properly belongs to the third stage. The main interest at this stage lies in the practical application of the insights of the Liturgical Movement to the parish and community situations.

At Chicago in 1940 the first National Liturgical Week was held, bringing representatives of all sections of the Roman Catholic Church together. This has been an annual event ever since. In France, the 'Centre de Pastorale Liturgique' was

11. In addition to the work mentioned, see also *John Knox's Genevan Service Book,* 1556, Edinburgh, 1931; and *Concerning Worship,* O.U.P.

founded in Paris in 1943. Of special interest among its publications is the periodical, *La Maison-Dieu*. This centre sponsors liturgical weeks and missions on the liturgy. The whole Liturgical Movement in France was given a boost with the establishment in 1941, under the patronage of the Cardinal Archbishop Suhard, of the Mission de France. Under the leadership of Abbé Michonneau this movement has tried to put into practice in French cities the insights of the Liturgical Movement. Abbé Michonneau describes the work in *Revolution in a City Parish*. There is a realism and expression of common sense about this Mission which must surely impress even the most die-hard Protestant. The mood in France created by these experiments must be reckoned as having been at least partially the impetus behind the worker-priest movement.

The Liturgical Movement in the Roman Church could be said to have become formally accepted with Pope Pius XII's encyclical 'Mediator Dei'. There is a note of caution in this, but Benoit suggests that this is inevitable in such a document. 'This, like most encyclicals, does not inaugurate a new movement in the Church; rather does it bear witness to the reality and vitality of a movement already in existence. It does not create it: it sanctions it and at the same time controls, harmonizes and limits it.'[12] The next important reform came in 1955: the revision of the Holy Week services and the restoration of the Easter Vigil. The most recent developments have been the growing emphasis on Biblical study in the vernacular (aided by the remarkable French translation of L'École Biblique de Jérusalem), leading to the official acceptance of the Revised Standard Version in the Roman Church (a fact which must mean that it will be finally accepted in non-Roman English-speaking Churches, rather than the New English Bible). More recently still, the approval given at the second Vatican Council to the use of the vernacular for at least part of of the Mass, illustrates how far the Roman Church has moved in half a century.

In the United States, there have been interesting experiments in the parish of Holy Cross, St. Louis. In England, the Movement has still not yet gathered fire, though there are

12. Benoit, op. cit., pp. 7of.

signs that the younger clergy are becoming 'restless', and Fr. Clifford Howell[13] admits as much. When he was still a priest, Charles Davis soundly berated those who would hold back.[14]

'When we take stock of our situation in the light of what is being achieved elsewhere, we cannot but notice the superficial character of so much of our apostolic effort . . . It never seems to occur to us that people sometimes do not listen because what we tell them is not worth their attention and does not meet their legitimate needs and desires.'

Perhaps one sign of hope is that the book, according to the author, sold well among English Roman Catholics!

Some of the most interesting practical experiments are being made in the non-Roman Churches. In America there are the Inner City Protestant Missions of New York, Chicago, and Cleveland, where members have accepted the churches' immediate neighbourhood as their responsibility—their liturgy. Many of the books with the most radical suggestions about the method of the mission are emerging from America—such as the writings of Harvey Cox, Peter Berger, Colin Williams, Gibson Winter, and Paul Van Buren.[15]

In Scotland there has been in existence the Iona Community, where worship and work are openly recognized as dual aspects of the liturgy. In Ralph Morton this community has as its deputy-leader a man who, along with the Anglican Mark Gibbs, is nationally known for his identification with the movement—parallel to the Liturgical Movement—to bring the laity to a deeper understanding of what it means to be the people of God. Experiments in mission have been made through the 'Tell Scotland' movement, especially in the parish of North Kelvinside, whose minister, Tom Allen, has described his work in *The Face of my Parish*.

In Germany there have been various manifestations of the

13. In an article, 'The Liturgical Situation in England', in *Heiliger Dienst*, II, 50.

14. C. Davis, *Liturgy and Doctrine*, Sheed and Ward, 1960, p. 17.

15. Harvey Cox: *The Secular City* now published by S.C.M. Peter Berger, *The Noise of Solemn Assemblies*, Doubleday, New York, 1961. Colin Williams, *Where in the World?* and *What in the World?* now published in England by Epworth. Gibson Winter, *The Suburban Captivity of the Churches*, Doubleday, 1961; and *The New Creation as Metropolis*, Macmillan, New York, 1963. Paul van Buren, *The Secular Meaning of the Gospel*, S.C.M., 1963.

Movement's influence. There has been the publication, with typical German thoroughness, of the five volumes of 'Leiturgia', and the work of the Lutheran Liturgical Conference. There has also been the Kirchentag movement, which attracts hundreds of thousands to its main meetings. Most important of all, perhaps, have been the attempts to see life in industry as part of the liturgy: and on the one hand the Social and Evangelical Academies, and on the other the work of Horst Symanowski at the Gossner Mission in Mainz-Kastel show the extent to which this has been reached throughout the country. In a recent article[16] Symanowski concludes by quoting Bonhoeffer: 'Dietrich Bonhoeffer wrote from prison, "I don't want man in his worldliness to be made to feel a worm, but to be confronted with God at his strongest point." The place for that with the non-churchgoer is his place of work. That is his strongest point.'

We have here moved away from the narrowly ecclesiastical aspect of the Liturgical Movement to one which many Roman Catholics, at least, would no doubt reject. But the two are interconnected, and we shall be suggesting that much of the modern expression of 'outreach' takes its inspiration from the Liturgical Movement.

In England the most widespread effect of the Movement has been the Parish and People Movement, with its aim of making the Parish Communion Service, rather than Mattins, the main act of Sunday worship. R. H. Martin, in his thesis *The History of the Parish Communion*, rejects the idea that the Parish and People Movement began as a direct consequence of contact with those working within the context of the Liturgical Movement on the Continent. He suggests that Sir Edward Hoskyns's visit to Maria Laach after the First World War no doubt encouraged him but was not the main influence which motivated him to establish a Sung Eucharist with general communion in the chapel of Corpus Christi College, Cambridge. He feels that Heiler may well have had a strong influence on many of the English, but nevertheless sees this movement as basically an indigenous thing arising out of the English situation, and

16. *Over the Bridge* (Magazine of the South London Industrial Mission, ed. R. J. Billington), April 1965, p. 10.

related to earlier movements and trends in the Church of England. If by this he is implying that the majority of Anglican leaders have given scant recognition to the work of the Movement on the Continent one can only agree. Bishops like Henry De Candole are too rare on the Anglican scene.

There have, however, been several important experiments in the missioning aspect of the Liturgical Movement. In the parishes of Halton in Leeds and Greenhill in Harrow (described by Ernest Southcott and Joost De Blank in their books, *The Parish Comes Alive* and *The Parish in Action* respectively) house churches have been formed, with discussion, Bible study, Holy Communion, and daily offices in people's homes. In Greenhill the parish has been divided into areas, responsibility for which—amounting to a genuine pastoral responsibility—has been given to the laymen. One of the great contemporary questions raised by the Liturgical Movement is to what extent forms of worship—perhaps totally different in structure—must be devised for use in places like homes and factories, alongside those used in centres of public worship.

The most far-reaching experiment, because it is comprehensive of so many aspects of the Liturgical Movement, which has yet manifested itself must surely be that of the Taizé Community in Burgundy. In Max Thurian they have one of the most eminent of living liturgiologists, and their Daily Office, an English translation of which was completed after some three years and must be taken into account in any revision of the Book of Common Prayer, is a landmark in the history of Christian worship, while its Eucharist has a greater expression of vitality and joy than any comparable liturgy. In their development of a common liturgical life ('at the frontier of the Church and the world'), their ecumenical spirit towards both Protestantism and Rome (the local Roman Catholics far outnumber Protestants at the daily office, and also even at the Eucharist for the Ministry of the Word), their mission to the neighbourhood and beyond, their theology and their emphasis on Christian art, they present a rare phenomenon. We cannot do better than close this brief history of the Movement with this quotation from Roger Schutz, Prior of the Taizé Community:

'One thing is certain. All contact with God leads to one's neighbour. The sign of all genuine, inner life, that is to say of all contact with Jesus Christ, is discovery of one's neighbour. And if our neighbour disappears from our relations with Christ, then our love of God is directed to a mythical deity our of touch with our human condition and not to the Christ of the Gospels. With a godless man the soul is devoured by love, with the Christian it is stifled if love of God cuts out love of one's neighbour.'[17]

Love of God and of one's neighbour; worship and witness; Eucharist and Word: these are our liturgy, and it is to this that the Liturgical Movement is pointing us.

Although the above outline of the three stages is the normally accepted pattern, it should be noted that Max Thurian of Taizé, in an address to the Section on worship at the Montreal Faith and Order Conference in 1963, observes four stages.[18] First, as we have noted, there was the 'romantic' stage, as a reaction against the sterility of rationalism and the subjectivity of pietism, and an emphasis on the 'mystery' of the liturgy. At this stage, Thurian notes, the movement remained somewhat emotional and individualistic, with undue concentration on an aesthetic form of piety. The second stage was the result of the interest in Biblical and patristic studies, which stressed the need to understand the liturgical sources. At this stage the emphasis was on worship as the expression of the whole Body; the communal replaced the aesthetic. The third stage was marked by genuine liturgical studies, scientifically pursued. In the fourth stage the movement no longer has an independent existence but is part of the life of the whole Church.

'The liturgy can no longer be regarded as the sphere reserved for initiates; it has become a natural, ordinary expression of the Church's life. The only liturgy admissible is a liturgy whose theological significance is clearly explicit, which expresses a genuine sacramental life, which links the local congregation with the Church of all times and places, and which builds up a holy people so as to arm it for its presence and mission in the world through worship and intercession.'[19]

17. R. Schutz, *This Day Belongs to God*, Faith Press, 1961, p. 32.
18. *Studia Liturgica*, Vol. III, No. 2, Autumn, 1964, pp. 107ff.
19. Thurian, op. cit., p. 108. (The appearance of this ecumenical quarterly is itself a sign of the extending effects of the Liturgical Movement.)

This is a more sophisticated outline than the normal historical one, but it links the bare historical facts of the movement to the various insights which have emerged during its history, with which we must now concern ourselves.

C. THE INSIGHTS OF THE LITURGICAL MOVEMENT

(a) The Nature of the Church as the Body of Christ

There are many metaphors used to describe the Church in the New Testament, but none which are mentioned so frequently, or given such clarity of expression, as that of the Body (soma). This is particularly true of the Pauline writings. In 1 Corinthians 12, Ephesians 4, and Colossians 1 (assuming these last two to be either Pauline or expressions of St. Paul's thought) we have the doctrine enunciated. St. Paul's teaching bears witness to his Jewish heritage: the belief that God has raised up a community of His chosen, through whom His will and purpose for mankind will be revealed. Against the background of individualism in such Roman religions as Stoicism, he outlined the great mystery of the union of individuals with each other through their common relationship with, and dependence on, their Lord, who was their Head. 'We are to grow up in every way into him who is the head, into Christ, from whom the whole body, joined and knit together by every joint with which it is supplied . . . makes bodily growth and upbuilds itself in love.'[20] The only major study on this theme in English is by John Robinson in *The Body*. In the introduction to this he states:

'One could say without exaggeration that the concept of the body forms the keystone of Paul's theology. In its closely interconnected meanings, the word σῶμα (*soma*) knits together all his great themes. It is from the body of sin and death that we are delivered; it is through the body of Christ on the Cross that we are saved; it is into His body the Church that we are incorporated; it is by His body in the Eucharist that this Community is sustained; it is in our body that its new life has to be manifested; it is to a resurrection of this body to the likeness of His glorious body that we are destined.'[21]

20. Ephesians 4:15f.   21. J. A. T. Robinson, *The Body*, S.C.M., 1952, p. 9.

The rediscovery of this status through the Liturgical Movement is a natural parallel to the sociological tendencies of the last century. The Victorian Age, particularly in this country, was one of intense individualism. It was a time of outstanding and gifted leaders in a large number of spheres of thought and action, and in culture and religion too. As an inevitable corollary to this, it was also an age in which the vast majority of the people were subjected to harsh if not brutal treatment. The twentieth century has reacted against this, with less gifted leaders but with more rights and a better life for the masses of the people. The influence of communism must not be underestimated. Benoit states:[22] 'We are tending towards a mass-civilization, in which living shoulder to shoulder is a reality, and even a necessity. Everywhere the social spirit claims its rights.'

But the community of the Church is spiritual rather than physical (despite the early attempts of the Church to found a communist society). It expressed itself in common action in the Eucharist, and in a common expression of the nature of Christ in society. It is a redeemed community, living in communion together, seeking to communicate its common experience to all mankind. The Liturgical Movement has shown how the Church's worship and witness express this. 'The liturgy expressed the essentially social nature of man . . . it implies, confirms and consecrates a particular anthropological view.'[23] The Church is not merely an accidental assembly of individuals but a corporate priesthood, unitedly and symbolically offering the oblation of Christ's body and of herself as the Body of Christ. The whole becomes more than the sum of the parts, and the worship of any assembly of people, while it includes each individual offering, is more than the sum of these, and becomes a thing of mystery, in which the individuals are caught up and lifted out of themselves.

Similarly in the Church's witness: the individual goes among his fellows, there to be as it were Christ's representative; but in doing so he is ineffably strengthened by the knowledge that he is supported by the other members of the body. His suffering

---

22. Benoit, op. cit., p. 110.
23. Fr. Chenu, 'Anthropologie et liturgie', in *La Maison-Dieu* No. 12, 1947, IV, p. 53. (Quoted by Benoit, op. cit., p. 110.)

will be their suffering, his victory their victory. (We are now completely in the world of thought expressed in 1 Corinthians 12.) In the most recent years this aspect of the body has been adumbrated further. The motive inspiring the contemporary emergence of team and group ministries is essentially that of the body: how can the Church truly be the Church? The rediscovery of the nature of the laity is another indication of this. We shall reflect in the final chapter on the developing possibility that the Church of the future will comprise strong centres, with a mixed team of clergy and laity, dedicated to their task and accepting the discipline of the group, and reaching out alongside the other laymen who are associated with the Church into the secular structures at all levels.

This is not to say that individualism within the Church is now dead. On the witnessing side, most Churches have hardly begun to understand what it is to be the body of Christ in the world. There remains in the minds of many the conviction that the Christian's task is to be a 'personal evangelist', aiming at inducing his fellows to join his Church, armed with a Bible or Prayer Book. This is particularly the case in those Free Churches, where the influence of the 'Billy Graham' approach is keenly felt. And there are still large numbers, Roman, Anglican, and Free Church, for whom the Church's worship expresses a personal need unrelated (at times even indifferent) to others who may be worshipping alongside.

Nevertheless, the insights of the Liturgical Movement concerning the body are taking an increasingly firm hold of the thinking of the worshipping community, and influencing their whole attitude to what takes place in the church building week by week. Private Masses are less popular in the Roman Church; the Parish Communion is drawing Anglicans closer together in one body; and the increasing use of genuine liturgical worship in the Free Churches is causing their members to think about the nature of the Church and its worship much more deeply than ever before. And as an important consequence of this all sections of the Church are coming to appreciate more and more that if a body is divided against itself it must be to its own harm: the different members need one another. Mascall states:[24] 'The supreme service which the Church performs for society is one that society *cannot* perform for itself—the maintenance in the midst of society of the new human race in which all the mysteries of God are fulfilled.' In other words, the Church constitutes in itself a piece of prophetic symbolism—a portrayal of mankind as it will be in the Kingdom of God, with all barriers removed and mutual love springing from a divine love greater than and over and above, their own; a love which maintains the harmony between people of different cultures, races, classes, and nationalities. But if the very people who are called upon to represent this dramatic portrayal are themselves unable to come organically together, are they not contradicting in themselves the very thing they are called upon to manifest to others?

(b) The Rediscovery of Worship as an activity of the whole congregation

Bouyer writes:[25] 'The liturgical movement is the natural response arising in the Church to the perception that many people have lost that knowledge and understanding of the liturgy which should belong to Christians, both clergy and laity, and in consequence, have lost the right use of the liturgy also.' A general summary of the weak state of the Church's worship prior to the Liturgical Movement (and which still exists in many areas and congregations) would be that on the one hand the liturgy had become an activity conducted by the priest which the congregation were invited to observe without necessarily understanding or participating in what was happening; while on the other hand all sense of liturgy had been sacrificed to the didactic element in worship, so that the congregation spent most of their time listening to one man's voice, without any sense that they were themselves making a positive contribution to the worship.

Before we can consider how the Liturgical Movement is causing the more fundamental elements of worship to be manifested, we must first consider the nature of worship, what it is. The English word affords us a clue to its meaning. To worship

24. E. L. Mascall, *Corpus Christi*, Longmans, 1953, p. 46.
25. Bouyer, op. cit., p. 39.

is to acknowledge the inherent worth of the person or object concerned. There are a variety of contexts in which the word can be used, but Christian worship is different in kind from all other uses of it for this reason: all other uses arise from an assessment of the worthiness of the person, or thing. The subject of the worshipping decides, after due consideration on his own part, that the object can have his respect and praise. In Christian worship, however, there is no assessment, only acknowledgement. The Christian does not worship God because, all things considered, this seems a reasonable thing to do; he does not work out the respective claims of potential objects of worship and conclude that God's claims are strongest: *he worships God because He is God*. This is the first, and basic, hallmark of Christian worship: the acceptance by the worshipper of his status as creature, bending low before his Creator, without whom his very worship would be impossible for he would not be in existence. The Greek words indicate this status: 'proskunein' means literally to fall down, and 'latruein' to serve. The opening of the Te Deum expresses this thought perfectly: 'We praise Thee O God, we acknowledge Thee to be the Lord.' It is found in Romans where Paul writes: 'O the depth of the riches and wisdom and knowledge of God! How unsearchable are his judgements and how inscrutable his ways! ... I appeal to you, therefore, brethren, by the mercies of God, to present your bodies as a living sacrifice, holy and acceptable to God, which is your spiritual worship.'[26] The worship of God consequently must be undertaken as part of the natural order of life: the worshipper himself cannot avoid it. He worships, and not because he himself will be the better for worshipping, even though this may well be the result (because of this, the well-known definition of worship by William Temple, 'To worship is to quicken the conscience by the holiness of God ... to purge the imagination by the beauty of God . . .',[27] is totally inadequate). As Benoit says:

'The liturgical movement represents a reaction against a sentimental anthropocentric egotism. It does not pander to men's desires, or the special devotions of this or that individual or section. Its aim is to set the glory of God firmly in the centre once

26. Romans 12:1.   27. W. Temple, *The Hope of the World*, p. 30.

more. "The liturgy," writes Fr. Doncoeur, "has as its first and sovereign object the glory of God." Man is not in the centre of it, with his aspirations and his wants, his states of mind and his scruples.'[28]

If this were all that could be said, there might be little to distinguish Christian from Muslim worship. The Christian approach to God is coloured at all times by the knowledge of God which he has in Christ, and which becomes a personal awareness through the Holy Spirit. God is not just the Jahweh of Mount Sinai: He is a personal, loving being, who Himself has taken the initiative in bringing His people to an understanding of Himself. In the natural order of things man is a creature and God the Creator: the slave before the omnipotent. But God has made it quite clear that this relationship, factual though it is, will not be the mood or motive behind His dealings with men. Instead, all those who approach Him through His Son, who are thereby identified with Christ, receive the same treatment as the Son and are accepted in that status. 'For you did not receive the spirit of slavery to fall back into fear, but you have received the spirit of sonship. When we cry, "Abba! Father!" it is the Spirit himself bearing witness with our spirit that we are children of God, and if children, then heirs, heirs of God and fellow heirs with Christ.'[29] Consequently Christian worship is motivated not only by a sense of awe, but also of love; it takes place in and through the presence of Christ, who is the supreme revelation of love, revealing both the nature of the Father and the way for all those who are identified with Him to follow. 'Christ, as God incarnate, Immanuel, God with us, brings the presence of God into the world, and so must be the focus of our worship. It is in the presence of Christ in the midst of those who are gathered together in His Name that Christian worship takes place.'[30] We here see how Christian worship is fundamentally linked with the Christian life in the body of Christ; for the worship is that of the body, guided and inspired by the Head.

We may say, therefore, that worship is an act of praise and thanksgiving to God, offered by the representatives of the Mysti-

28. Benoit, op. cit., p. 111.   29. Romans 8:15–17a.
30. W. Nicholls, *Jacob's Ladder*, Lutterworth, 1958, p. 27.

cal Body of Christ in any one place. Other elements in worship follow from this. Because no group of human beings is worthy to make such an offering, there must be the expression of penitence as early as possible in the worship, followed by the assurance and acceptance of God's forgiveness. There must be the bringing before God of the needs of the world to which the worshippers belong, along with their own needs, in intercession and petition. There must be the expression of oblation and dedication, whereby the congregation manifests its reliance upon, and commitment to the God revealed in Christ. And running through all these as an expression of the fundamental mood of the worshippers is adoration. Benoit says:[31] 'Adoration disposes the heart to contemplation. Our contemplation is directed less towards the invisible God than to Jesus Christ who has revealed Him to us, and who in his humanity became one of us.'

From this definition of worship we can see how several principles or corollaries emerge.

I. WORSHIP IS OBJECTIVE

This follows logically from the expression of worship as acknowledging God to be God. The theme is 'Thou', not 'I', and even the 'we' is only incidental. This is reflected in the prayer of oblation: 'Here we offer and present *unto Thee*, O Lord, ourselves, our souls and bodies, to be a reasonable, holy, and living sacrifice *unto Thee*.'

In other words, the worshipper when entering a church building on a Sunday morning should be doing so with the sense of having a contribution to make, rather than with the thought of having an inspiring hour, with his feelings stirred. To treat the validity of worship as depending on the extent to which this happens to the worshipper is to surrender in the end to individual whim—and allows for the excuse that because a particular person does not 'feel' like worshipping he might just as well stay away. Subjectivism like this has its inherent shallowness in contrast to the words of one of the few great hymns of adoration: 'Lo, God is here: let us adore, And own how dreadful is this place.' The fact that few congregations

31. Benoit, op. cit., p. 63.

could enter into the spirit of that hymn indicates how subjective our worship is.[32]

Slightly different, but still a form of subjectivism, is the belief that 'koinonia' (Christian fellowship) is the aim of worship. One often sees notices outside a church building stating that 'this is a friendly church', but too often one finds that the friendliness has turned in on itself and a cliquish spirit has arisen which is a barrier to any stranger who may turn up. This is, of course, much more of a problem for the Free Churches who have always emphasized this spirit of friendship than for the other communions. It is worth recalling that 'koinonia' is not an end in itself: it is a bi-product of a community's sharing in a common task, whether worship or witness. The first attitude leaves the depth of the 'koinonia' too dependent on the feelings of the people concerned towards each other; whereas genuine 'koinonia' is possible even between people who are naturally antipathetic to each other. As a congregation offers itself in sacrifice to God, the sense of joy which springs from sharing in the common life of worship and witness is 'koinonia'—Christian fellowship. It is the consciously experienced blessing of the Holy Spirit on the corporate Church. But this is not found by members' looking at one another, but by their looking to God.

This point has, perhaps, been over-laboured. This is because lack of objectivity in worship is probably the greatest obstacle to the expression in Methodism of the Liturgical Movement's insights. Indeed, there are many other ways whereby our congregations consciously or otherwise make this objectivity difficult, such as their attitude to hymns or to the preachers. In the context of Roman Catholicism this would not seem so important an aspect of the Liturgical Movement's findings simply because, whatever else it may lack, the Mass does not militate against objectivity; quite the reverse. But in Methodism, as we shall see, our worship as we have received it makes this extremely difficult to achieve.

32. Cf. this advertisement in the *Methodist Recorder*, 26 October 1965: 'Coming on holiday to ————? ENJOY holiday worship at ———— Methodist Church —Plush tip-up seats—Real Methodist fellowship—Lively singing led by organ and piano—Evangelical preaching featuring "The Centralaires" close harmony Gospel Singers.' And Green Shield stamps too, no doubt.

II. WORSHIP IS A DIALOGUE: IT EXPRESSES
GOD'S INITIATIVE AND MAN'S RESPONSE

In *Worship and the Oneness of Christ's Church*, the Report of
Section IV of the Montreal Faith and Order Conference,
the section on 'The Nature of Christian Worship' states:

'In Christian worship, God comes to us in Christ through the
Holy Spirit, sustains us through His grace, establishes us in fellowship with Him and with one another, and empowers us for His
service in the world. In worship we come to God in Christ, the
True Worshipper, who by His incarnation, by His servanthood,
His obedience unto death, His resurrection and His ascension, has
made us participants in the worship which He offers. In Him,
truly God, we have access to the Father; in Him, truly Man, we
are restored to our true nature as worshippers of God.'[33]

This dialogue may be summarized as God's initiative and
man's response; it is expressive of the two-way relationship
between God and man which gives worship its fundamental
character. It is epitomized in the two parts of the Eucharist:
the Ministry of the Word, and the Ministry of the Upper
Room. The two are not rigidly separated into initiative and
response, but the distinction is clear. In the ministry of the
Word the congregation hears again the recounting of the mighty
deeds of God: His creation, providence, and whole purpose for
mankind, revealed in the ministry of Jesus. The first two of
these will be given utterance particularly in the psalms and Old
Testament lesson; the third in the Epistle and Gospel, which
will recount the coming and ministry of Jesus, His death and
the redemption won thereby for those committed to Him, His
Resurrection and the new life which is now possible in Him,
and his Ascension and present glory. The hymns and prayers of
praise and thanksgiving will at this part of the worship continue
to adumbrate this theme. This is one of the justifications for
continuing to worship at all: not that God cannot be enthroned
and glorified in the rest of daily life, in the world He made;
but such is the sin of man that this is rarely possible, either
consciously or unconsciously. And those occasions when it is
possible would become rarer if a group of people did not

33. *Studia Liturgica*, Vol. II, No. 4, December 1963, p. 244.

regularly meet to be reminded of all that God has done, and to make a symbolic response.

The link between the first part of the service with its emphasis on God's Acts, and the second with its stress on man's response, is the sermon. This should embrace both aspects: it should take one of the elements in God's plan of redemption and draw out its significance as the preacher understands it. But his sermon, if it is doing its job, will also turn to consider what this means in the lives of the congregation, what their response to this particular facet of God's nature and works should be. Their response is then symbolized in what follows in the worship. The response of faith is expressed in the Creed (though this may also be linked with the first part of the service, as it recounts God's mighty acts). Their response of sacrifice is made in the offertory (a sacrifice caught up in Christ's own). And of course the communion itself involves the response of love, and gratitude, and obedience.

This dialogue is not just two long monologues; within each section the dialogue is continuing; indeed in a sense there can be no response without initiative, or vice versa, so that at every point the two are present. Especially is this true at the actual moment of communion. But it does not seem too artificial to see each part of the service making one or the other particularly clear. Luther recognized this centuries ago when he said, 'The event which we call worship consists simply in this, that our well-beloved Lord Himself speaks to us by His Holy Word, and we, for our part, speak to Him by our prayers and our hymns of praise.'

The link between this point and the foregoing is clear, for the dialogue is not one between God and a group of isolated individuals but between God and the body, meeting together in the name of the Head. It is also worth mentioning here a point which will be considered at greater length in a later chapter; that although the Eucharist makes the dialogue especially clear, it is in no way obviated in an act of worship without communion —indeed, if that worship is to be valid (and in the Free Churches at least we must accept that this style of worship will be with us for a long time yet) then it *must* have this pattern. Benoit expresses it thus:

'This dialogue is communion. Behind the words of the dialogue there are living realities. God's Word is not mere discursive intellectual explanation intended to enlighten our minds; it is an act of God, a creative word, a sovereign *Fiat*. It is a word which breaks, which overthrows, which lays hold on man and calls into being that which does not exist. God's Word is inseparable from his grace; for the soul which hears it, it is the gift of grace. In its full sense, the Word of God is God himself communicating himself and giving himself to us.

'Man's reply to God is also a living word, a word that expresses realities, a word which is a giving of ourselves, so that the dialogue of worship becomes an effective encounter by the community with God, the community offering itself to God in its weakness and nakedness, and God coming to the community in self-giving power.'[34]

III. WORSHIP IS THE CORPORATE ACT OF THE WHOLE CONGREGATION

This, more than anything else, is the great truth about worship brought home to the Roman Catholic Church by the Liturgical Movement. It was one of the main points in the encyclical 'Mediator Dei'; and it springs logically from a genuine awareness of what it is to be part of a body, rather than one of a number of isolated individuals meeting together for momentary inspiration.

It does not need a Protestant to point out what has appeared to be a grave weakness in Roman worship, the fact that many of the worshippers seem to be little more than spectators (and not always attentive ones at that) observing the priest performing the objective sacrifice of the Mass: many Roman Catholics are themselves quite aware of this. However, having a Roman Catholic wife has given one more opportunities to witness this than would otherwise have happened: large numbers of the congregation (particularly in Ireland) waiting outside the Church until the ministry of the Word is over; gross inattentiveness during the service (a woman suckling a child during the Epiclesis seemed startling at the time, but on reflection was not so irreverent as the blasé attitude of many others); the majority of the congregation leaving immediately after communion, so that the reading of the Johannine Prologue (now

34. Benoit, op. cit., p. 59f.

unfortunately fallen into disuse) was done to a small minority of the congregation. Above all there was the obviously prevalent attitude in the minds of many that the whole thing was rather like queuing at the post office for one's weekly pension; rather a bore but one cannot manage without it.

This describes the worst types of Roman congregational attitudes. Elsewhere, particularly in France, Belgium, and Germany, the influence of the Movement is already beginning to be quite manifest. Pope Pius himself declared in his encyclical: 'The people must take part in the Eucharistic sacrifice not passively or negligently or with a distracted mind, but with such active devotion as to be in the closest union with the High Priest . . . with him to surrender themselves.'[35] He urged them to realize that, although this was the sacrifice of Christ that they were contemplating, they must mystically die with Him in the Mass; they were to be crucified with Him.

How in practice did the Church of Rome set about restoring this corporate nature of worship? First, by the position of the priest during the Mass: instead of facing the Holy Table with his back to the congregation, apart from an occasional glance, in many places the eastern or 'basilican' position was restored (restored because it was the earliest practice of the Church). Automatically, this practice makes the Holy Table less of an altar and the whole communion more of a family meal, with the members of the family gathering around. This is not normally done by moving out the High Altar—at any rate in the Roman Church. Instead—and one has seen many examples of this in France—a second Table is placed more in the body of the congregation, so that the High Altar falls into disuse. (In one church in Rheims the High Altar was so covered in dust as to indicate complete disuse over a long period.) This restoration of the basilican position was, of course, not just motivated by antiquarian ideas. The aim was to make participation in the sacrament a living and real experience for all the worshippers.

Not unnaturally, these practices did not go uncriticized. Paul Claudel, who revealed in his poetry a profound understanding of symbolism and Biblical imagery, and a deep

35. Quoted in Benoit, op. cit., p. 72.

awareness of the meaning of the Cross for the world, reacted violently and described it as 'the Mass back to front'. In an article with this title he wrote:

'The new liturgy detracts from the dignity and rights of Christian people. It is no longer the people saying the Mass with the priest . . . all we have is a curious crowd watching the priest at his work. Unbelievers may very well compare him to a juggler performing his act in front of a politely amazed audience.'[36]

It is clear from this that Claudel never visited Taizé! Had he done so, he, with his absolute honesty, must have been arrested by the utter reverence of the Eucharist there, with the celebrant facing the people. His objections to the transformation of the altar with its liturgical ornaments into a simple table might also have been overcome. The simplicity of that table, bare but for the essential vessels, in no way hides from the congregation that it is, above all, a *holy* table. Perhaps it was the suddenness of the change, with its stark and immediate contrast with previous practice, which caused his strong reaction. One can appreciate how to people with a colourful imagination like his it must have seemed that the mystery of the sacrament was simply being dispelled. One of the insights which the Liturgical Movement is bringing home to those with this mentality is that the mystery does not need to be artificially created by elaborate structures. There have been many communion services in people's homes where the mystery has been manifest.

A second way in which the attempt is being made to help congregations to participate more positively in the Mass is by the use of the vernacular. Since the end of the Second Vatican Council this has gone ahead with considerable speed. The objections to it from Roman Catholics are interestingly enough similar to Protestant objections to modern versions of the Bible —that it is bringing the world of the sacred far too much into that of the common. But since the language Jesus spoke, during His ministry and at the Last Supper, was the common language of the day, this argument can hardly be sustained.

A more valid objection is that by allowing each nation to use its vernacular in the Mass the Church's sense of unity will suffer, for hitherto the use of Latin, though a dead language, has

36. In *Figaro Littéraire*, 29 January 1955; quoted in Benoit, op. cit., p. 83.

been universal in the Roman Church. One of the great difficulties facing English-speaking Catholic liturgiologists is that even in English the Mass is not necessarily going to be uniform throughout the English-speaking world. Thought-forms and structures which are acceptable to the English will not always suit the Americans or Australians. However, since the Latin would continue to be strange to almost all participants, and since the majority of worshippers in, for example, a German Church are likely to be German, this argument also cannot be maintained. The result is that today, even in English Roman churches, most of the Mass is in the vernacular, with only some of the great historic parts like the Kyrie and the Sanctus remaining in the original Greek or Latin.

Another practice which is being increasingly encouraged (arising naturally from the encyclical) is the communion of the laity. It comes as a surprise to many Protestants to realize that until quite recently the majority of Roman Catholics have not been likely to actually take communion any more frequently than themselves. Alongside this (and paralleled in the Church of England) has gone the desire to have real bread rather than wafers. (It always seems strangely illogical to Free Churchmen that Anglicans who insist—justifiably—on having genuine wine rather than the non-alcoholic grape juice specially concocted by the Free Churches to salve total abstinence principles, should specially concoct these unnatural wafers.) There are even some in the Church of Rome who are seeking to introduce communion in both kinds for the laity. It is too soon yet for this to happen, but it is clear that alongside the doctrine of the Mass as a sacrifice is growing that aspect of it which is a family meal.

In general, the attempt is being made to give members of the congregation more awareness that while the only essential person to be present at a Eucharist is the priest, the presence of a vocal, actively participating congregation is almost equally desirable. So the offertory procession has been introduced (which would be a startling innovation to many Free Churchmen); private masses are playing an increasingly diminishing part in the worshipping life of the Church; and, in a unique manifestation of the influence of the Liturgical

Movement, the new liturgy for Holy Week makes tremendous demands on the congregation as well as the priest. To the Free Churches all this is all the more remarkable because it is occurring in a Church which many had come to believe was quite immovable, unchangeable in both its theology and its worship. Such a judgement had, it seems, discounted the Holy Spirit.

This desire for corporateness in worship has been evinced in other communions too. We have referred to the Parish Communion. There are still many changes which could be made in this which could make for a greater sense of all participating at every point (which will not happen until the Book of Common Prayer is drastically revised). But the Parish breakfast which often follows the Eucharist is a clear sign that the traditional reserve among Anglicans, amounting to what seemed to some Free Churchmen an indifference towards each other, is breaking down.

There seems little doubt that the Church in general is becoming increasingly aware that being 'in Christ' involves not just a personal experience, but also being incorporated into a worshipping community. The World Council of Churches' Report, *Ways of Worship*, puts it more strongly: 'There is a growing sense that worship is not to be thought of as a gathering of individual pious Christians but as a corporate act in direct relation to the Lord of the Church.'[37] It was not for nothing that Jesus taught His disciples to pray, '*Our* Father'.

IV. WORSHIP ON EARTH IS LINKED WITH WORSHIP IN HEAVEN

Congregations of all communions rise week by week to declare: 'I believe . . . in the Communion of Saints'; it is only in very recent years that the meaning of this has been enunciated in a way that is helpful to the average congregation.

Yet it has always been present in the New Testament. First, and basic, is the picture of Jesus given in the letter to the Hebrews: the risen and exalted Son, our great High Priest, who has passed through the veil and entered *the* Holy of Holies, which is Heaven itself, where He remains the Mediator of the

37. *Ways of Worship*, p. 21.

New Covenant.[38] The author sees the link between the Christ who has gone before—'prodromos'—and the people who worship in His name in Heaven, and those who are still running the 'race set before (them)'.

We have already seen how the Book of Revelation expresses this thought, and pursues it further. In chapter 14: 1–3 it gives a picture of heavenly worship, where the Lamb has with Him the 144,000 'who had his name and his Father's name written on their foreheads'. This, as Hebert has pointed out, refers the reader back to chapter 7:2–3, where the angel proclaims that Judgement cannot begin before God's servants have been sealed on their foreheads.[39] Chapter 7 then proceeds to speak of the 144,000 who constitute the Church Militant on earth; and clearly they are the same group as those described in chapter 14, except that now they have come through the 'great ordeal'. But it seems clear that the author of the Apocalypse was indicating that there was an essential link between the 144,000 and those who would 'Believe through them'.[40] The link is Christ who even in the heavenly congregation and when standing before the throne of God is still the Lamb as it had been slain (Revelation 5:6).

'Though exalted into heaven, Christ remains the One who had sacrificed Himself to redeem mankind. In the imagery of the final consummation (Revelation 21f) the Lamb is the bridegroom of the people of God (21:9), and likewise the Lamb, i.e. the Christ of Calvary, is, together with God Almighty, "the Temple" (21:22; 22:3), . . . Thus, the heavenly Christ is and will always be the Christ of the Cross and Resurrection.'[41]

From this, two things follow. First, worship which remains earthbound, limiting its sights to Christ as He lived on earth, is not genuine Christian worship for it does not penetrate to the liturgy of heaven. Christian worship is only possible through the death *and victory* of Christ, now exalted and enthroned in Heaven, and it should never lose sight of this. It needs no

38 Hebrews 9:5.
39. A. G. Hebert, 'Liturgical Prayer'; in *Studia Liturgica*, Vol. II, No. 3, September 1963, p. 163f.
40. Cf. H. Riesenfeld, 'Worship and the Cross and Resurrection of Christ', *Studia Liturgica*, Vol. II, No. 2, June 1963, p. 100.
41. Riesenfeld, op. cit., p. 106.

artificial atmosphere or liturgical gimmicks to make this manifest in worship; the liturgy must convey this *per se*, just as the meaning of the Cross must come home to the mind of any Christian worshipper without his necessarily having a Cross before him as a symbol. We shall follow out the implication of this in the next subsection.

Second, the Apocalypse suggests that Christian worship is only possible through passing through the great ordeal. Many who have lived their lives in tribulation—from the early martyrs to the victims of Nazism in this century (and no doubt many of those in Eastern Europe today)—will testify to the intensifying of the spirit of worship which takes place in such circumstances. But it is not the fault of multitudes of worshippers in the western world that they do not live in such conditions. What is their great ordeal? The answer emerges from the liturgy: their ordeal is to share Christ's sacrifice. His sufferings must symbolically be their sufferings, His crucifixion theirs. The cup He drank they also must drink. This is the theme which Pope Pius XII enunciated so clearly in 'Mediator Dei'. Whether or not he would have accepted this exegesis is irrelevant: but he would no doubt have pointed out the obvious link between the lack of any sense, among the majority of modern worshippers, of sharing the great ordeal, and their lack of genuine spirituality and strength of witness.

It is because of what we have said about sharing in Christ's ordeal, so that we may also share His victory, that Fr. Hebert[42] argues that the central festival of the Church's year is the night of Easter Eve, when the congregation are surrounded with the symbolism of light, but hear again and, if they will, enter into the experience of their redemption, the 'Christian Exodus from Egypt'. 'All this is enacted in liturgy that it may be lived out in the daily life of the believing community which is called to be God's witness in the world.'[43] We may note here, though strictly it applies to a later subsection, that the condemnation of those who worship the beast and its image, contained in Revelation: 14:9–11, is the first suggestion in the Apocalypse

42. Hebert, op. cit., pp. 164 and 165.
43. Hebert, op. cit., p. 165; cf. *Liturgy and Society*, pp. 59 and 66.

that there will be nothing but judgement on those who try to maintain their worship in isolation from the world and its needs. This is adumbrated further in the city imagery of chapter 19, where worship has become life itself (how far removed is this thought from Temple's definition! And how far removed is it from any ideas of worship as the 'highest thing we do'!). This leads to the further reflection (unrelated though it is to the field of this study) that perfect worship will be possible only when God's will has been accomplished for all who will be saved. And then worship in the conventional sense will no longer be necessary; for all life, all being, all existence, will be praise.

V. THE ESSENTIAL MOOD OF WORSHIP IS JOY

This follows from the previous thought. It is unfortunate that traditional worship in the Western world has lacked this mood. The reason for this is clear: our worship has over-emphasized the earthly ministry of Christ, concluding with, and reaching its consummation in, His death: it has not stressed with anything like enough frequency or clarity the Resurrection and Ascension, with their concentration on Christ's present enthronement and glory, and the link He thereby forms between earth and heaven. The Eastern Church has not so neglected this aspect of the faith; and the consequence is, or so it appears after attending the Eastern liturgy only once, that there is a stronger mood of joy, born of this emphasis on light and victory. It is not just coincidence that the period in which the Western Church is beginning to realize that it has concentrated too much of its devotion on the Cross, and not enough on what followed Christ's death, has gone hand in hand with a rediscovery of the earliest liturgies, and a growing link with the Eastern Church.

Perhaps this is over-simplifying. But to anyone reared on the Book of Common Prayer it must be intensely difficult to escape from the mood of sin, penitence, and atonement. How much longer are twentieth-century Anglicans, who share with their contemporaries in other communions and beyond an extremely slight sense of guilt, to continue to accept a liturgy which seems incapable of escaping from this sense and—even worse—of accepting the fact that God actually does forgive? Why should we have Cranmer's guilt complex cast on us week by week? How long will congregations endure an unnatural and unnecessary ordeal: standing up for the last communal act of the Eucharist and again, in words similar to those used at the beginning of the Liturgy of the Upper Room, begging for mercy? In the Taizé Eucharist confession is put in its proper place: outside the church before the main liturgy begins.

Perhaps through the impact of this element in the Liturgical Movement congregations will be encouraged to sing the hymns of joy and victory, rather than the morbid products of guilt-ridden Victorians. Even the best of this type of hymn, written much earlier and by a man different in kind from the Victorians, 'When I survey the wondrous Cross', does not fit the ethos of our time. Any attempt to produce this feeling of guilt must be adjudged artificial—though artificial ways such as those adopted by Billy Graham are the only ways likely to bring this about.

Probably it is expecting too much to imagine that just singing Easter hymns will alone bring back the mood of joy. Benoit suggests that it springs rather from the realization of the communal character of the Church. Whatever is the reason, the fact remains that in the various types of liturgical experiment undertaken since the first days of the movement there has been this mood of joy and vitality embodied in the liturgy; which is one cause of the movement's popularity. In any case, it is only a false approach—or an insincere one—to the Cross which views this as purely tragic. Benoit writes:

'The memory of death and the joy of thanksgiving are by no means irreconcilable. The primitive Supper could very well contain that note of joy and gladness to which these Historians' (those who see two types of Eucharist in the New Testament—one of joy based on Easter and one of sorrow based on Paul) 'are pleased to point, although it also recalled the Lord's death: indeed, just because it recalled his death. It is only when faith becomes weak, and is replaced by a false sentimentality, that the theme of the Passion, instead of awakening grateful joy in the heart, becomes a funereal theme.'[44]

44. Benoit, op. cit., p. 65.

61

Perhaps if this sense of joy could be recaptured in our weekly worship the number of those who turn up once but never again might begin to be replaced by those who find within the Christian community a vitality which, in this country at least, seems sadly lacking in the community at large. And then the worship would be an act of witness in itself.

VI. WORSHIP MUST BE RELATED, OR RELEVANT

This point is really concerned with the relationship between worship and witness, which will be treated later as a section on its own. At this stage there are three things to be said.

1. *It must be related to the congregation*

Clearly there is, and will continue to be, a basic liturgy for all congregations. But already it is becoming clear that within the liturgy there is room, and need, for alterations of emphasis to suit the situations and needs of particular communities. The use of the vernacular in the Roman rite is evidence of the realization of this need; the use of modern versions of the Bible another. An imaginative use of prayers of intercession is an obvious way in which this can be—and is being—achieved. Prayers concerning people and situations related to the congregation can make them feel that they have a growing part to contribute to the liturgy. (We shall ask in our final chapter to what extent this can be taken: do we, for instance, look for new forms of liturgy relevant to house worship, or worship in factories?)

2. *It must be related to worship in other communions*

The fact that this is becoming increasingly manifest—in, for example, the use by 'Prayer Book' Churches of extemporary forms of prayer, and vice versa—is one of the most important practical results of the Liturgical Movement. Worship needs to comprise the best in all traditions, and because the movement has resulted in scholars of the different communions' studying as never before the liturgy of other communions than their own, the cause of ecumenicity is being served. Max Thurian expresses this point thus:

'The liturgical movement has brought out the ecumenical character of worship, in the sense that all liturgy should unite us with the Church in all times and places. That does not mean statism or uniformity in the liturgy. The liturgy can and must be adapted to circumstances, while remaining true to the basic structures. The liturgy may create an ecumenical unity of the Churches everywhere, in the diversity of rites which manifest the integration of the basic structures in the different cultures.'[45]

3. *Related to the world*

This will be considered in some detail later in this chapter. At this point our only concern is the effect this has on Christian worship—ideally, if not always in practice. The basic idea is that when a company of Christians meet together to celebrate the Eucharist, they do so not as those who would escape from the world and their commitments in it, but as people who seek a deeper meaning for what they do through the ministry of the liturgy. They do not come to worship in order to escape from the world: rather the worship becomes a piece of prophetic symbolism, an eschatological event, in which the world as it might be under the total sovereignty of God is revealed. To this extent, the more completely the worshippers are caught up in their worship with Christ's sacrifice and triumph, the more, paradoxically enough, what they do is related to the world beyond the church's walls. Clearly, there are parts of the liturgy —like the sermon or the intercessions—where this relationship is explicit. But far more significant is the fact that the world which God made and loves is implicit—and a motivating factor—in the entire Eucharist.

Worship, we may finally add, is thus seen to be related to the entire personality—to the feelings, the mind, and the will. There has always been the tendency to cater for one of these in particular and to neglect the others as a result. There have been Churches which aimed primarily to stir up the emotions in their worship, with 'conversion' as the ultimate aim; others have concentrated on being intellectual in their worship, with the aim of appearing reasonable to society as a whole; still

45. Max Thurian, 'The Present Aims of the Liturgical Movement', *Studia Liturgica*, Vol. III, No. 2, Autumn 1964, p. 112.

others have made the *raison d'être* in their worship the 'Social Gospel' to which the members were bidden to apply themselves with vigour during the period before next meeting together. It is clear that the most perfect worship will meet all these needs: the congregation's emotions will be caught up in an intelligent appraisal of what Christ has done, so that they will be encouraged to play their part as His witnesses in the world. Worship does not deal with part of man, or an imitation man, or even imaginary man: it is for man as he is, and the extent to which man can worship in the context of a particular liturgy brings a judgement both on the man and on the liturgy.

(c) The Meaning and Centrality of the Eucharist

I. WHY HAVE A SACRAMENT AT ALL?

There are branches of the Christian Church—though not many of them—which cannot accept that there is any need for sacraments in the life of the Church. William Booth removed the Eucharist from Salvation Army worship for two reasons: first, because he saw that it was at the Lord's Table that many of the most deep-rooted divisions between the various denominations were most clearly manifest; and secondly because he found that the alcoholic wine often rekindled a taste for alcohol among ex-alcoholics who had been converted by his ministry. The Quaker objection is a more theological one—the 'scandal of the particular'. They believe that whatever the Eucharist may be taken to mean is—or can be ideally—equally true of every other facet of life. The unity before God of 'all sorts and conditions of men' is true everywhere, not only at the Lord's Table; the presence of Christ in the Body is true everywhere; the atoning power of the love of God as revealed in Christ is everywhere, whether the sacrament is observed or not. Thus, they state, every meal can be a communion meal, the whole of life an acceptance of the Lordship of Christ leading to the rendering of oneself in sacrificial obedience to Almighty God.

There is an easy answer to this, which leads on to a more important point related to the theology of a sacrament. This is the simple recognition that ideally what they say is true. In terms of baptism, for instance, God is not limited by the sacrament: a child can be recognized as a child of God even if he has not been sprinkled by the water. Unfortunately, such is the human condition that what is theoretically true is not always—some would say is seldom—realizable in the daily situations of life. Every meal can be a communion: but how often do families manage to bear this in mind at meal-time (even Quaker families)? Christ is Lord over all personal relationships and the uniter of all races, nationalities, ages, sexes, and classes: but in how many of life's encounters can this possibly always be expressed? When the Kingdom of God is finally established among men there will be no need to state these truths: they will be experienced as an established fact. Then all sacraments—and no doubt worship in any way isolated from daily life—may be dispensed with. But until then, man is so made that unless he puts aside certain times and places to bring himself face to face once more with the 'ground of his being' he is likely to lose sight of many of the truths which are declared and made real on those specialized occasions. The Eucharist, and Baptism, are dramatic expressions in time and at a certain place of what is ideally true everywhere all the time. But experience demonstrates that the second will never be fully comprehended unless the first is faithfully observed.

Reference to 'the scandal of the particular' leads on to the basic point about sacraments; that they exist because man, however 'spiritually-minded' he may be, is at root a physical being in the sense that it is through material things that the spiritual is made known. This is true, for instance, in the sphere of friendship which is possible between two people without the necessity for either to *smile* at the other. But it is the smile of welcome or understanding which conveys the fact of the friendship from one to the other. (The same is true of the sexual side of marriage.) What distinguishes the Christian Faith from all other religions is that it alone recognizes this truth: and it is epitomized in the incarnational teaching of Christianity.

'The Word became *flesh*'—here is the basic answer to those who doubt the desirability of having sacraments. If the above Quaker argument is true, should it not be equally true that the incarnation was unnecessary because everything which this conveyed could be apprehended 'spiritually'—that mankind in its sinful condition can be instinctively (or by the operation of the Spirit of God) aware of this state? In the same way man could know and accept the forgiveness of God, and live a triumphant and joyful life in the glad assurance that God is with him and will remain so throughout eternity. Fortunately God understood human nature better than some human beings seem to understand it themselves. It may be too bald to declare, 'He died that we might be forgiven'—as though God only became a forgiving God after the Incarnation; but this is surely only poetic licence (or the demands of the metre) for, 'He died that we might *know* we are forgiven'. In the Old Testament writings (and in the writings of contemporary religions) the hope, sometimes amounting to the expectance, of forgiveness emerges; there is never, and in man's present state in this way never can be, the certainty of it. In this sense it is not too bold a thought to describe Christ Himself as the one sacrament, from whom all other sacraments take their validity and efficacy. He became flesh, and ministered to men, and died and rose again in order to reveal, at one point in time and in one place, what could be true everywhere always but which faithless man would —or could—never accept short of seeing it for himself. The demand of Thomas to see and feel the wounds of Christ is not so unreasonable: and in the Eucharist his wish—and that of all those who feel like him—can be fulfilled.

One may add here one final thought. While it is not our purpose to consider in detail the validity of our Lord's words, 'Do this . . .', whatever answer be reached (and Jeremias[46] has given strong reasons for accepting that these words reveal His intention) there can be no question that within a few years of those words being spoken the Church was interpreting them to mean meeting regularly and celebrating the sacrament. Considering that this command, along with the Shema, repre-

46. J. Jeremias, op. cit., discusses the objection that the command 'Do this' is found only in Paul and Luke (and here it is said only over the bread). He argues that as far as the other Evangelists were concerned there was no need to repeat the command, because it was being fulfilled in every celebration in the early Church. He quotes the words of Benoit: 'On ne récite pas une rubrique, on l'exécute.'

sent the only two direct charges by Jesus on His followers, it is not to be wondered at that the main branches of the Church have continued to observe the Eucharist for two thousand years.

Unfortunately, they have not always appreciated its true meaning; and it is one of the gifts of the Liturgical Movement that this is in the process of being rediscovered in our own time.

II. THE SIGNIFICANCE OF THE EUCHARIST

The clearest outline of this in modern times has been given by one of the great Protestant pioneers of the Liturgical Movement, Archbishop Brilioth of Sweden.[47] An indication of the importance of his writings is offered in the way Louis Bouyer, though a Roman Catholic, quotes Brilioth with approval. We shall therefore use Brilioth's five suggestions about the Eucharist as the basis of this section.

1. *The Eucharist as a Thanksgiving*

This is of course the meaning of the word eucharist (used interchangeably in the Gospels with 'eulogein', to bless). Although not found so starkly in the New Testament, by the second century 'eucharist' had become the name regularly used for the rite. In time, as the note of sacrifice came into increasing prominence, this custom ceased. Brilioth summarizes the process thus:

'It is one of the tragedies of the history of the liturgy that the ancient order of the eucharistic prayer was lost; the canon of the Latin mass laid the whole emphasis on the sacrificial idea. And when the Lutheran Reformation condemned the false popular conception of the eucharistic sacrifice, it failed to restore the act of thanksgiving in its true proportions. . . . Praise and thanksgiving were left chiefly to the ante-communion service. . . .

'It must be a primary object of the liturgical revival of our own day to recover the objective expression of corporate faith and worship in the service whose name means the *Thanksgiving*. The eucharist must take its place as the central act of congregational praise.'[48]

47. Y. Brilioth, *Eucharistic Faith and Practice, Evangelical and Catholic*, S.P.C.K., 1930.
48. Brilioth, op. cit., p. 278.

Earlier Brilioth had[49] quoted Bishop Gore as saying: 'Early canons suggest that a Christian eucharist in the first age must have frequently resembled a modern harvest thanksgiving.'[50] The Clementine liturgy, for instance, includes the chant, 'One is holy, one Lord Jesus Christ, to the glory of God the Father, who is blessed for ever,' followed by the Gloria in Excelsis, the Benedictus, and the Hosanna, with prayers of thanksgiving after communion.

In the sacrament, the bread and wine typify all created things, for which the congregation must be thankful to God. They also typify the divine condescension of God, who came into the world of the physical that all men might be saved. Bouyer reminds us of the extent of man's grounds for thanksgiving:

'It is a thanksgiving to God for all His gifts, including in one view the whole of creation and redemption. . . . But this element of thanksgiving, the jubilant acknowledgment that everything is a grace, and that the grace of God is marvellous . . . pervades the whole Eucharistic service. . . . In conjunction with the Christian sacrifice, (it) is, in a still deeper sense, a new attitude of man, as he stands before God in the Church, an attitude which springs from the exultant faith which receives and drinks in the divine agape as it flows from its source in the Holy Spirit.'[51]

It is an indication of the widespread effect of the Liturgical Movement that in most, if not all, of the major modern experiments in the liturgy, the great Prayer of Thanksgiving is, even among traditions where this element has not previously been conspicuous, being restored to its rightful place at the heart of the liturgy. This is true for the Liturgy of the Church of South India; of the Experimental Liturgy; of the Taizé Eucharist; and of the American Lutheran 'Service Book and Hymnal'. One 'invariable preface' suggested for the Anglican rite may be quoted here, simply because it not only includes thanksgiving for the death of Christ but includes material from the Prayer Book prefaces for Christmas, Easter, and Ascension Day, and also a reference to the creation:

49. Op. cit., p. 26.　　50. Gore, *The Body of Christ*, p. 172.
51. Bouyer, op. cit., p. 78.

'It is very meet, right, and our bounden duty, that we should at all times and in all places give thanks unto Thee, O Lord, Holy Father, Almighty, Everlasting God, Creator of all things visible and invisible;

'Because Thou didst give Jesus Christ Thine only Son to be born for our salvation; who, by the operation of the Holy Ghost, was made very man of the substance of the Virgin Mary his mother; and that without spot of sin, to make us clean from all sin;

'For he is the very Paschal Lamb, which was offered for us, and hath taken away the sin of the world; who by his death hath destroyed death, and by his rising to life again hath restored to us everlasting life;

'And hath ascended up into heaven to prepare a place for us; that where he is, thither we might also ascend, and reign with him in glory;

'Therefore with Angels and Archangels, and with all the company of heaven, we laud and magnify thy glorious Name; evermore praising thee and saying, Holy, holy, holy . . . etc.'[52]

2. *The Eucharist as a Memorial*

It is at this point that the inadequacies of the English language are revealed. Whether, in translating 'anamnesis', we use the word memorial, or commemoration, or recalling, or recollection, the English word and its associations must inevitably lead to misunderstanding. It led Zwingli's successors to view the service as little more than a remembrance of One who had once lived among men, and should be constantly remembered lest His words and deeds, with their resultant impact on the human race, should be forgotten. It is this antonym—to forget—which epitomizes the main problem. It suggests that if the Eucharist were not constantly celebrated, with its dramatic repetition of Jesus' acts at the Last Supper (and to repeat an event with its actions is a penetrating way of enforcing the point, as the Masonic ritual illustrates) it would be forgotten who Jesus was.

But this is too shallow an interpretation of the word. A brilliant exegesis of it is given by Max Thurian.[53] He points out that the word 'mneia' is used only in the Pauline Epistles, and six times out of seven is connected with prayer. In four

52. S. M. Gibbard, 'Liturgy as Proclamation of the Word'; *Studia Liturgica*, Vol. I, No. 1, March 1962, p. 20.
53. Max Thurian, *The Eucharistic Memorial*, Part 2, Lutterworth, 1961, pp. 30–32.

of the seven it is accompanied by the verb 'poieo', to make; and in five of them the remembrance is made within the context of thanksgiving. Typical of the passages is Philemon 4f: 'I thank my God always when I remember you in my prayers, because I hear of your love and of the faith which you have toward the Lord Jesus and all the saints.'[54] Thurian concludes from these passages:

'In all these passages "remembrance" is conceived to be an act of prayer before God and in particular a thanksgiving. In all instances St. Paul "makes remembrance" of the faithful before God in his prayer or thanksgiving. The word "remembrance" therefore in these passages has not just the subjective sense of "recollection", it does signify an objective action consisting of placing in prayer before God the remembrance of those for whom one prays and gives thanks. This is close to the idea of the memorial, *mneia* being a derivative which has preserved a quasi-liturgical meaning, for "remembrance" in the prayers of St. Paul is a recollection which becomes a memorial before God. . . .'[55]

Referring to 1 Thessalonians 1:2f, Thurian says:

'The activity, labour and constancy of this church became the content of the memorial to the apostles before God; they form the content of their prayer of thanksgiving. But if this "work" can be presented in a prayer of thanksgiving before God, it is not because it has a value or a merit of its own. It is the work of Christ himself in the church at Thessalonica or the work of the Thessalonians in Christ, and this can be a legitimate and acceptable offering in thanksgiving to God.'[56]

Thurian concludes by quoting from the Didache:[57] 'Remember, O Lord, Thy Church, to deliver her from all evil, and to perfect her in Thy love, and gather together from the four winds her that is sanctified into Thy Kingdom which Thou didst prepare for her.' His conclusion[58] we can take as definitive: 'For Christians "to remember" or "to make remembrance" is the equivalent of "to pray", and, for God, it is the equivalent of "to hear, to grant, to show mercy".'

The Eucharistic memorial is clearly the memorial of the Cross, and the whole redemptive purpose and power of God which was revealed thereby to mankind. But the Cross cannot

54. Cf. Romans 1:9; Ephesians 1:16; Philippians 1:3; 1 Thessalonians 1:2; 2 Timothy 1:3.
55. Op. cit., p. 31.   56. Thurian, op. cit., p. 32.
57. Op. cit., p. 33; Didache 10, 5.   58. Op. cit., p. 33.

be seen in isolation from what preceded it, and followed it. It includes, as Bouyer points out,[59] the sacrifice of Abel, and of Melchizedech; and the offering of Abraham, and beyond them the whole history of God's People. It includes the Resurrection and Ascension, with their resultant outpouring of the Holy Spirit, the formation and building up of the Church, and the eschatological hope of the consummation of all things in the divine love. 'In this way, we can understand the apparent strangeness of some ancient liturgies which make the anamnesis not only of Christ's sitting at the right hand of the Father, but also of His coming again to judge the living and the dead, just as St. Paul speaks of us as already risen again and seated in heaven with our Lord.'[60]

It is this aspect of the Eucharist in particular which demonstrates the link between the Word and the Meal. The Scriptures recall the divine plan for mankind, from Creation to Judgement. It is significant that the Liturgical Movement has brought about in the Roman Church a much greater emphasis on the authority of the Bible than was previously found: and that in the non-Roman Churches it has induced a growing awareness that the fulness of the divine plan cannot be found in the New Testament alone; consequently in the modern liturgies—as opposed to many of the earlier ones—provision is made for the reading of three, rather than two, lessons. Brilioth states:

'It is necessary to emphasize the inestimable value of the preservation of Scripture-lessons in the Christian liturgy. The remains of the rational and didactic service of the synagogue stood in the Christian service side by side with the sacramental mystery. So long as this was the case, Christian piety could never quite slip its moorings in Scripture.'[61]

It is remarkable to read these words by a Roman Catholic:

'The meal needs the readings to point out to us the way to see it aright, not as a separate event of today, but understandable only in reference to a decisive action accomplished once and for all in the past. . . . The whole Mass is a single liturgy of the Word, Who began by speaking to man; Who continued speaking to him more and more intimately; Who finally spoke to him more

59. Bouyer, op. cit., p. 78. 60. Op. cit., p. 79.
61. Brilioth, op. cit., p. 38.

directly as the Word-made-flesh; and Who now speaks from the very heart of man himself to God the Father through the Spirit.'[62]

We may add—and we shall concern ourselves at greater length with this in the next section—that the following of the Church Year was another way, in addition to the Liturgy itself and the Scripture readings, whereby the full memorial was maintained in the life of the Church.

Among the various modern liturgies, it is perhaps not surprising to find the Memorial most clearly enunciated in that for which Max Thurian was himself primarily responsible, the Taizé Eucharist:

'Wherefore, O Lord, we make before Thee Thy Memorial of the Incarnation and the Passion of Thy Son, His Resurrection from His sojourn with the dead, His Ascension into glory in the heavens, His perpetual intercession for us; we await and pray for His return.

'All things come of Thee and our only offering is to recall Thy gifts and marvellous works.

'Moreover we present to Thee, O Lord of Glory, as our thanksgiving and intercession, the signs of the eternal sacrifice of Christ, unique and perfect, living and holy, the bread of life which cometh down from heaven and the cup of the feast in Thy Kingdom.

'In Thy love and mercy accept our praise and our prayers in Christ, as Thou wast pleased to accept the gifts of Thy servant Abel the righteous, the sacrifices of our father Abraham, and of Melchizedek, Thy high priest.'[63]

3. *Eucharist as Communion*

(Communion with fellow-Christians)

We saw in an earlier chapter how the Lord's Supper originated in the early Church as a shared meal—as the title 'breaking of bread' (Acts 2:42) suggests; this is not in any way weakened by the suggestion of some scholars[64] that from the start there was only a symbolic meal. To the Jews, a common meal was the supreme way in which people identified themselves with each other—hence the uproar because Jesus 'ate and drank with publicans and sinners'. If, as has been suggested, the earliest communion services were in fact in remembrance of the common meals the disciples had shared with their Risen Lord,

62. Bouyer, op. cit., p. 79.
63. *Eucharist at Taizé*, Faith Press, 1962, p. 47f.
64. Cf. the reference made by Brilioth, op. cit., p. 28, note 1, to Batiffol, *Études d'histoire et de théologie positive*, II, p. 157.

the point is further substantiated. Testimony to the strength of this thought is given in I Corinthians 10:17: 'Because there is one loaf, we who are many are one body, for we all partake of the same loaf.' This has its parallel in the prayer of the Didache already quoted.

One of the great miracles of the early Church was the way people who in society generally were completely divided from each other—master and slave, Jew and Greek, male and female —were united at the Lord's Table. Thus did the communion meal become a piece of prophetic symbolism—a dramatic foretelling in miniature of the Kingdom of God in all its fulness.

This emphasizes what the Free Churches today need to be constantly reminded of: that the relationship between the worshipper and his Lord is not just a matter of personal faith and experience. The koinonia means communion with other people in a common partaking of the same gifts. Bouyer, in what is otherwise an inadequate assessment of this aspect of the Eucharist, puts this point admirably:

'This use of the word combines the two different meanings of the Latin phrase "communio sanctorum" and explains each by the other: that is "communio sanctorum" (taking sanctorum in the masculine) as meaning the communion among the saints, which is brought about by "communio sanctorum" (taking sanctorum in the neuter), that is, communion *in* the holy things. Thus, the element of "Communion" means that the Eucharist is a meal, a community meal, in which all the participants are brought together to have a common share in common goods, these common goods being first of all the bread and wine of a real human meal, whatever their deeper significance.'[65]

If this were more completely understood among the Free Churches, there would be less of the unfortunate practice whereby the sacrament—or a garbled version of it—is held as an optional extra after the 'main' service. We are seeing the results of the growing understanding of this aspect of the meal in the increasing emphasis in the Roman Churches on the actual communion of the faithful; in the Parish Communion followed by breakfast (a kind of 'agape'); and in the house

65. Bouyer, op. cit., 76.

churches, where this element of fellowship, because of the more intimate nature of the meeting-place, can become more real.

(With other denominations)

But the communion does not begin and end with the worshippers actually gathered in one place. Fundamentally the Eucharist is what Max Thurian calls 'a sacrament of unity': it is a communion between all the faithful, of all traditions and all countries, simply because they are all taking part in the same ritual with the same purpose and motive. The scandal of our divisions is made vividly manifest at the Lord's Table.

'The Eucharist unifies and joins together the members of the Body of Christ; those who have been baptized are joined together in unity and can but seek the deepening, extension and fulfilment of their unity. As the sacrament of unity, the Eucharist is the sacrament of charity which it supports and extends. Hence, in the quest for the unity of the Church, intercommunion should be seen not as an end but as a means of recognizing and living the fact that Christ establishes the unity of His Body in the communion of His eucharistic body . . .'[66]

This approach has, of course, been adopted by the Anglican and Methodist Churches in their quest for full organic unity.

(With the Church Triumphant)

Further, the communion expressed at the Eucharist is not only within the Church Militant, but is between the Church Militant and the Church Triumphant. We have tried to express this thought in the sub-section on worship in general. Summing up these three aspects of communion, Brilioth writes:

'We cannot be members of Christ's body without being at the same time members one of another; and thus the unity of the brethren is lifted up into the mystery of union with God. This fellowship knows no limits narrower than the whole universal Church of Christ; it begins with the circle round our own local altar, it extends to the fellowship of the whole Church on earth, and it embraces not only the living but also those who are gone hence in the Lord. Thus it passes into Mystery—the Mystery of christian fellowship; for these two aspects of the sacrament are in-

66. Max Thurian, op. cit., p. 124.

separable, even though we are bound to study them separately. Finally, this fellowship is unreal if it does not find expression in life as well as in liturgy, and deepen and sanctify daily intercourse.'[67]

If only those words could be written at the front of every Prayer Book and Hymn Book!

(Communion with Christ)

As we have indicated, this communion of the faithful is a communion with their common Lord. He is present with the worshippers, and meets them in the Eucharist. Symbols the bread and wine may be, but they are symbols of a Christ who is with the congregation, not of a Christ who is absent. This leads on to a doctrine of the Real Presence, which many non-Romans would find untenable. Nevertheless, it has received clear expression in the writings of a Reformed minister, Max Thurian. He writes:

'The real presence of His body and blood is the presence of Christ crucified and glorified, here and now, under concrete signs. The meaning of every corporal presence is to attest concretely the presence of that person that he may enter into a concrete communion. By the real presence of His body and blood, the Church knows that Christ is there concretely in the midst and it receives Him by means of a concrete sign. The substantial presence of Christ does not denote a material presence, in the natural sense, but the presence of the profound reality of the body and blood of Christ crucified and glorified.'[68]

He states that how this happens—that Christ is both glorified in heaven and present in the Eucharist—is a mystery of the work of the Holy Spirit. We do not need to express *when* in the liturgy this takes place. 'It is by means of the liturgical action, and especially by the whole eucharistic prayer.' He favours having an Epiclesis, but is not adamant about where it should occur. In fact he has no objection to the inclusion of two Epicleses, as, for instance, in the Alexandrian Liturgy of St. Mark. Christ is consequently objectively present in the bread and wine; this does not depend on the faith of the communicant. The difference made by a lack of faith is that while he certainly meets Christ, he 'does not receive the fruits of this encounter.'[69]

One finds it difficult to find fault with this doctrine; and as

67. Brilioth, op. cit., p. 279.   68. Thurian, op. cit., p. 121.
69. Op. cit., p. 123.

we shall see, it is given clear adumbration in the writings of the Wesleys, and particularly in the Eucharistic Hymns of Charles Wesley.

4. *Eucharist as a Sacrifice*

The idea of sacrifice is written deeply into Jewish theology, from local shrines to the High Priest entering the Holy of Holies on the Day of Atonement. The symbolism of Jesus' actions at the Last Supper, and the meaning of the words He spoke, could not fail to impress men so steeped in sacrificial ideas as were the first disciples.

Arising from this, a sacrificial interpretation was eventually so strongly interwoven into the Eucharist, that all other interpretations of it faded into comparative insignificance. It was this which was one of the major causes of the 'great divide' at the Reformation, and which still, or at least, as we shall see, until quite recently, kept the Romans sharply contrasted with all other Western denominations.

No student of human nature need express surprise that the two points of view tended to be expressed extremely. The Roman Catholics, especially during the centuries when congregations were not encouraged to communicate, began to teach that the sacrifice of Christ was actually repeated at every Mass; while the Reformers and their successors (especially the latter) in contrast suggested that the idea of sacrifice could be altogether omitted from the Eucharist on the grounds of the all-sufficiency of Calvary. F. J. Leenhardt expresses his concern about the deficiences of both these extremes:

'The protests of reformed theologians would seem to be legitimate insofar as there is talk of a sacrifice which obtains from God graces which He would not have bestowed without it. This effect *upon God* of the sacrifice of the altar necessarily issues in the devaluation of the sacrificial work of the life and death of Christ Jesus, no matter what one says to the contrary.'[70] On the other hand: 'The reaction against the sacrificial interpretation of the Lord's Supper (among some Reformers) issues in a refusal to see in it anything but a commemoration, a recalling, an evocation, an acted preaching. The unique character and the unique efficacy of the sacrifice of the Cross are thus perfectly safeguarded, but at the price of a

70. F. J. Leenhardt, 'This is my Body': in *Essays on the Lord's Supper*, p. 57.

remoteness of the Cross in time; the sacrifice loses all its contemporaneity by dint of our concentration on its beneficial effect.'[71]

Is it possible to express a theory of sacrifice which will satisfy both Romans and non-Romans? We can both begin by stressing the sacrifice of themselves that any congregation must make in fully entering into the communion. The bread and wine at the offertory procession may then be seen, in part, as symbols of this sacrifice—the offering of the physical necessities of this life, symbolic of one's time, talents, and possessions. This is expressed in the prayer of oblation (which, if it were said immediately after the offertory procession, or at least before communion, would make this more clear); '. . . Here we offer unto Thee, O Lord, ourselves . . .'. Some, under the influence of Barthian theology, would object that this would not be a sacrifice worthy of the God we worship; even the offering of our lives would not bring us any merit. But the idea of gaining merit is not necessarily linked with such an idea of sacrifice. To offer oneself in love to God, is automatically to accept the necessity of sacrifice. The one is not possible without the other. Bouyer makes this point, then proceeds:

'This is, of course, to say that the meal which expresses and, as it were, incorporates that agape, is itself and in all its details sacrificial in the highest sense. Thus, not only are the eating and drinking in this meal sacrificial, but so, too, is the sanctifying prayer which is said over the food; and when we understand it in this way, this prayer becomes the perfect form of that sacrifice of pure lips which the teaching of the Prophets had already so strikingly outlined. But, since the Christians have partaken in the meal of agape, the whole Christian life of each individual is now imbued with that sacrificial virtue.'[72]

Bouyer then gives the remainder of Paul's daring words in Colossians 1:24, 'Now I rejoice in my sufferings for your sake, and in my flesh I complete what is lacking in Christ's afflictions for the sake of his body, that is, the church.'

It seems therefore reasonable to say that in the Eucharist the sacrifice of the congregation is in some way taken up in Christ's eternal sacrifice, inasmuch as they are acknowledging their total commitment to Him. This is not at all the same thing as

71. Op. cit., p. 58.   72. Bouyer, op. cit., p. 77.

to say that they 'offer Christ'. There seems no ground for using that phrase, with its hint of a man-made Calvary rather than one of Jesus' choosing, unless we mean by this what Max Thurian describes by 'memorial'. But if that is what is meant, it would be better to say so.

This leads to the heart of the problem: is Christ sacrificed again or not? If so, must we adopt a doctrine of transubstantiation? If not, must we relegate Calvary to a historical event? What we need to resolve the conflict is a deeper understanding of the word 'repeat'. To illustrate: Handel's 'Messiah' was composed once and for all two hundred years ago; but that is no reason why we should not talk about having 'repeat performances' of it: repetitions in which players and audience enter, to a limited extent perhaps, but to a certain extent none the less, into the mind and mood and purpose of the composer when actually putting pen to paper. To quote Leenhardt again:

'What gives to the sacrifice of Christ, in His life and in His death, its full meaning is that it is the point in history where the sacrifice of God in search of His creatures emerges. The bread, which Christ stretches out to His disciples, saying, "This is my body", recreates for each believer the sacrificial initiative which God took in His only Son.'[73]

The same point has been expressed by Bishop Aulén:

'If the sacrifice offered once for all is eternally valid and relevant, and if it is one with Christ who is himself the sacrifice, then the presence of Christ in the sacrament includes the effective presence of this sacrifice. It is not a question of recalling something which happened 2000 years ago on Golgotha. The past is here too the present as the Lord himself makes the past and eternally valid sacrifice contemporaneous with us. As the Lord on that last evening of his life presented the sacrifice which was momentarily to be made, and which signified the last act in his total sacrificial activity, and as he included his disciples in his sacrifice and united them with it, so also he includes his present disciples in the sacrifice which is eternally valid and eternally effective, and makes them partakers in the blessings flowing from the sacrament. . . . The real presence and the sacrifice belong together. *This sacrifice is present because the living Lord is present. But the living Lord cannot be present without actualising his sacrifice.*'[74]

73. Leenhardt, op. cit., p. 63.
74. G. Aulén, *Eucharist and Sacrifice*, 1958, pp. 192–3. Quoted in 'The Eucharistic Offering' by A. M. Allchin, *Studia Liturgica*, Vol. I, No. 2, p. 106.

A growing number of Roman Catholics would accept this approach; and it is significant that in recent years the doctrine of transubstantiation has not loomed so large in joint discussion. The safeguard for non-Romans who object on principle to any talk of sacrifice is given by Brilioth:

'The way to guard the evangelical fullness of eucharistic doctrine is not the "reducing-method" of Puritanism. The eucharist is menaced at every point, and not at this point only, by the danger of degradation to a pagan level; and the danger becomes serious whenever any of the aspects of the eucharist is held in isolation from the rest.'[75]

There are a few other doctrines of which that last comment could be made!

It appears that in the end, disagreement on this doctrine springs from disagreement about the nature of the Church. Those who hold firmly to a doctrine of the Body as previously outlined, would agree with these words:

'The real presence means that the sacrifice on Calvary is eternally in Christ's Church, till He comes, in the form of the bread and wine of the new covenant feast, and makes it possible for His disciples to have a part in His sacrificial passage through death to life.'[76]

Those who hold a more individualistic interpretation of the nature of the Church will be unmoved by this, or by any other quotations in this section.

The signs are that a *modus vivendi* is being found, where a generation ago there seemed to be only a focal point of disagreement. It is one of the minor miracles of our times, brought about to a great extent by the impact of the Liturgical Movement. That this is part of a process which will not easily be halted is suggested by the fact that the report of the Montreal Faith and Order Conference itself expresses this 'co-ordinating theology'.[77]

5. *The Eucharist as Mystery*

This aspect of the Eucharist is not so much an extra element added to the others, as one that infuses them all. It is the

75. Brilioth, op. cit., p. 48.   76. Allchin, op. cit., p. 110.
77. *Studia Liturgica*, Vol. II, No. 4, p. 261.

recognition that the human mind is fallible, and that it is ultimately presumptuous to imagine that we can give clear-cut definitions of the ways whereby God confronts men. To recognize this requires humility; it is for this reason that the rediscovery and expression of this point of view is one of the great signs of hope for the unity of the Church: for there can be little progress until all sides have expressed their own inadequacy, if not sinfulness, in the outlining of their doctrines.

The first, and greatest, name associated with the 'Mysterientheorie' was that of Dom Casel of Maria Laach. His ideas were taken up by Brilioth, and later by Bouyer. Now they are influencing the Church at large, and it is not written how much they will continue to do so.

It is not our purpose to give an exposition of Casel's teaching. Suffice to quote his own definition of his intention:

'The main intention of the mystery-teaching is to set out clearly once again the Church's mysteries, above all the Eucharist, but the other sacraments as well, each according to its measure and place, as the sacramentum redemptionis; that is to say, to show them as the presence of the oikonomia in the Church; not to reduce the sacraments to mere "means of grace".'[78]

The divine plan in the Church's midst: who can presume to explain, define, outline all that this means? Is not the automatic response of man to accept this with humility and gratitude and to respond with obedience? This is what Casel suggests: that the Christian community should take part in the cultic rite of the Eucharist, naturally never ceasing the attempt to understand, but recognizing that in the end they cannot comprehend the riches of divine wisdom and love; all she can do is faithfully to obey. Bouyer outlines the sort of faith which is needed:

'She believes that Christ is present in an ineffable way in the celebration; she believes that what she does today, He himself is doing and through her; she believes that this action of today, which is His as it is hers, is, finally, the one saving action of God in Christ throughout history. That is to say, that the Mass is the Cross, but the Cross always seen in the whole perspective of which we spoke when we were discussing the Memorial.'[79]

78. Quoted in 'Towards a Theology of the Liturgy', by L. M. McMahon; *Studia Liturgica*, Vol. III, No. 3, p. 149.
79. Bouyer, op. cit., p. 79f.

This approach to the sacrament is, of course, akin to the approach the Christian must make to other doctrines of his faith: to the Incarnation, with which, as we have seen, the Eucharist is closely connected; to the Atonement, and the mystery of divine forgiveness, which cannot be proved but must be apprehended by faith: 'By grace you have been saved through faith; and this is not your own doing, it is the gift of God.'[80] It is paralleled by the mysteries of the Resurrection, the Holy Spirit, and the Holy Trinity. Death itself is a mystery (I Corinthians 15:51); Jesus spoke of 'the mystery of the Kingdom of God' (Mark 4:11); and Paul refers to the 'mystery of the Gospel' (Ephesians 6:19),[81] and all this finds an echo in everyday life in the mystery of a little child. Concerning the Eucharist, Brilioth sums it up thus:

'We do best if we affirm the truth of the real presence as "focussed" in the elements, and endeavour to avoid the crudity of our expression of it by balancing it with the other two modes of the eucharist mystery: the thought of the personal presence of the Saviour "in the midst", as Priest, Lord and King, and that of the mystery of the body of Christ which is his church, and the equally mysterious presence of Christ in the hearts of our brethren.'[82]

Because of this, and because the very word implies something understood only by initiates, it follows that the Eucharist must be seen as an action carried out by the worshippers, the initiates. Ernest Koenker says:

'The ancient understanding of the Christian mystery was of an altogether concrete, visible, tangible and audible reality, the actuality of which consisted not only in concrete circumstances, but in an *action* which transpired before the eyes of the spectators, in which they themselves took part actively.'[83]

This emphasis on action in which the congregation participate, the fact that something is not only done in the Eucharist, but is seen by all the people present to *be done*, is motivating many of the liturgical experiments of our time. Bishop J. A. T. Robinson has made this clear in *Liturgy Coming to Life*. In this

80. Ephesians 2:8.
81. Cf. 1 Corinthians 4:1; Ephesians 1:9; 3:3; Colossians 1:26; 1 Timothy 3:9 et al.
82. Brilioth, op. cit., p. 287f.
83. E. Koenker, *The Liturgical Renaissance of the Roman Catholic Church*, University of Chicago Press, 1954, p. 108.

he shows how the action in the Eucharist is linked with action by and in the name of Christ in the world:

'The Eucharist is *the* Christian action, the heart of all Christian action in the world, because it mediates and makes present . . . the great saving act of God in Christ . . . For all Christian action in this world is nothing else than the finished work of Christ becoming operative through His body, the Church. And the Eucharist is *the* point where that finished work is constantly renewed to the Church. . . . This is the crucible of the new creation, in which God's new world is continually being fashioned out of the old, as ordinary men and women are renewed and sent out as the carriers of Christ's risen life.'[84]

Dr. Robinson proceeds to suggest that this is why, in the early Church, they spoke of 'doing the eucharist' as opposed to the modern parlance of 'saying' or 'hearing' mass, or 'holding' a communion. The expression 'to celebrate the eucharist' is apt; unfortunately the type of service which it describes hardly lives up to this optimistic description. We need, in the words of Abbé Michonneau, to 'let the liturgy be splendid': and before this will happen throughout this country generally, and in Methodism in particular, there are considerable and far-reaching changes which must be made in the liturgy we use. The basis for an outline of the action of the liturgy has already been suggested: the four actions of the Last Supper—'took', 'blessed', 'brake', and 'gave'. It is significant that in the Eucharist conducted at Clare College, which according to Dr. Robinson had the notes of exultation and joy which are normally so rare, they outlined the action clearly in this four-fold way. The same is true at Taizé; to attend their Eucharist ought to be prescribed regularly for those—apparently increasing—numbers of Christians in this country who are finding that the zest has disappeared from their religious practices.

This section can well be concluded by quoting Benoit's apposite description of the difference in his country between the Eucharist as conducted a generation ago, and as, under the influence of the Liturgical Movement, it is celebrated today:

'I recall without joy the services of the Lord's Supper in the big Protestant town in which I spent my childhood. After the sermon there was a general exodus. There remained to take part

84. Robinson, op. cit., p. 22.

in the Communion only a few aged women, almost all in mourning, and even fewer men. The atmosphere was funereal. Today our members are finding their way back to the Holy Table. Services of Holy Communion are more frequent; instead of four celebrations annually . . . the Lord's Supper is celebrated at least once a month. More and more are coming to it, and the proportion of young people is a joy to see, especially in the urban churches.

It is understandable that such a revival of Eucharistic life should have called for a revision of the Eucharistic liturgy. In its turn, a Eucharistic liturgy that is less didactic, more lively and joyful, attracts young people to the Lord's Supper and teaches them to love it. Holy Communion is no longer an extraordinary and exceptional act, simply because of being so infrequent, an occasion for which one spent several days . . . in preparation, examining one's conscience, and which one approached in fear and trembling. It is becoming a normal act of Christian life, just as normal as eating and drinking are for the life of the body.'[85]

If this can happen to the continental Reformed Churches, is there not some hope that it may happen in British Methodism too?

(d) The Return to Basic Christian Teaching

Perhaps that title puts the situation too baldly, or not quite accurately. What we mean by it is that in the Roman Catholic Church there has been increasing dissatisfaction with the vagueness in the minds of many worshippers about the central truths of the Christian faith; while in the non-Roman Churches there has been the desire expressed to concentrate more of the people's attention on the central truths rather than on the more peripheral elements in Christian teaching.

The Liturgical Movement cannot of course claim exclusive credit for this. During the last century the world-wide Biblical Movement had begun to affect Christians of all traditions with the desire to understand the Bible more completely. There can hardly be a theological student, present or former, in the Western world today who has not been influenced to some extent by this movement. Through them, congregations have also been affected. But while the Biblical Movement prepared the way, it is the contribution of the Liturgical Movement that insights of the Biblical Movement have been applied in the

85. Benoit, op. cit., p. 53.

local situation, that they have not remained in the vacuum of specialized research. It is with this fact that we are here concerned.

I. IN THE ROMAN CATHOLIC CHURCH

In a sentence, the Roman Catholics are rediscovering the place of the Word of God in worship and the Christian life, whether the written or spoken word. Discussing the Scriptures, Cardinal Béa, who played no small part in the meetings of the Second Vatican Council, said:

'The holy books are the Word of God. . . . In them it is not man who speaks—it is the Holy Spirit. . . . Every move to make the Scriptures better known, read, studied and used, deserves our best praise, our full approval, and sincere encouragement.'[86]

Béa expresses a concern to recover an insight which Thomas à Kempis expressed: that in the liturgy there are two tables, one bearing the holy mysteries of the bread and wine, the other the mystery of the Word. He suggests that congregations need to be led to the second table as well as to the first.

His words—and those of others like him—are already bearing fruit within the Roman Church, not only in France, where such *avant-garde* ideas may be expected, but in this country, where one anticipates more resistance to change. One hears of increased emphasis on the reading of psalms and Scripture in the liturgy; of Bible-study groups meeting more informally; of a genuine desire to understand the faith more.

We have already quoted Charles Davis's strictures on the Roman Catholic Church in this country for failing to keep abreast of much of the thinking which is taking place. The very fact that he said this when he was still a Roman Catholic is itself a sign of the growing realization of the truth in what he says.

'The inadequacy found in so many current popular accounts of Catholic teaching is the inadequacy of the out-of-date. It is being overcome in the Church by various forces of doctrinal renewal, among which the liturgical movement is prominent. . . . Many must have heard the cry that went up for a kerygmatic theology.

86. In *La Maison-Dieu*, Nos. 47–8, 1956, IV, p. 149. Quoted by Benoit, op. cit., p. 92.

Rightly understood, this is not a new branch of theology but an attempt to bring the work of theology into closer touch with what is required for the proclamation and teaching of the Christian message or *kerygma*. . . . Our complacency must be shattered; we must realize that all is not well in this matter.'[87]

In words which must surely startle many Protestants by their boldness, Davis continues:

'We should be acting like ostriches, were we to ignore the inferior quality of belief in so many of our people. They have little hold upon truths that are central to the Christian message and cling to what is peripheral. Often they have been given but a lopsided and impoverished presentation of Christian truth.'[88]

As a consequence of this renewed interest in the Bible for its own sake there has grown up a deeper understanding of the sermon, as the means whereby the eternal truths revealed in the Scriptures can be brought to bear on the situations which Christians face in their daily lives. Benoit quotes with approval[89] Bouyer's definition of a sermon: 'It is not for us to make known our own ideas, not even some abstract doctrine: we have news to tell, the greatest news, the *good* news.' There is a consequent growing impatience with the 'sermonette' type of utterance badly prepared, poorly expressed, and hardly worth saying anyway. (One feels that not a few Anglican churches need to take a close look at themselves in this respect.)

This is not to suggest that there is not still a long way to go. The Roman Catholic emphasis on the Church as the sole guardian of Christian truth, sound though it is in itself, tends to blot out the more individual prophetic word. An even bigger drawback is their attitude to tradition, in which are found additional dogmas to those in the New Testament: such as the Marian dogmas, prayers to the saints, and Purgatory. These will always be a stumbling-block to Protestants, but one of the signs of developing ecumenicity of spirit in the Roman Church is that such doctrines as these do not obtrude in conversation and discussion to the extent that they did a generation ago. Instead it is interesting to see emerging a different attitude to tradition, not dissimilar to the approach of other denomina-

87. C. Davis, op. cit., p. 17f.   88. Ibid., pp. 18f.
89. Benoit, op. cit., p. 94

tions. This attitude states that while there is an absolutism in New Testament teaching, it is developed and put into practice in any particular Church according to its tradition. Tradition, on this definition, does not supplement the Bible but interprets it from age to age. Benoit writes:

'It is as it were the atmosphere through which God's Word comes to us: it is, in Fr Bouyer's own words, "the treasure of living interpretation in which the mystery which is at the heart of the Divine Word blossoms and becomes explicit, at the same time being continually renewed and made real." '[90]

One of the major benefits of serving in an ecumenical team ministry is to realize the truth of this statement: to find that on many of the most important problems with which the Church is confronted, members of different 'traditions' have different insights, whether from the Anglican, Methodist, or Presbyterian standpoints. The sum total of these makes for a depth of understanding denied to anyone relying solely on the insights granted to his own denomination.

A summary of the main doctrines about which the Liturgical Movement is bringing greater light in the Roman Church is given by Charles Davis:

'A new understanding of Christ, and, in particular, of the significance of his resurrection and the role of the glorified humanity; a sense of the history of salvation; an insight into the mystery of the Church as expressed and realised in the liturgical assembly; a fresh approach to the mystery of Christ's saving work and its permanent presence and efficacy in the liturgy; a richer theology of the Eucharist and the sacraments; a reawakening of a fuller eschatological hope: these are some of the doctrinal insights on which the liturgical movement rests.'[91]

He therefore concludes:

'We need to set to work to spread abroad the doctrinal insights that motivate the desire for liturgical reforms in those who are leading the movement. Serious reflection is required on our part to make our own the doctrinal progress that underlies the liturgical movement, a progress which is bringing about a welcome reorientation in Catholic piety.'[92]

90. Ibid., p. 96.   91. Davis, op. cit., p. 98.   92. Ibid., p. 99.

II. IN THE NON-ROMAN CHURCHES

If the new understanding of doctrine in the Roman Church springs from a growing appreciation of the Word, in the non-Roman Churches it springs, paradoxically enough, from a growing understanding of the liturgy. This does not mean that the non-Roman Churches did not need, or have not benefited from, the Biblical Movement; it is simply that by tradition the Word has always played a major role in these Churches' life, even if it has not always been fully appreciated, while the meaning of the liturgy has not been so clear in their understanding.

The Liturgy is itself an expression of the great Christian truths. Benoit writes:

'The Liturgy moves in the serene and majestic domain of the great dogmatic affirmations. It is prayer woven with dogma. Sunday by Sunday it proclaims the great basic truths of Christianity: the holiness of God, the judgement of sinful man, redemption in Jesus Christ, salvation by faith. And if to the forms of Sunday worship are added those for Baptism and Holy Communion, one finds that in this service-book one has the Gospel—in brief, of course, but nevertheless the whole Gospel.'[93]

As a testimony to the way the realization of this is growing in the non-Roman Churches, we have the various books on the meaning of worship, and increasing study in the field of liturgy, mentioned in the first chapter; we have the increasing sense that the Eucharist must not be relegated to an occasional after-service, as we quoted from Benoit in the previous section; and, just as important, there is the growing amount of work being done in the sphere of Baptism: that this is something more than simply the seal of God's love, but that in a mysterious way it is a representation of the Christian's sharing with Christ in His death and Resurrection because in the baptismal liturgy is reproduced the whole redemptive drama of Calvary. There is, in short, the growing awareness that the more people come to know Christ and to commit themselves to Him, the more they will find Him present in the liturgy; conversely, the more the liturgy is performed in its fulness and with understanding, the

93. Benoit, op. cit., p. 56.

greater becomes the awareness of Christ and one's consequent commitment to Him.

'The dogmatic revival has also brought into the foreground the Person and work of Christ, and here again there is seen to be a close concordance between the doctrine of the Church and its liturgy. Christ fills the liturgy altogether; he is its centre. It is through Jesus Christ our Lord that the Church speaks to God. The greater the fervour for Christ, the more living the liturgy becomes.'[94]

Two other points may be made here. First, the increasing understanding on the part of the non-Roman Churches (more especially of course the Free Churches) that one's understanding of the faith can be deepened not only by what is taught and preached but also by what is *done* in the context of the Church, is evinced by the growing stress in these Churches on the observance of the Church Year: not only the main festivals like Christmas, Easter, and Whitsuntide, but also the great seasons, such as Advent, Epiphany, Lent and Eastertide. To observe all these with fidelity is to ensure through the year none of the great doctrines of the faith is ignored.

Secondly, as we have already indicated earlier, this emphasis on doctrine in the liturgy is militating against the unfortunate tendency in the Free Churches to make the aim of worship the stirring up of the individual emotions. There are still a few who openly declare that the aim of any act of worship is to see teen-age girls weeping at the communion rail; but this idea is by no means so widespread or so frequently expressed as it once was, and one can only see in this one of the most healthy effects of the Liturgical Movement. For the liturgy, in Benoit's words,

'. . . shows a certain modesty, avoiding the display of the soul's secrets. It prefers to leave discreetly in the shadow what passes between the soul and God, throwing over this mystery the veil of its imagery and solemnity. It turns its back on expansive self-expression and spiritual prattle. Liturgical worship may for this reason seem to some to be dry and cold, and pietistic circles are usually averse to it. There is, however, a deep concordance between dogma and liturgy, between the doctrinal bias of our time and the "truth clothed in prayer" which is what liturgical worship is.'[95]

94. Ibid., p. 57.   95. Ibid., p. 57.

(e) Meaningful Symbolism and
Church Architecture

So far, in discussing the insights of the Liturgical Movement, we have concerned ourselves chiefly with theories and the possible effect these might have—and sometimes are having—in practice. At this point we turn to a subject which—while there are theories *about* it—is intensely practical: the visual element in the Church's liturgy, as summed up in the word symbolism; and the sort of building that is required in order to bring out or clarify the liturgical principles of those who occupy the building.

I. CHRISTIAN SYMBOLS

Not all symbols are visual. The Apostles' Creed is a symbol; it articulates the Christian doctrines. How then are we to define a symbol? There is a sense in which, if we could say exactly what it was, we should hardly need it; but the attempt must be made. It is clearly something that stands for, represents, or denotes something else, not by exact resemblance, but by (sometimes vague) suggestion or by some accidental or conventional relation. Gilbert Cope[96] points out that a symbol is not consciously thought out like an allegory, and is therefore an important link between the conscious and the unconscious. Clearly those symbols which are used in worship must be as consciously meaningful as possible; while there are symbols which are personal to the individual, this would not be suitable in corporate worship. A simple, succinct definition is given by two architects, Robert Maguire and Keith Murray:[97] 'They *articulate and present* meaning.'

Symbolism plays a large part in every aspect of life, for man is a symbol-maker and a symbol-user. The algebraic and road signs are symbols; so also is a salute, a bow, a wedding-ring. Modern advertisers are well aware of the nature of symbolism and use it to sell goods. One American car manufacturer planned to use a blatantly phallic symbol on one of his makes of

96. Gilbert Cope, *Symbolism in the Bible and the Church*, 1959.
97. 'Architecture and Christian Meanings': *Studia Liturgica*, Vol. I, No. 2, p. 117.

car; this was withdrawn, but we often see cars which are advertised as an expression of masculinity. A symbol can often express a meaning more effectively than explaining it could do: the handshake is now more a formality than a symbol (the original meaning being that it showed that the person concerned did not carry a weapon); but to refuse a proffered handshake is a gesture whose meaning cries out clearly and sharply.

The danger with symbolism—and with religious symbolism in particular—is that of forgetting that a symbol is only valuable to the extent that it presents the meaning of that which it symbolizes. There is always the tendency to give the symbols some kind of magical quality in themselves. It is fine, and reasonable, for one man to say that he worships God through an ikon; where his belief begins to turn into superstition is when he declares that another man cannot worship God without the ikon. (This argument is surely relevant to the symbolism of the historic episcopate.) A more precise understanding of this (and more detailed knowledge of symbolism in the Old Testament, like Jeremiah with the yoke around his neck) could have prevented many of the barren debates between Christians, often with their resultant divisions. (Both extreme Zwinglianism and transubstantiation arise from a grossly inadequate understanding of symbolism. Or perhaps these are the result of our Western, logical minds: a thing must be one thing or another, it cannot be both; the Jews with their different mentality understood—they did not laugh at Jeremiah, they broke his yoke.)

When considering Christian symbolism it is worth while bearing this further related point in mind: virtually every ritual practice in Christianity has a parallel in one or more other religions; for example, virgin birth of gods, the death and resurrection of the gods re-enacted in death-and-resurrection rites of believers (often at puberty), the baptism of believers, the eating of the god in symbol by believers in order to acquire some of his properties. While this is no reason for the Church not to use her traditional symbols, it does seem a reason for not making them an essential part of Christianity (in the sense of writing off those who try to do without them: we criticized the Quaker view earlier, but many try to exclude them from any definition of the Church) or for saying that our symbols are 'true' while somebody else's are 'false'.

The contribution of the Liturgical Movement to the Church's use of symbols is the insistence that they should be clear in their meaning and relevant in their context. Max Thurian writes:

'Admittedly, the liturgy assumes that (the faithful) have received instruction in the Bible, in catechetics and symbols. The liturgy cannot be directly comprehensible to the man in the street. A form of liturgy which conformed to this criterion of being immediately understood would have to be emptied of all biblical and traditional substance, and would very soon be obsolete. On the other hand, the liturgy must never pander to man's natural taste for the esoteric. The modern liturgical movement must exorcise this tendency to the esoteric. Some extreme examples could be given here, such as the custom of commixing in the Roman Mass—dropping part of the consecrated host into the chalice, a gesture which had theological and symbolic meaning in the Early Church but which has now lost any such significance. The use of certain liturgical vestments or ornaments, such as the maniple, has also lost all meaning today. We could give examples from the protestant liturgies also.'[98]

Brother Max is perhaps too polite to say what is there to be said: but as examples of outdated or false symbolism in the Free Churches we have the Introit sung by the choir *after* the minister has reached the pulpit; the Bible (and hymn book) carried by a steward into the pulpit roughly five minutes *before* the service is due to begin; obsequiousness on the part of the preacher (otherwise known as the 'pulpit voice'—an unconscious attempt, perhaps, to introduce an element of mystery which is lacking where the service is entirely in the vernacular; it is certainly interesting that in personal experience the Roman priests use a completely normal voice in saying the Mass in Latin); and, most amusing of all, the attempt of a respected colleague to represent two schools of churchmanship at the time of the blessing: pronounced with right hand raised high in an episcopal manner, but ending with the fully Protestant, 'be with *us* all'.

In the symbolism of the Eucharist there are certain obvious elements about which Christians have always had their beliefs: the bread and wine as symbols of the whole of creation, or of

98. Max Thurian, op. cit. in *Studia Liturgica*, Vol. III, No. 2, pp. 109f.

man's possessions, or the Body and Blood of Christ, or the sacrifice of the congregation, and so on. Not all traditions have held these ideas at the same time, but they have been prominent throughout the Church's history. In the light of the Liturgical Movement a new form—or rediscovery, in part, of an old form —of symbolism is, as we have seen, emerging: the four actions of the Eucharist. So we are today seeing more of an offertory procession; the bread is actually broken (and many people are urging the use of real bread); the Eucharistic prayer is being placed more prominently in modern experimental liturgies; and congregations are being encouraged to communicate more frequently. Other pieces of symbolism which are re-emerging are the Peace (found in the Church of South India's liturgy, Taizé, etc.) and the Little Entry, giving the Bible its place alongside the Sacrament as one of the twin pillars of the liturgy.

Much of the rethinking of symbols in our time is taking place around the Service of Baptism. The different forms of symbolism surrounding, or finding expression in, this service through the history of the Church and in different areas makes intensely fascinating reading[99] but is too involved for us to discuss here. The water is generally taken to symbolize cleanliness, but it also symbolizes unformed chaos in general, the unknown out of which we were born (intra-uterine fluid), the unknown to which we go after death (cf. the river of death) and the mysterious depths of the unconscious—besides of course the more well-known crossing of the Red Sea, Noah on the waters, and the baptism in Jordan. The font has been made to symbolize a boat (safety in the water), a womb, (safety again, together with birth) a cradle and a coffin. It is uncertain what the font in Coventry Cathedral is supposed to symbolize—perhaps the unwitting reference is to Moses smiting the rock!

In modern baptismal rites[1] the thought of the sacrament as a dying and rising with Christ, following St. Paul,[2] is predominant. For this the most expressive symbol is the waters themselves.

'But if you want to make water explicit as a symbol you need quite a lot of it. It is no use having a teacupful in a bird-bath. And

99. Cf. J. G. Davies, *The Architectural Setting of Baptism*, Barrie and Rockliff, and (of course) J. G. Frazer, *The Golden Bough*.

1. E.g. C.S.I., Taizé.   2. Romans 6:3–4.

if you have a lot of water, you can make it symbolically explicit either by putting your water in an expressive architectural context, or by using it expressively in the rite. Or, or course, both.'[3]

We shall see in the next chapter how Baptism as initiation into the family of God, the body of Christ, is becoming more articulated in Methodism today.

The presence of candles is another very clear symbol—one that has been central in the Church's tradition—of light. Jesus often used it;[4] it was found in the carrying of a lamp during the Jewish Berakah; there was the paschal candle; there is the baptismal candle, lights carried at the Gospel, candles on the altar, and lit by worshippers as an expression of prayer. Maguire and Murray point out that a candle makes a more immediate impact than electric lights, probably because it conveys warmth as well as light.

The use of robes and vestments is another example of symbolism in the liturgy. The idea here is, presumably, that of dressing up for a special occasion, besides helping to add to the sense of the Mystery; dignity and reverence are also included. It is unfortunate that the Reformed tradition has opted for *black* robes; the white cassocks worn by the Taizé community add a sense of joy and exultation to their worship. On the question of vestments, one must reserve judgement. Some of the liturgical colours are clear: black for death, white for purity, green for fruitfulness (not always really relevant); but it is often difficult to understand the significance of golden or purple vestments—and if a symbol has to be explained it loses its usefulness.

However, in so far as the Liturgical Movement is causing an increasing amount of research and practical debate on the whole question, the liturgy, as a genuine expression of the worship of the entire congregation gathered together, can only benefit.

II. ARCHITECTURE

The insight of the Liturgical Movement on this theme is that the Church building should, as far as possible, serve the liturgy.

3. Maguire and Murray, 'Architecture and Christian Meanings'; in *Studia Liturgica*, Vol. I, No. 2, p. 123.
4. E.g. Matthew 5:14, 16; 6:23; John 8:12; 9:5, and especially the Prologue.

The building itself, it is realized, along with its furniture (and more particularly the placing of it) can vividly express a theological viewpoint which will affect the entire liturgy. Thus the typical medieval-style Roman (or Anglican) church with its High Altars as the central feature, focal-point of the congregation's devotion, contrasts with the typical Free Church church, with its huge central pulpit, and tiny communion table almost out of sight underneath, probably dominated by vases of flowers; and both of these indicate which element in the liturgy these Churches considered predominant. It is one of the signs of the ecumenicity of our times that in many modern churches, especially on the Continent, it is becoming less easy to guess the particular tradition to which the building belongs. Gilbert Cope writes:

'The reason is, on the one hand, that Catholics are rediscovering the importance of a proper ministry of the Word and are stripping away from the Mass the devotional accretions and extra-liturgical practices which obscure its true character. On the other hand, Protestants are recovering the sacramental pattern which was excessively disrupted at the Reformation and are realising that man does not live by words alone.'[5]

There is a growing desire in both traditions that the building shall contain Holy Table and pulpit not as Big and Little Brother, or vice versa, but as equal partners. To these must of course be added the font, and possibly a lectern with the Bible (though this could be kept on the Altar/Holy Table.) Cope points out that the places where this is best understood seem to be those where institutes have been established for the purpose; and it is significant that in his own University an Institute for the Study of Worship and Religious Architecture has been established (1962).

In the building itself there are various tensions to be resolved, which have been highlighted by the emphases of the Liturgical Movement. The first is the tension between this-worldliness and other-worldliness. Should the building direct the worshippers away from the issues that face them day by day to the Christian mysteries? To what extent should the architect build

5. G. Cope, 'Trends in Modern European Church Architecture'; in *Studia Liturgica*, Vol. II, No. 4, p. 286.

a church which is 'open' to the world? This is being done in some buildings by putting in plenty of plain glass; but symbolically sound though this no doubt is, the activities seen through the window may well distract rather than remind the worshippers of the theological and liturgical principle. H. R. Blankesteyn expresses another aspect of this tension:

'A church should be built to receive all faith, doubt and also unbelief, but must it be a place where unbelief can find its shape? The question lying behind this, therefore, is whether or not a church is a place where the "church" and the "world" meet each other.'[6]

He proceeds to add a further aspect of the tension:

'Should the doors of our churches be as inviting as possible . . . suggesting a minimum area between the inside and activities without, or should the doors be a testimony to the hardship implied in faith?'[7]

Related to this is the tension between the liturgy as koinonia, communion of the congregation with each other, and sacrifice. The objection expressed in some quarters to the 'basilican' position was that it increased the sense of the former only at the expense of the latter. But from the other side it could be argued equally strongly, that simply to celebrate from a westward position is not being revolutionary enough in the quest for the sense of the congregation as the body: the placing of the chairs in a rectangular, or even semi-circular, form around the Table would help to get rid of the sense of being at a public meeting. (It is interesting that on the stage, another area of drama, many of today's leading directors are asking for this type of theatre, akin to the amphitheatres of ancient Greece.)

Other tensions are also present: is the church primarily the House of God, or the meeting-place of His people? Should it be lofty and magnificent, expressive of the former, or lower and simpler, of the latter? There is the question of the relation of the 'other rooms' to the actual worship-room; the problem of the extent to which a church building should reflect its age and follow the pattern of neighbouring buildings or deliberately,

6. H. R. Blankesteyn, 'Vis-à-Vis'; in *Studia Liturgica*, Vol. III, No. 3, p. 173.
7. Ibid., p. 174.

by being quite different in style, contrast with these; there is the question of the ethics of spending large sums of money on buildings which may within a decade be white elephants because the population has moved away (Dr. Robinson has suggested the building of plastic, sectionalized churches to cope with this problem.)[8] Should the church be so designed as to indicate that this is only a stopping-place on the way for the Christian pilgrim, or that it is the end of the journey? (The place of Christian art is involved in any answer to that.)

It is not possible to answer these questions; there is something more permanent about a church building (and more costly!) than the details of the liturgy: these can be changed, and changed back again; not so a building. Consequently much more study and thinking must be done, with a wider area of general agreement, before any absolute principles can be formulated. The German *Documents for Sacred Architecture* by Cardinal Lercaro and Theodore Klauser contains many fine ideas; but its complete certainty about every aspect of the subject seems somewhat unrealistic in an age of fluidity.

What we can be sure of is that whatever experiments are made in this field in the future will come under the judgement of the ideas and principles which have emerged through the Liturgical Movement; we have already seen this in the general disappointment expressed in many quarters over the lost opportunity of Coventry Cathedral. Meanwhile what is needed is more research into what people want in their church buildings—and this involves sociological research. Gilbert Cope sums this up:

'There are many different ways of designing the worship-room for truly corporate worship and there are many different ways of relating the "other rooms" . . . to one another and to the worship-room, and there is a marked trend for all denominations to give increased attention to the sociological implications of these fresh insights into the essential character and work of the Church. Now, while there is much to admire in many church-centres of this kind, one still senses the need for much more sociological research into the spiritual and cultural condition of the people who make up the vast populations which are being settled in new large groupings all over Europe. Too little is known concerning the behaviour

8. In a sermon at St. Mary's Church, Woolwich—and probably elsewhere!

patterns of the uprooted persons who move (or are moved) into new centres of population and there is no doubt that the Churches must do much more work in the field of Christian sociology. The Church, as a whole, will be able to function effectively in the world only in so far as it understands the world, and, as a farmer must know both his seed *and* his land, so must churchmen encourage and develop the sociological studies which are now being established.'[9]

(f) The Relationship between Worship and Witness

The point at issue in this section may well be introduced with a quotation from the Evanston Report, *Christ the Hope of the World.*

'It is the very nature of the Church that it has a mission to the whole world. That mission is our participation in the work of God, which takes place between the coming of Jesus Christ to inaugurate God's Kingdom on earth and His coming again in glory to bring that Kingdom to its consummation. "I have other sheep that are not of this fold; I must bring them also, and they will heed my voice." This is His word to us; this is His work in which He is engaged and in which we are engaged with Him. For He whose coming we expect is also He who is already present. Our work until His coming again is but the result of our share in His work which He is doing all the time and everywhere. The Church's mission is thus the most important thing that is happening in history.'[10]

We have already suggested that the major functions of the Church, the body of Christ, are twofold; to worship and to witness. These have never been lost sight of throughout the history of the Church; but the difficulty has been keeping the two in harmony. There has always been the tendency among Christians to be either so heavenly-minded that they are no 'earthly' use, or so earthly-minded that they have no use for heaven. A. C. Lichtenberger expresses the former, and what will be for our purposes treated as the major, danger thus:

'Unfortunately, a man may worship and yet be turned inward upon himself, a parish may become parochial, a Church a sect. This, of course, is not the product of Christian worship itself, but is the result of a particular view of the relationship of God to His

9. Cope, op. cit., p. 289.
10. Quoted in C. Williams, *Where in the World?*, p. 21.

creation and, following from that, the perceived purpose of worship. This, in general, is the subjective view of Christianity in which the emphasis is largely upon personal piety and individual personal morality, and where a sharp line of distinction is drawn between the natural and the supernatural, the secular and the sacred.'[11]

Our purpose at this point is not so much to produce a blueprint whereby this distortion might be removed, as to demonstrate how, under the influence of the Liturgical Movement, increasing insight is developing throughout the Church into the truth that the body exists not by worship alone, nor by witness alone, but by the two together, each enriching and motivating the other. We have already outlined some of the experiments in mission which are taking place throughout the world as a result; here we shall quote in some detail from various writers who, since the war, have expressed this viewpoint.

One of the earliest to express himself—in fact before the war—was Fr. Hebert:

'We have not only to consider what to do with Christ in the Church, but what He wills to do with us in the street. The Church has indeed the key of the street. Too often she seems inclined to use it to lock herself in.'[12]

Akin to this, from the Roman side, are these words of Louis Bouyer:

'The world of the sacraments, the world into which the liturgy introduces us, is not a world in its own right, standing aloof from the world of ordinary living. It is rather the meeting-place of the world of the resurrection with this very world of ours in which we must live, suffer and die. And this fact implies that liturgical life, far from taking us out of real life, far from making us indifferent to or uninterested in real life, on the contrary positively sends us back into it in order to carry out fully in it the mystery which has come to us through the sacraments.'[13]

The difficulty of putting this into practice has been vividly expressed by John Robinson. He first quotes with approval

11. A. C. Lichtenberger, 'The Social Implications of the Liturgical Renewal', in *The Liturgical Renewal of the Church*, p. 103.

12. A. G. Hebert, *Liturgy and Society*, Faber, 1935, pp. 191ff. Quotation from p. 182.

13. Bouyer, op. cit., p. 266.

Vidler's phrase summing up the Christian tension—'holy worldliness'—and comments:

'Holy worldliness involves constantly walking on a knife-edge: it is only too simple to slide off into becoming too worldly or too other-worldly—and neither is holy, though the latter has often been hailed as sanctity. To be concerned but not involved is just as great a temptation for the Church as to be involved but not concerned.'[14]

A classical statement of the answer to the dilemma is given in the Epistle to Diognetus:

'Christians are not distinguished from the rest of mankind either in locality or in speech or in customs. For they dwell not somewhere in cities of their own, neither do they use some different language, nor practise an extraordinary kind of life. . . . But while they dwell in cities of Greeks and barbarians as the lot of each is cast, and follow the native customs in dress and food and the other arrangements of life, yet the constitution of their own citizenship which they set forth is marvellous and confessedly contradicts expectation. They dwell in their own countries, but only as sojourners; they bear their share in all things as citizens, and they endure all hardships as strangers. Every foreign country is a fatherland to them and every fatherland is foreign. . . . Their existence is on earth, but their citizenship is in heaven. They obey the established laws, and they surpass the laws in their own lives. . . . In a word, what the soul is in a body, this the Christians are in the world. . . . The soul is enclosed in the body, and yet holdeth the body together; so Christians are kept in the world as in a prison-house, and yet they themselves hold the world together. . . . So great is the office for which God hath appointed them, and which it is not lawful for them to decline.'[15]

We have quoted at some length from this Epistle because of its simplicity and directness—and nearness to the mark. One feels that this could profitably be included in any church lectionary; there would be several answers to the question as to what passage it should replace!

The New Testament word which perhaps sums up the thought of this passage is Jesus' description of His followers as the leaven, taken up by St. Paul. Abbé Michonneau pursues this thought:

14. Robinson, *On Being the Church in the World*, S.C.M., 1960, p. 18.
15. *Selections from Early Church Writings*, H. M. Gwatkin, Macmillan, 1937, pp. 13–17.

'The first question we want to treat is whether or not we are really producing the leaven that St. Paul talks about. After all, we do have to form and insert the leaven which will spread through the whole mass around us; that is our vocation. And, if we are going to give so much of our time and of ourselves to this task, we should be able to procure proportionate results. They will come only when we do mould men and women capable of becoming sowers of the seed, leaders, magnetic Christians. A necessary condition for this result is to see that the leaven is in contact with the group which needs leavening; it must become an integral part of the group it is to influence.'[16]

Joost de Blank describes how this leavening can be expressed in one obvious way: the influencing of public opinion:

'Sometimes to our shame the Church has lagged behind public opinion. Sometimes it has not woken up to a local problem until other groups have taken action or expressed their opinion. But the Church must always be awake and alert to everything that is going on in the local situation; it must be alive to the needs of the neighbourhood; it must be alive to those things that are threatening its best interests. The Church should not follow public opinion, it should lead it, and in so doing the Church should ever have as its aim the raising of the whole community to a new level of service and friendship. In spite of the cloud that has fallen over Blake's great hymn it still remains true that the Church has no right to rest till it has "built Jerusalem in England's green and pleasant land".'[17]

Tom Allen describes his own attempts to bring his church to see that it must not be an irrelevant, escapist clique, making no impact on the community:

'Gradually three principles became articulate for me. . . . The first is that the solution to the vast problem of communicating the gospel to the masses who live outside the sphere of Christian fellowship is inextricably bound up with the local church—that the key to evangelism lies in the parish. Secondly, that the Church can only fulfil its function and penetrate the secular world when it is exhibiting the life of a genuine and dynamic Christian community—the koinonia of the New Testament. And thirdly, that in all this the place of the layman is decisive.'[18]

16. Michonneau, *Revolution in a City Parish*, Blackfriars, 1949, p. 60.
17. J. de Blank, *The Parish in Action*, Mowbrays, 1954, p. 61.
18. T. Allen, *The Face of My Parish*, S.C.M., 1954, p. 66.

Abbé Michonneau strongly iterated—as opposed, for example, to Godin, in *France Pagan?*—the first point, the importance of the parish structure in the carrying out of the Church's mission:

'The parish can play this part . . . firstly, because it is already existing. Whether it plays its role or not, hic et nunc, the parish is a fact. It is, by right if not in reality, that tiny cell of Christianity, of the Incarnation, about which we are talking. Whatever be its future, the parish is, right now, the one concrete element of the task of evangelism. . . . Every community has its own. . . . So it is something that the parish *is* and that there is no question about its existence, or right to existence. . . . And that is not all, for a parish is equipped. It has its priests, and parish clergy have always been the mainstay of the Church's force. . . . They live in the midst of those whom they are evangelising. They are, or can be, or should be, in permanent contact with their people. . . . And if, besides considering the number of these priests, we realise the actual set-up in each parish, we shall see what power and influence these parish priests and curates—all occupied by the same sort of problem, and all striving in different places for the great goal of the apostolate—could wield. Unfortunately, we say "could" and not "do".'[19]

This idea of a revolutionary parish is pursued by Ernest Southcott:

'When the parish is a community in which God is discovered and rediscovered, in which Christ is shown forth, in which the Holy Spirit is experienced, it is revolutionary and dynamic. It is a community in which people see more and more of the love of God and do more and more about it. Maritain has said that every age has its relative pattern of holiness and the relative pattern of holiness for today is community. The Church is *the* community.'[20]

This is the second of the two convictions Tom Allen reached; he describes his attempts to act upon it:

'We are all familiar with the dreadful anonymity which exists in any city parish. I have tried to show how, in my own parish, I did not find a community, but a broken, divided, inchoate mass of people. And in this situation our congregations are as often as not mere aggregates of individuals who have little more than a nodding acquaintance with one another. If we believe that the parish—or the congregation—should be what one writer has called

19. Michonneau, op. cit., p. 13.
20. E. Southcott, *The Parish Comes Alive*, Mowbray, 1957, p. 17.

"the local and universal seat of the redemption"; if we believe that the Christian community should be in some way a constant "representation of the Incarnation", then it is clear that our traditional set-up is inadequate and badly in need of overhaul.'[21]

Perhaps the sphere in which most progress has been made is that of Mr. Allen's third conviction: the absolute involvement of the laity in the Church's mission. Far too often the whole burden of this mission—in terms of visiting, contacts in industry and elsewhere, and evangelism generally—has been left to the ordained man. Far too many of the clergy have unthinkingly taken this burden upon themselves; and far too many laymen have let them. Often, even where laymen have been prominent, they have been a species of 'clericalized laymen'— important men, holding positions of authority in the organization of the Church. This has nothing whatever to do with the real ministry of the laity; the doctrine of the Priesthood of all Believers does not mean the right of laymen to take over ecclesiastical duties—though they may well do that—but that every layman and woman is a priest of God, that is, God's representative, an expression of the Nature of Christ, in the sphere he occupies in daily life.

Shands expresses this thought, in what must be a rather lengthy quotation, extremely well:

'There is a great need for a relevant lay spirituality in this way of life the Church is beginning to discover today. We need a spirituality which sees action and religious devotion as one and the same thing. Many of the hymns we use regularly express a point of view which is hopelessly inadequate to the task of being a layman. Judging by the devotional practices of the laity in some of the mission churches in France, one suspects that the foundation of this approach has already been laid. Here you find people standing to pray with the full consciousness of those around them. Outwardly it gives the impression that devotion is not something to be left in church. They seem to be longing to translate prayer into action in the Body.

'This spirituality ought to connect up the daily round in the local neighbourhood or office, the liturgy, and the mission. Laymen should be able to see these three as one whole. They must see the holiness and sacredness of the most ordinary situations of everyday

21. Allen, op. cit., p. 69f.

life. And unless they possess this sort of spirituality, it is impossible for them to see what they are really doing in being laymen. . . .

'The self-giving love of Christ's priesthood will be the key to this spirituality. This is what will connect worship and the world. Thus the Parish Communion in which the laity come together to make their weekly offering will be essential. They will be offering back to God the world renewed by the operation of the Holy Spirit in them. God's love for the world and theirs will be marvellously united.'[22]

It will be argued that this is essentially a Protestant concept. Abbé Michonneau demonstrates that this is not so:

'We have lay-movements; let lay-people take charge of them! Let them realise that this is *their* movement, and that they do not have to be constantly worrying about what the parish priest will think; . . . we must leave them alone in their organising, in their formation, so that they can require a necessary sense of responsibility.'[23]

For this type of work, many laymen will require a degree of training not normally found in church life. It is here that the main contribution of the clergy will be made; and because this training involves a knowledge of the secular structures, it is felt in some quarters that the training of the clergy must be considerably broadened, so as to include, for instance, sociology, with especial reference to the industrial world and Trade Unions. In other quarters this thought has been taken further in the concept of the worker-priest, especially in France, but to a certain extent in this country also.[24] All this can be seen as an attempt to make the Church's mission real, and springing ultimately from a growing understanding of this aspect of the liturgy.

In one area of thought a distinct new development has begun to emerge in the past five years, especially from the United States: that of the Church as the Servant Community. It is argued that the essence of a servant is not that he invites people to enter his house in order to be served, but that he leaves home in order to serve people where they are. This has led to the question whether it is right to gear the strategy of the

22. Shands, op. cit., pp. 52f.   23. Michonneau, op. cit., p. 181.
24. Cf. an article in *The Guardian*, 22 April 1965, by Geoffrey Moorhouse: 'Worker Priests in England'.

Church's Mission to the end of getting people to 'come to church'. An experiment on opposite lines, where service to the community is the central motive, is the East Harlem Protestant Mission in New York, vividly, if perhaps in somewhat extravagant terms, described by Bruce Kenrick in *Come Out the Wilderness*. (This book illustrates a feature of so many of these descriptions of modern experiments, including some of those from which we have quoted: inevitably the authors choose the most interesting aspects of their work; equally inevitably, the work itself seems, when one sees it at first hand, somewhat humdrum.)

This 'servant' concept with some of its implications is given clear expression by Colin Williams:

'When the Church sees itself as a piece of the world used by God to approach the world which He would redeem, it is also rescued from the temptation to think that God speaks only within the institution of the Church. Knowing that God's purpose enfolds the whole world, and that the Church is a segment of the world which exists for the world, it also knows that God is at work in the rest of the world outside the Church; that He speaks to the world also through pagan witnesses, and that the Church must therefore watch for the signs of God's presence in the world, ready to reach out to work with God at the points where He is at work and to be open to "humble dialogue with pagans".'[25]

One of the ways in which the Church is not only expressing the desire to listen, but is finding it practicable, is by the development of team ministries, with key members of the church closely working with the team, and including ordained men who undertake secular employment while still remaining closely linked with the team. Thus whatever insights he gains from his 'listening-post' can be fed into the team, and through it to the life of the church as a whole. This is not as far as some would go, but it is a step in the process. Peter Berger outlines what this listening implies:

'Christians must enter into dialogue (with non-Christians) with all their cards on the table. They must relinquish the idea that, in inviting both Christians and non-Christians to such communication, they will subject the latter to some subtle religious manipulation. They must not merely say, but honestly realise themselves, that they cannot know the answers to most of the problems

25. C. W. Williams, *Where in the World*, Epworth, p. 48f.

arising in the dialogue. They must abandon the rhetorics of moral authority which too many contemporaries have learned to recognise as empty and pretentious verbiage. In many ways this approach represents a new posture of the Church, quite different from the kerygmatic posture so dear to many of our theologians. This posture has been called that of the listening Church. But it would be erroneous to regard this posture as a new expression of quietism. Listening in this context is a most active undertaking indeed. It means the concentration of every intellectual faculty upon the task of understanding, of grasping the nuances of what is said, and of taking painstaking care that every human interest in the situation is heard and understood by all the participants. This process is far removed from the technology of "group dynamics". There is no intent of manipulating the psychology of the situation. The only technology involved has to do with providing the physical and social circumstances within which free communication can occur.'[26]

This expression of the mission of the Church in non-evangelical terms—or at least in terms different from those normally adopted by those concerned about the Church's task in the world—is expressed with intense clarity by Paul Van Buren:

'The mission of the Christian is the way of love upon which he finds himself, the way towards the neighbour, not the way of trying to make others into Christians. His mission is simply to be a man, as this is defined by Jesus of Nazareth. It is not particularly appropriate in our time, when the Church has talked far too much to the world, for him to tell his neighbour why he is "for" him. It is quite enough that he practise the liberty for which he has been set free. It is for this reason that we agree when Barth says that theology is done by the Church, takes place within the Church, and is for the Church. It is also for this reason that we questioned earlier the concern with evangelism and preaching to "modern man" which informs the theology of Bultmann and Ogden.'[27]

Some may suggest that we are here departing far from the Liturgical Movement. This seems a shallow view. Inasmuch as one of the insights of the Movement can be summarized as that the Church must 'be Christ' in the world, it seems right to view the teaching of Van Buren (and others like him, such as the Methodist John Vincent) as a development of this; for in the passage we quoted, as elsewhere in his prophetic book, it is the

26. Berger, op. cit., p. 152f.   27. Van Buren, op. cit., p. 191.

parallel with our Lord's own ministry which he is seeking to express in terms of the Church's mission today.

This will lead of course (and has already led in many areas) to tension. In the words of Gibson Winter:

'The most disturbing experience for church members in our time is to find their confessional assemblies divided over public and economic issues. Men and women today look to the local congregation as a haven from conflict and tension. Clergymen view their work as the maintenance of harmonious relationships within the flock; the frictionless machine is the ideal image of the congregation. The creation of such *harmonious enclaves* is an indication of the utter dislocation of the Church in our society. The Church is intended to be a *suffering body* in the world, showing forth the Lord's death until He come. This community in Christ is not called to sacrifice its ministry of reconciliation in order to preserve its inner tranquillity. This body is called to bear within itself the sufferings imposed upon it by a ministry of reconciliation within the broken communications of the world. Reopening broken communication will inevitably tear and disrupt the internal life of the Church, but that inner suffering is the essential nature of the authentic presence of the New Mankind in the world. The work of the clergyman is not to spare the ministering fellowship from internal suffering by diverting it from its ministry; his task is to open new possibilities of ministry to which the servant Church is summoned, deepening the reflection of the prophetic fellowship in the course of its sufferings. There is no Church without such a ministry.'[28]

Thus, by a strange paradox which can only instil in the observer or listener a renewed belief in the continuing activity of the Holy Spirit, a movement which began as a reform of the liturgy, with all the priestly associations attached to this in the minds of many, has led eventually to a rediscovery of the prophetic nature of the Church, introducing a vital note which has for too long been unsounded in the Church's life.

But is not this in fact a return, or relapse, to humanism? To answer this, we turn, not to the more obvious revolutionary ideas emerging from America, but to a source which, whatever accusations can be made, cannot include that of being humanist —Louis Bouyer:

'Let us notice how every easy-going method of reconciling the world with Christianity makes light, not only of Christianity, but of the world as well. To think that the world would be redeemed,

28. Winter, op. cit., p. 127.

that salvation would have been achieved for mankind, that the preparation for the Kingdom would be so complete that, for all practical purposes, things would be as though it had already come, all this simply as a result of the fact that the majority of the people on earth were practising Christians, or that legislation all over the world had become open to Christian considerations, or that states and civilisations reflected Christian ideals—to suppose all this is to avoid the major issues of secular life as well as of Christian. . . .

'We do not get to the heart either of the problems of the world or of the task of Christianity until we seriously face the problem of sin and accept, not the way of some illusory reconciliation with the world, but the way of conflict which is the way of the Cross, the way of voluntary death in and with Christ. . . .'[29]

Bouyer proceeds to show the inadequacy of humanism, deriving from its lack of understanding of human nature, particularly its ignoring the fact of sin, and the devastating consequences, in terms of human suffering, arising from this, to which only the message of the Cross and Resurrection can give any ultimate answer. He proceeds:

'But if we are all to accept and understand this truth fully, we must never forget the other truth on which we have meditated already in connection with the fact that the Mystery does not bring the Cross into the world, but finds it there. . . .

'In everything that he does, in his work, his study, his relaxation, the Christian finds joy, which is greater because purer than that which the man of this world knows, because' (arising from his belief in eternal life) 'his achievements here and now can bring him joy even though he is quite aware of their lack of permanence . . .

'The Christian knows that he can love forever those whom he loves here on earth, for the reason that he does not love them any longer for himself alone. Therefore, although the Christian is a man of sacrifice, the priest of all creation, he cannot accept—as do so many idealists of this world only—any plan for the salvation even of the whole world which would necessitate innocent death or suffering. . . . And this is what brings the Christian finally and unavoidably to the Cross, because when a man refuses to shift the burden of his pain to other men, he cannot avoid taking the burden of their pain upon himself. But this fact also is what causes the Christian to love the world with the love of Him who "so loved the world that He gave His only-begotten Son. . . ." '

29. Bouyer, op. cit., p. 267. 30. Ibid., p. 270f.

One feels that there is no dispute between this teaching and that of those previously quoted. The Liturgical Movement has, by emphasizing the presence of the Mystery in the world, brought in its wake the timely reminder that because this is God's world, it is not the function of Christians—as they have too often in the past suggested—to despise or deride the world. What God has called holy, they must not call unholy.

We have completed our study of the various insights of the Liturgical Movement. Obviously the different ideas which have emerged cannot naturally be fitted into such water-tight compartments as the outlining of six separate sections suggests. Nor can one always carefully delineate where the influence of the Liturgical Movement ends, and that of other great movements—Biblical, Ecumenical, Missionary, Lay, Christian Stewardship[31]—begins. But we need not be unduly concerned; logic is the creation of the inventive mind of man, not part of the natural order of things.

31. An outline of these different movements, and how they are inter-related, is given in the British Council of Churches' pamphlet, *All in Each Place,* 1964, pp. 4–8.

CHAPTER THREE

THE IMPLICATIONS
FOR METHODISM

A. THE METHODIST HERITAGE

(a) Wesley

MUCH has been written about John Wesley; some would say too much. Until relatively recently, in Methodist circles at least, while the sacramental side of his teaching was not totally lost sight of, it was certainly not given a great deal of emphasis. This of course reflected the Methodist churchmanship of the period. Wesley was seen primarily as the great evangelist, one in the line of the 'Evangelical Succession' from Paul to Augustine, thence to Luther and so to Wesley. It was his stress on the need for personal experience and faith, on the assurance of forgiveness which the Spirit gives, on the desire for perfect holiness which must be a natural corollary of this experience, which received almost all the attention of Methodist biographers up till Methodist Union in 1932. Added incentive to this approach was given by the general antipathy of the Anglicans to Wesley's enthusiasm. They were the inheritors of a 'theology of reason', so that the emotion stirred up in the Methodist meetings appeared *infra dig*, if not positively embarrassing. The snobbery and class distinction which abounded in the Church in the eighteenth century did not encourage the majority of the clergy to feel warmly inclined towards Wesley's more general appeal.[1]

Since Methodist Union there has been an attempt to redress this imbalance. Credit for this must go chiefly to a strong opponent of the union, Dr. J. E. Rattenbury.[2] In more recent

1. There were of course exceptions to this, as Bowmer indicates on p. 6 of *The Sacrament of the Lord's Supper in Early Methodism*, Dacre, 1951.
2. Particularly in *The Eucharistic Hymns of John and Charles Wesley*, Epworth, 1948.

times, in his book *The Sacrament of the Lord's Supper in Early Methodism*,[3] John Bowmer, the present connexional archivist, has made a definitive study of what has emerged as a second side of Wesley's teaching and practice—his sacramentalism. In 'The Proceedings of the Wesley Historical Society' there has been increasing evidence in recent years of interest in this side of Wesley.

Nineteenth-century Anglicans were never so blind to this, as the title of one book by W. H. Holden suggests: *An Old Methodist: John Wesley in Company with High Churchmen*.[4] This point of view was given stark expression by Evelyn Underhill:

'Methodism . . . began, not as a revolt from institutional worship, but as an attempt to restore the continuity of the full Christian life of realistic adoration within the Anglican Church. . . . It is difficult to say whether early Methodism as its founder conceived it was more catholic or more evangelical in tone.'[5]

Against this may be quoted the words of Henry Bett:

'With regard to the sacraments of the Church, Wesley's attitude was mainly pragmatic. He found that, as a matter of fact, these hallowed rites brought blessing to the believing soul, and therefore he urged them upon his people. This is the truth, and practically the whole truth, of the matter. It is, of course, easy enough to make out that Wesley was a sacramentarian if you go through his writings and select and stress every reference to the duty of receiving Holy Communion, and the blessing which attends it. But it creates a false impression if you isolate those references, and give them a unique emphasis. . . . A great deal that has been written on Wesley's supposed sacramentarianism is entirely beside the mark. . . . It is easy to quote a multitude of references as to the duty and privilege of attending at the Lord's Supper. It would be equally easy to quote as many allusions (or, indeed, more) to the duty and privilege of attending meetings for preaching and prayer and fellowship. . . . Wesley often tells the Methodists in general . . . that if they neglect to attend their Classes and Bands it will be at the peril of their souls' salvation.'[6]

3. Mention should also be made of Ryder Smith's *The Sacramental Society*, Epworth, 1927.

4. Cf. also, *John Wesley and the Church of England*, by W. J. Sparrow-Simpson, London, 1934.

5. E. Underhill, *Worship*, Nisbet, 1936, p. 303.

6. H. Bett, *The Spirit of Methodism*, Epworth, 1937, p. 58. It could be argued that Dr. Bett fell into the error he condemns in others: choosing to quote only from those aspects of Wesley which suited his own thesis!

Strangely, Dr. Bett did not pursue his thinking one stage further. The real point at issue is not whether Wesley was *either* a sacramentalist *or* an evangelist (nobody denies the latter, even though it has perhaps been underplayed by some of the proponents of the former as an entirely natural reaction to the picture of Wesley as an evangelist purely and simply) but whether he was not, in fact, both. Can we say with M. Piette that Wesley would have been more at home in the modern Salvation Army than in Methodism, or Anglicanism?[7] Or can we say with Dr. Rigg[8] and many others, that while Wesley was a High Churchman with strong sacramental ideas before his conversion in 1783, he changed his attitude after this experience?

To decide on the answer to these questions requires some consideration of Wesley's teaching and practice. This has already been done in great detail by John Bowmer and, more briefly and with special reference to the doctrinal aspects of the question, by John Parris.[9] We cannot possibly discuss the matter at such length; but what we can and must do is to demonstrate what Wesley said and did, and in particular consider whether he remained constant throughout his life. We shall therefore consider three periods: the pre-conversion period (roughly 1725–38); the post-conversion period (1740s); and the period at the end of his life (1780s). We shall deal at greatest length with the second of these. About the first there is little argument; and for the third we need only look for signs of confirmation of earlier ideas and practices. The main authorities we use are the Sermons[10] and the Journal;[11] in addition, for the doctrine of the sacrament, where relevant, we use Charles Wesley's 'Hymns on the Lord's Supper'[12]—the hymns which received his brother's strongest approval.

7. M. Piette, *John Wesley in the Evolution of Protestantism*, London, 1937. (Translated from the French, *John Wesley, Sa Réaction dans l'Evolution du Protestantisme*, Brussels, 1926, which Bowmer considers to be much better.)

8. J. H. Rigg, *The Churchmanship of John Wesley*, London, 1878.

9. J. Parris, *John Wesley's Doctrine of the Sacraments*, Epworth, 1963.

10. *Sermons on Several Occasions*, in Three Volumes (Wesleyan Methodist Book Room; no date).

11. *The Journal of the Rev. John Wesley*, in Four Volumes; Nos. 105–8 in the Everyman Library, Dent, 1906.

12. Printed in full in Rattenbury, op. cit., pp. 195–249.

I. PRE-CONVERSION

While there was a considerable amount of nonconformity in Wesley's ancestry, the nearest family influence—his parents—was predominantly High Church. His mother was the daughter of a staunch nonconformist, but being of independent mind had thought the matter through and decided for the Church of England. His father, Samuel Wesley, had published a treatise entitled *The Pious Communicant Rightly Prepared or a Discourse Concerning the Blessed Sacrament*; it seems that both John and Charles were profoundly influenced by their father's attitude, which laid much more emphasis on the sacrament than did that of the majority of his colleagues at that time.

At Oxford and in Georgia John was clearly much impressed by the Nonjurors (the small but influential company of Churchmen who had refused to take an oath of allegiance to William and Mary on the grounds of their loyalty to the Stuarts and who were distinguished by High Churchmanship with particular emphasis on the external forms of worship) and the Caroline Divines with whom, in many respects, they may be linked. The book of one of the Nonjurors, William Law, *A Serious Call to a Devout and Holy Life*, made a profound impression. It has been noted that on the voyage to Georgia[13] the books Wesley read were almost all by Nonjurors, Roman Catholics, or Caroline High Churchmen. One of the Oxford Methodists, Benjamin Ingham,[14] stated that on board ship Wesley and his friends celebrated the sacrament daily among themselves, and every Sunday from October 19th, 1735 onwards for all on board.[15]

The influence of the early Church on Wesley's practice in Georgia is indicated by this entry in his 'Journal':

'I began dividing the public prayers, according to the original appointment of the Church: (still observed in a few places in England). The morning service began at five. The communion

13. Listed by Bowmer, op. cit., p. 30f.
14. Tyerman, *The Oxford Methodists*, London, 1878, pp. 68f.
15. Cf. Journal for 21st December 1735 (Vol. 1, p. 18): 'We had fifteen communicants, which was our usual number on Sundays: on Christmas Day we had nineteen; but on New Year's Day fifteen only.'

office (with the sermon), at eleven. The evening service about three. And this day I began reading prayers in the Court-house; a large and convenient place.'[16]

Wesley's Diary, which supplements material in the Journal at this stage, reveals that communion was also observed on saints' days, such as St. Andrew's Day, The Conversion of St. Paul, The Purification of the Blessed Virgin Mary. The entry in the Journal for Palm Sunday 1737, is:

'Sun. April 3, and every day in this great and holy week, we had a sermon and the holy communion.'[17]

At this early stage, therefore, all the indications are that Wesley was a High Churchman, strongly influenced by others like-minded, seeking to put into practice, both for himself and for those in his pastoral charge, what he believed to be the principles and practices of the early Church. A major facet of this was the celebration of the sacrament.

II. THE POST-CONVERSION PERIOD

During the period prior to his conversion and in the immediate post-conversion years Wesley came strongly under the influence of the Moravian Brethren—an influence which began on the ship to Georgia when Wesley was overwhelmed by the joy and courage of a group of the Brethren on board, who, unlike himself, showed no signs of fear or doubt in the midst of a frightening storm. Headed by Count Zinzendorf, the Moravians were keen missionaries, and one of these, Peter Boehler, encountered Wesley in London in 1738. They distrusted doctrinal formulae, believing rather in the 'witness of the Spirit'—the fact that a Christian is not one who simply 'goes through the motions' of religion, but who must have a definite experience of 'justification' of which he is consciously aware. Conversation with Boehler along these lines prepared Wesley, mentally and spiritually, for his own conversion on May 24th, 1738.

For some eighteen months after his conversion, Wesley continued to meet with the Moravians in their meeting-house in Fetter Lane, London. Then, in October 1739, Philip Henry

16. Journal Vol. 1, p. 29: entry for 9 May 1736.
17. Ibid., p. 46.

Molther arrived, and began to teach a strange doctrine of 'stillness'. He taught that no ordinance of the Church—prayer, Bible-readings, church services or sacraments—were of any avail without faith, and that until they had faith (as described in the previous paragraph) they were to be 'still'; that is, they were to abstain from all the ordinances, especially the Lord's Supper, because they were not means of grace, Christ Himself being the only means. 'Stand still, and see the salvation of our God' might be taken as the watchword.

Wesley hesitated before withdrawing from the society at Fetter Lane, for he owed much to the Moravians; but this teaching was contrary to some of his profoundest convictions, and he withdrew, taking with him those who agreed with him, on July 20th, 1740. His preaching around this period gives some indication of his feelings. On June 27th he wrote in his Journal:

'I preached on, "Do this in remembrance of me".
'In the ancient Church, everyone who was baptised communicated daily. . . .
'But in latter times, many have affirmed, that the Lord's Supper is not a converting, but a confirming ordinance.
'And among us it has been diligently taught, that none but those who are converted, who have received the Holy Ghost, who are believers in the full sense, ought to communicate.
'But experience shows the gross falsehood of that assertion, . . . Ye are the witnesses. For many now present know, the very beginning of your conversion to God . . . was wrought at the Lord's Supper. Now one single instance of this kind overthrows the whole assertion.
'The falsehood of the other assertion appears both from Scripture-precept and example. Our Lord commanded those very men who were then unconverted . . . who (in the full sense of the word) were not believers, to "do this in remembrance of him". Here the precept is clear. And to these he delivered the elements with his own hands. Here is example, equally indisputable.'[18]

The entry for July 18th itself significantly and simply states:

'A few of us joined with my mother in the great sacrifice of thanksgiving; and then consulted, how to proceed with regard to our poor brethren of Fetter Lane: we all saw the thing was now

18. Ibid., p. 279. Cf. the entries for the 28th and 29th. In the former Wesley gives what appears to be a summary of his sermon on constant communion; and in the latter, equally an attack on 'stillness', a sermon on good works.

come to a crisis, and were therefore unanimously agreed what to do.'[19]

In organizing his own societies, Wesley followed, with class and bands, a pattern often employed by the Moravians; but the rules were somewhat different: on Christmas Day 1744 the rules for bands were formulated:

'Constantly to attend on all the ordinances of God, in particular: to be at Church and at the Lord's Table every week and every public meeting of the bands, etc.' [20]

To find a fuller outline of Wesley's sacramental beliefs at this period, we must turn to his sermons. On Sunday March 18th 1741, his Journal states that he preached on 'The Use and Abuse of the Lord's Supper'. Bowmer comments that the essence of this, and other sermons on a similar theme which the Journal states he preached at the time, is almost certainly contained in the Standard Sermon XII: 'The Means of Grace'.[21] The text of this sermon is significant, in the light of the controversy with the Moravians: 'Ye are gone away from my ordinances, and have not kept them'—Malachi 3:7.

Beginning with a reference to Acts 2:42, Wesley proceeds to show how easily the means can become an end, and that this happened to the Church in later centuries, though it was an abuse rather than a despising of the ordinances which was most predominant. In the second part of the sermon he proceeds to examine which are the means of grace, beginning with what must be a classical definition:

'By "means of grace" I understand outward signs, words, or actions, ordained of God, and appointed for this end, to be the ordinary channels whereby he might convey to men, preventing, justifying, or sanctifying grace.'

He discusses first prayer, then 'searching the Scriptures', and, finally, receiving the Lord's Supper.

19. Ibid., p. 281. On p. 282 we have, in the entry for July 20th, a full description of the final encounter, of how Wesley read a statement with his reasons for leaving clearly outlined, concluding, ' "I have borne with you long, hoping you would turn; but as I find you more confirmed in the error of your ways, nothing now remains but that I should give you up to God; you that are of the same judgement, follow me." I then, without saying any thing more, withdrew, as did eighteen or nineteen of the Society.'

20. Quoted in Bowmer, op. cit., p. 43.   21. Sermons, Vol. 1, pp. 185–201.

He quotes 1 Corinthians 11:23ff, emphasizing the imperatives in v. 28: 'Let him eat; let him drink', commenting:

'. . . words not implying a bare permission only, but a clear, explicit command; a command to all those who either already are filled with peace and joy in believing, or can truly say, "The remembrance of our sins is grievous unto us, the burden of them is intolerable." '

He then deals with various objections; first, that one cannot use the means without trusting them. He answers with asperity: 'I pray, where is this written? I expect you should show me plain Scripture for your assertion: Otherwise I dare not receive it; because I am not convinced that you are wiser than God.' He then demands: 'But what do you mean by "*trusting* in them?"'—looking for the blessing of God therein? believing, that if I wait in this way, I shall attain what otherwise I should not? So I do. And so I will, God being my helper, even to my life's end.'

Secondly, there is the objection that this is salvation by works. Wesley answers this by describing what Paul meant by works in this context—the Mosaic law. Then he deals with the Quietist argument: that Christ is the only means of grace. His answer to this is a perfect piece of reasoning: 'When we say, "Prayer is a means of grace", we understand a channel through which the grace of God is conveyed. When you say, "Christ is the means of grace", you understand the sole price and purchaser of it; or that "no man cometh unto the Father, but by him." And who denies it?' This leads to another objection: that Christians are told to be still and *wait* for salvation. Wesley says, 'But how shall we wait? If God himself has appointed a way, can you find a better way of waiting for him?' The retort which quotes the text about standing still and seeing God's salvation Wesley deals with by Biblical exegesis. The final argument he deals with refers to Colossians 2:20: 'If ye be dead with Christ, why are ye subject to ordinances?' Wesley shows that to identify these 'ordinances' with the means of grace, and not the Jewish ordinances, is a bare-faced abuse of the verse, and of Paul's teaching generally.

Wesley then demonstrates his belief in the sacrament as a 'converting ordinance' by listing it, alongside prayer and Bible study, as one of the ways to bring a sinner through repentance to a sense of sin forgiven. He concludes with four warnings: first, to remember that God is above all means; second, following from this, the warning that there is no power in the ordinance: 'It is, in itself, a poor, dead, empty thing: Separate from God, it is a dry leaf, a shadow. Neither is there any *merit* in my using this. . . . But, because God bids, therefore I do. . . . Settle this in your heart, that the opus operatum, the mere *work done*, profiteth nothing; there is no power to save but in the Spirit of God, no merit, but in the blood of Christ; that consequently even what God ordains, conveys no grace to the soul if you trust not in Him alone.' Thirdly, and as a consequence of the second warning, the people should always look beyond the ordinances to the God who ordained them: finally, he reminds the people that, because of the primacy of God, there is no cause for self-congratulation after having taken part in the ordinance.

We have quoted at length from this particular sermon simply because it states Wesley's strongly sacramental ideas with great clarity; but we receive in this sermon a hint of that other side of Wesley's nature—the evangelical. In seeing that Holy Communion may be a converting ordinance he was doing for sacramentalism what he was doing for evangelism in laying down the rule about weekly observance of the Lord's Supper for those meeting in bands. He was linking the two together, and we shall see that this was the contribution made by Wesley which is of most relevance to the current situation. He may be accused of a certain degree of illogicality in this sermon, as in his teaching generally; but one wonders whether the evangelical and sacramental aspects of the Church will ever be so logically interwoven that they will satisfy the legal mind. It is worth recalling what was said previously, but this time with a different emphasis: man is not all feeling—but he is not all mind either.

Two other sermons are worth noting. The sermon on[22] 'The Duty of Constant Communion' is self-explanatory. In it, Wesley covers much of the ground of the sermon on the means of grace, but in considerably greater detail. He argues in this sermon that to receive communion constantly is to recover the pattern of the early Church:

22. Sermons, Vol. III, pp. 147–156.

'. . . the first Christians, with whom the Christian Sacrifice was a constant part of the Lord's Day service. And for several centuries they received it every day:[23] Four times a week always, and every Saint's day beside. Accordingly, those that joined in the prayers of the faithful never failed to partake of the blessed sacrament. What opinion they had of any who turned his back upon it, we may learn from that ancient canon, "If any believer join in the prayers of the faithful, and go away without receiving the Lord's Supper, let him be excommunicated, as bringing confusion into the Church of God."'

Because of this, and because it is God's command, it is the Christian's plain duty to receive the sacrament as often as he can—and Wesley takes pains to emphasize the meaning of that phrase.

In addition to the objections to the sacrament considered in the sermon on the means of grace, Wesley deals with others, which are not unheard of in our own time. First, the argument that one is not worthy. Wesley replies that God is a forgiving God: what more can He do but offer us pardon? But even if this were not so, there would still be the direct command, Do this; and the Christian must obey, unworthy or not. It might be argued that a Christian 'cannot live up to' frequent communion, because of the implications of what he must say and do. Wesley replies (and the theme of the sermon, it will be recalled, is *constant* communion) that if a person has no intention of even attempting to live up to the service, he would be better to absent himself from it altogether, for this argument applies to communion only once a year, as much as to constant communion.

Another argument is that communion demands more time of preparation than it is possible to give. Wesley replies that the only preparation needed is to repent and have faith. Others argue that constant communion 'abates our reverence for the sacrament'. Wesley admits that in time some of the reverence of the first communions will pass; but a different reverence, born of experience, will take its place; in any case, there is still the charge, Do this. Others protest that, after frequently receiving the sacrament, they found no benefit. Again, this is no reason for refusing the Lord's command; but those who

23. Wesley was surely mistaken here.

obey will find benefit; if not, it was their own fault. Finally,
Wesley considers the suggestion that the Church enjoins the
sacrament only three times a year. He replies that it would
make no difference to the fact of God's command if the Church
enjoined it not at all: adding that the three occasions annually
was a minimum below which a person could be excluded from
the Church. He then quotes a direction of the Church to all in
Holy Orders: '. . . in Cathedral and Collegiate Churches, and
Colleges, where there are many Priests and Deacons, they shall
all receive the Communion with the Priest every Sunday at the
least . . .' (This does not sound a very convincing quotation; in
fact on this point Wesley had to tread warily. The common
practice in the Anglican Church was not to administer communion more than three or four times a year. There were, of
course, places where it took place monthly, and a few even
weekly, but they were comparatively rare. It was by precept
rather than by castigation that he hoped to revive a truly
sacramental ardour. But his example was not followed until the
Oxford Movement a century later.)

The only other sermon from which we need quote is another
of the Standard (forty-four) Sermons: Sermon on the Mount,
number six. When considering the petition: 'Give us this
day our daily bread', Wesley gives it a sacramental interpretation:

'By bread . . . we understand not barely the outward bread,
what our Lord terms "the meat which perisheth"; but much more
the spiritual bread, the grace of God, the food "which endureth
unto everlasting life". It was the judgment of many of the ancient
Fathers, that we are here to understand the sacramental bread
also; daily received in the beginning by the whole Church of
Christ, and highly esteemed, till the love of many waxed cold, as
the grand channel whereby the grace of His Spirit was conveyed
to the souls of all the children of God.'[24]

This interpretation of the Lord's Prayer would doubtless appeal
to the writer quoted on p. 24 who criticized Cranmer's placing
of it after communion in the 1552 Prayer Book Liturgy!

24. Ibid., Vol. I, pp. 327–343; the quotation comes from para. 11 (p. 338 in
our edition).

Two more witnesses to Wesley's sacramental view during the 1740s remain: the diaries, which supplement the Journal, and which were deciphered and published along with the Standard Edition of the Journal some sixty years ago (they are incomplete, but do include the period from June 1740 to May 1741); and the 'Hymns on the Lord's Supper' by Charles Wesley (to which John may have contributed, though this point is irrelevant, as we know that John had the highest possible regard for these particular hymns of his brother's).

A study of the diaries for the period under consideration confirms the impression gained from the Journal and the Sermons. Bowmer notes that during the twelve months mentioned they state that he communicated on forty out of the fifty-two Sundays.[25] As he was at St. Paul's on the remaining twelve, and as Charles Wesley reports that it was the regular practice to hold communion there, it is probable that these twelve can be added too. In addition to these, there were in this period fifty-eight week-day celebrations. A typical entry describing one of these is that for December 26th 1740: '9.15, many there, made communion'. Bowmer comments: 'The word "many" should not be exaggerated, for the Journal says "not above two or three men and as many women were present." Wesley was never slow to seize a favourable opportunity for "making a communion" with the companies who met with him.'

We cannot do better than quote Bowmer's own summary of Wesley's practice at this period:

'Thus, two years after his conversion, when the first flush of enthusiasm had had time to settle down into a steady purpose, John Wesley was in the habit of celebrating Holy Communion, on an average, just over once every four days—regularly on Sunday mornings and whenever and wherever opportunity allowed during the week.'[26]

The 'Hymns on the Lord's Supper' were first published in 1745, and indicate both the theories of the Eucharist held by the two brothers at this time, and also the emphasis they laid upon it: there are 166 of them. Their arrangement follows very

25. Bowmer, op. cit., p. 50.   26. Ibid., p. 51.

closely the outline of a tract by one of the Caroline divines, Dr. Daniel Brevint, *On the Christian Sacrament and Sacrifice*. His headings are:

I. The importance of well understanding the nature of this Sacrament.
II. Concerning the Sacrament as it is a memorial of the suffering and death of Christ.
III. As it is a sign of present graces.
IV. As it is a means of grace.
V. As it is a pledge of future glory.
VI. As it is a Sacrifice, and first, of the commemorative sacrifice.
VII. Concerning the Sacrifice of ourselves.
VIII. Concerning the Sacrifice of our goods.

Wesley reduced these eight sections to six:

I. As it is a memorial of the sufferings and death of Christ.
II. As it is a sign and a Means of Grace.
III. As a pledge of Heaven.
IV. The Holy Eucharist, as it implies a sacrifice.
V. Concerning the sacrifice of our persons.
VI. After the Sacrament.

Hymns on the importance of the sacrament are not placed in a special section but scattered throughout all the sections. His emphasis, seen in his preaching, on the given-ness of the sacrament, and also an echo of his debate with the Quietists, emerges in No. 86—not the best example of Charles's hymnology, and employing a rather crude piece of irony in v. 3:

> 1. And shall I let Him go?
> If now I do not *feel*
> The streams of living water flow,
> Shall I forsake the well?
> 2. Because He hides His face,
> Shall I no longer stay,
> But leave the channels of His grace,
> And cast the means away?
> 3. Get thee behind me, fiend,
> On others try thy skill,
> Here let thy hellish whispers end,
> To thee I say, *Be still!*
> 4. Jesus hath spoke the word,
> His will my reason is;
> *Do this* in memory of thy Lord,
> Jesus hath said, *Do this!*

Wesley understands anamnesis in the sense of re-calling, re-presenting, 'here and now operative by its effects'.[27]

> In this authentic sign
> Behold the stamp Divine:
> Christ revives His sufferings here,
> Still exposes them to view;
> See the Crucified appear,
> Now believe He died for you.[28]

On the sacrament as a means of grace, the hymns bring out what we have already seen as Wesley's belief in it as a converting ordinance:

> Sinner, with awe draw near
> And find thy Saviour here,
> In his ordinances still,
> Touch His sacramental clothes;
> Present in his power to heal,
> Virtue from His body flows.
>
> His body is the seat
> Where all our blessings meet;
> Full of unexhausted worth,
> Still it makes the sinner whole,
> Pours Divine effusions forth,
> Life to every dying soul.[29]

As something actually 'given' we have already seen evidence in the hymns; the thought is better expressed in No. 71:

> Draw near, ye blood-besprinkled race
> And take what God vouchsafes to give;
> The outward sign of inward grace,
> Ordain'd by Christ Himself, receive:
> The sign transmits the signified,
> The grace is by the means applied.

It is Wesley's expression of the Eucharist as a sacrifice which perhaps challenges most the thinking about the Eucharist in Methodism since. One wonders what some modern congregations make of these tremendous words,[30] contained (unlike most of the 'Hymns on the Lord's Supper') in the present Methodist Hymn Book:

27. Gregory Dix, *The Shape of the Liturgy*, p. 161.
28. Hymn 8, 2; Rattenbury op. cit.
29. 39, 1 and 2.   30. 116, 1 and 2.

Victim Divine, Thy grace we claim
While thus Thy precious death we show;
Once offer'd up, a spotless Lamb,
In Thy great temple here below,
Thou didst for all mankind atone,
And standest now before the Throne.

Thou standest in the holy place,
As now for guilty sinners slain;
Thy blood of sprinkling speaks, and prays,
All-prevalent for fallen man;
Thy blood is still our ransom found,
And spreads salvation all around.

Elsewhere[31] the contrast between an unrepeatable sacrifice
and the continued expression of it is clearly portrayed:

All hail, Redeemer of mankind!
Thy life on Calvary resign'd
Did fully once atone;
Thy blood hath paid our utmost price,
Thine all-sufficient sacrifice
Remains eternally alone:

Yet may we celebrate below,
And daily thus Thine offering show
Exposed before Thy Father's eyes;
In this tremendous mystery
Present Thee bleeding on a tree,
Our everlasting Sacrifice.

The sacrifice embraces men coming before God, and also
makes God known to man:[32]

With solemn faith we offer up,
And spread before Thy glorious eyes
That only ground of all our hope,
That precious, bleeding Sacrifice,
Which brings Thy grace on sinners down,
And perfects all our souls in one.

It is entirely indicative of the thought-processes of the Methodism of half a century ago that this seemed far too bold a
concept to allow normal congregations to ponder over. As a
result, in the present hymn-book the hymn which contains this
verse has been removed from the section on the Lord's Supper,
and placed in the Christian Fellowship section.

31. 124, 1 and 2.   32. 125, 2.

The concept of Christ as High Priest and Victim is expressed:

> Live, our Eternal Priest!
> By men and angels blest!
> Jesus Christ the Crucified,
> He who did for us atone,
> From the cross where once He died
> Now He up to heaven is gone.
>
> He ever lives, and prays
> For all the faithful race;
> In the holiest place above
> Sinners' Advocate He stands,
> Pleads for us His dying love,
> Shows for us His bleeding hands.[33]

The idea of the Church as the body, corporately presenting the sacrifice, is found:[34]

> Who Thy mysterious supper share,
> Here at Thy table fed,
> Many, and yet one we are,
> One undivided bread.
>
> One with the living Bread Divine
> Which now by faith we eat,
> Our hearts, and minds, and spirits join
> And all in Jesus meet.

The eschatological note is found in many of the hymns, of which this is typical:[35]

> How glorious is the life above,
> Which in this ordinance we taste;
> That fulness of celestial love,
> That joy which shall for ever last!
>
> The light of life eternal darts
> Into our souls a dazzling ray,
> A drop of heaven o'erflows our hearts,
> And deluges the house of clay.
>
> Sure pledge of ecstasies unknown
> Shall this Divine communion be;
> The ray shall rise into a sun,
> The drop shall swell into a sea.

33. 118.   34. 165, 2 and 3.   35. 101, 1, 3, 4.

Communion is seen as a link with the saints:[36]

> The church triumphant in Thy love,
> Their mighty joys we know;
> They sing the Lamb in hymns above,
> And we in hymns below.
>
> Thee in Thy glorious realm they praise,
> And bow before Thy throne;
> We in the kingdom of Thy grace,
> The kingdoms are but one.
>
> The holy to the holiest leads,
> From hence our spirits rise,
> And he that in Thy statutes treads
> Shall meet Thee in the skies.

Finally, in these hymns is expressed the doctrine of the Epiclesis:

> Come, Holy Ghost, set to Thy seal,
> Thine inward witness give,
> To all our waiting souls reveal
> The death by which we live.[37]
>
> Come, Thou everlasting Spirit,
> Bring to every thankful mind
> All the Saviour's dying merit,
> All His sufferings for mankind;
> True Recorder of His passion,
> Now the living faith impart,
> Now reveal His great salvation,
> Preach His gospel to our heart.[38]

We have quoted at some length from these particular hymns, not just because they are worth recalling for their own sake—although one feels that it would not be a disservice to modern worship if churches were to use most of them as a regular part of their liturgies—but because they reveal the amazing fullness of doctrine in the minds of the Wesleys, at a time when it was rare to find such profound thought being given to the Eucharist. Most of the elements we noticed in the previous chapter are to be found here: the anamnesis (if not so clearly understood as by some modern liturgiologists); the sacrifice—and here Wesley demonstrated that this was not only a Roman theory pure and simple, but completely evangelical too; the mystery (again evangelicalized to include the mystery of redemptive

36. 96, 2-4. 37. 7, 1. 38. 16, 1.

love); and communion, involving the real presence, though not in transubstantiationist terms, and the unity of the body. This last concept was especially necessary in the eighteenth century, when religion had become an extremely private matter. Parris comments:[39]

'There is an emphasis on the corporate character of the Supper. Communion was more than an individual experience. Just as the Love-feast, often used in the Methodist societies, illustrated the importance placed on corporate fellowship, so also in Methodist practice did the Lord's Supper. This was symbolised in the custom of the communicants' coming to the table, receiving, and departing together in groups. In an age when Communion was thought of in almost purely individualistic terms, this was a healthy redressing of the balance.'

III. OLD AGE

After considering the evidence for Wesley's sacramental ideas and practices in the middle period of his life, and discovering how it all paints the same picture—one of intense ardour and conviction—it would be surprising to find that there was any change in attitude over the years. There was not, as all the evidence again shows.

The fact that the Eucharistic hymns were reprinted eight times in Wesley's lifetime, and again just after his death, does not suggest a change of outlook. And while there are no sermons preached in old age from which to quote, we need no more than the brief note written by Wesley in 1788, when he edited and published his sermons, before the sermon on constant communion:

'The following Discourse was written about fifty-five years ago, for the use of my pupils at Oxford. I have added very little, but retrenched much; as I then used more words than I do now. But, I thank God, I have not yet seen cause to alter my sentiments in any point which is therein delivered.'[40]

From the Journal we take two passages to illustrate the latest practices; first, Sunday August 29th, 1790:

'Mr. Baddiley being gone to the north, and Mr. Collins being engaged elsewhere, I had none to assist in the service, [in Bristol] and I could not read the prayers myself; so I was obliged to shorten

39. Parris, op. cit., p. 95.   40. Sermons, Vol. III, p. 147.

the service, which brought the prayers, sermon and Lord's Supper within the compass of three hours.'[41]

Then the last Sunday but one recorded in the Journal: October 17th, 1790 (his last entry was for the 24th, though he did not die until the following March).

'At seven [in Norwich] I administered the Lord's Supper to about one hundred and fifty persons, near twice as many as we had last year: I take knowledge that the last year's Preachers were in earnest.'[42]

The diaries for the last eight years of his life are available, and they reveal the same picture: communion without fail on a Sunday morning, and frequently on Saturday evenings. (This latter was a former custom in the Holy Club at Oxford.) Bowmer[43] points out that it was clearly impossible for Wesley to communicate as often when he was travelling around the country as when he was at home in London. In the month of January in these last years he was always in London, and between 1783 and 1791 there was only one Sunday when, owing to illness, he did not communicate, while in addition he communicated even more frequently during the week. In 1785 and 1790 the average is once every other day.

The evidence is invariable for every period of Wesley's life: with all his evangelical fervour, he remained a devout sacramentalist. And the majority of his followers caught his enthusiasm. We read of communion services lasting four or five hours, so great was the number of communicants. We know how embarrassed many parish clergymen were by the regularity and insistence with which the Methodists sought communion. One of the reasons for the large number of hymns on the Eucharist was that they might have plenty to sing during the long periods of the actual administration.

Dr. Bett's comment that in this Wesley was just a pragmatist seems a trifle shallow. Certainly Wesley believed in the communion because, in his own experience, it 'worked'. But nobody who has studied carefully the hymns on the sacrament could really feel that this was the end of the matter. Nor, as was suggested earlier, need we feel that his sacramentalism

41. Journal, Vol. 4, p. 507f. 42. Ibid., p. 514.
43. Bowmer, op. cit., p. 52.

detracts in any way from his evangelism. The very hymns from which we have freely quoted were written to further the cause of evangelism. And what a way to evangelize! This dual emphasis makes Wesley unique among the great religious leaders, from the time of Augustine onwards. His recovery of the twin pillars of the liturgy—Word and Eucharist, Evangelism and Sacramentalism—was a truly prophetic act, and one which foreshadowed one of the basic discoveries of the Liturgical Movement.

It is worth mentioning in passing that Wesley's attitude on the sacrament of baptism was similar to that on the communion: it had Scriptural authority, and therefore should be accepted as the ordinary means of entry into the Church; but the moment it was held as essential for salvation, God's grace was being limited to a specific means of bestowal; and this Wesley could not accept. It is of course difficult to maintain these two points of view in harmony with each other; but Wesley managed to do this, probably because he did not pursue either theory in ruthless isolation from the other, as proponents of both sides have tended to do both before and after Wesley. Thus Wesley emerges as a pioneer of the Ecumenical Movement, for if his approach were adopted, both Catholics and Protestants would find that they had more in common with each other than they had previously imagined. The sermon on the Catholic Spirit[44] may not be irrelevant on this point:

'I do not mean, "Be of my opinion." You need not: I do not expect or desire it. Neither do I mean, "I will be of your opinion." I cannot; it does not depend on my choice: I can no more think, than I can see or hear, as I will. Keep you your opinion, I mine; and that as steadily as ever. You need not even endeavour to come over to me, or bring me over to you. I do not desire you to dispute those points, or to hear or speak one word concerning them. Let all opinions alone on one side and the other: only "give me thine hand."'

If this could be the attitude of Anglicans and Methodists concerning the interpretation of the proposed service of Reconciliation, one feels that more progress might be made than some

44. Sermons, Vol. I, pp. 492–504.

parties on both sides have so far been willing to commit themselves to.

It remains finally to consider two other related matters in Wesley's life and teaching which have a bearing on our present theme: his attitudes to the conduct of worship generally; and his ordinations.

IV. WESLEY ON WORSHIP

When contemplating early Methodist worship, most modern Methodists tend to think almost exclusively of the peculiarly Wesleyan innovations: the band and class meetings, the Lovefeasts, the open-air services. These of course had a place, and a very important place, in the devotional and spiritual life of Methodism. They were what Wesley himself described as 'prudential' means of grace, as opposed to the 'institutional' means, instituted by Christ. He believed that it was the task of the Church not only to maintain the received institutions, but also to construct other means suited to the particular age and customs.

'Wesley believed that "ecclesiolae in ecclesia"—small churches within "the great congregation"—were necessary to provide for the mutual training and care of converts for their Christian life in the context of the emerging town life of the eighteenth century. He therefore developed his class meetings, provided the members with definite disciplines, and produced rules which would help the converts to discover a "style of life" that was relevant to their eighteenth-century existence.'[45]

We know from the history of trade unionism in this country how the form of cell expressed in the class meeting became the pattern for local union meetings; and it does not seem to be claiming too much if we suggest that the 'house churches' described by Ernest Southcott and Joost de Blank are basically a rediscovery and re-application of the class meeting. It seems that Wesley was, as usual, instinctively right when he spoke of the need for 'ecclesiolae in ecclesia', and we shall return to this when considering the emerging pattern of church life today.

Nevertheless, it must be stressed that Wesley saw these meetings, and also the Methodist Sunday services which of

45. Williams, op. cit., p. 62.

course became more frequent throughout his ministry, as but supplementary to church worship (that is, in the Anglican Church). Even as late as the Conference of 1766, when it was discussed whether Methodists were Dissenters, a clear-cut answer was given: 'As we are not Dissenters from the Church so we will do nothing willingly which tends to a separation from it. Therefore let every Assistant so order his own Circuit that no preacher may be hindered from attending the church more than two Sundays in the month. Never make light of going to church either by word or deed.'[46] Then came an illuminating question and answer:

'Some may say: "Our own service is public worship." Yes, in a sense, but not such as supersedes the church service. We never designed it should. We have a hundred times professed the contrary. It presupposes public prayer like the sermons at the university.... If it were designed to be instead of church service it would be essentially defective for it seldom has the four grand parts of public prayer, deprecation, petition, intercession and thanksgiving. Neither is it, even on the Lord's Day, concluded with the Lord's Supper. But if the people put ours in the place of the church service, we hurt them that stay with us and ruin them that leave us, for then they will go nowhere but lounge the Sabbath away without any public worship at all. I advise, therefore, all the Methodists in England and Ireland who have been brought up in the Church, constantly to attend the service of the Church at least every Lord's Day.'

Two years later, at the 1768 Conference, Wesley declared that those who leave the Church leave the Methodists, and that preachers must always go to church on Sunday mornings, and afternoons too when possible. In the last years of his life, when the attitude of the majority of the Anglican clergy to what was by then a large number of Methodists made it unlikely that the majority would in fact attend church, it was usual to use Wesley's own abridgement of the Book of Common Prayer. This was first prepared for use in American Methodism in 1784. In introducing it to the American Methodists, Wesley wrote:

46. The quotations on this page are taken from an article by Maldwyn Edwards on 'Remembering our Methodist Heritage', in the *Methodist Recorder*, 27 October 1960.

'I have prepared a Liturgy little differing from that of the Church of England (I think the best constituted National Church in the World), which I advise all the travelling preachers to use on the Lord's Day in all the congregations. . . . I also advise the elders to administer the Supper of the Lord on every Lord's Day.'

At the Conference of 1788 it was agreed that local preachers should have 'a discretionary power to read the Prayer Book in the preaching houses on Sunday morning on condition that divine service never be performed in the Church hours on the Sundays when the Sacrament is administered in the parish church'. John Bowmer comments on this:[47]

'The fact that this was not always done, and that after Wesley's death a free service became the rule in the Connexion, does not invalidate the main evidence of where Methodism's original affinities lay.'

The fact that Wesley had the temerity to present even a modified form of the Book of Common Prayer for the strongly anti-liturgical (using liturgy here in the sense of a written order) Americans reveals as clearly as anything else he did where Wesley's heart was. As Rattenbury says, 'A Dissenter in Wesley's time would have destroyed the Prayer Book, not revised it.'[48] Bowmer[49] has made a careful study of the changes which Wesley made in the Communion Office, which indicate, perhaps, some of his liturgical principles.

Some of these changes were dictated by practical circumstances—the fact that the service was to be used in a Methodist and not Anglican congregation: this led to the omission of certain non-essential rubrics. Others were motivated by the cause of brevity: the omission of the exhortations, and of certain prayers including the second after communion. Style brought about two changes in the Lord's Prayer: 'who' for 'which' and 'on earth' for 'in earth' (both of which should surely be compulsory in any congregation today). Certain ceremonial rubrics were omitted, possibly to appease Dissenters. The Methodist doctrinal position is indicated by some of

---

47. Bowmer, 'Methodist Liturgies' in the *Methodist Magazine*, December 1964, p. 458.
48. Rattenbury, *The Conversion of the Wesleys*, Epworth, 1938, p. 216.
49. Op. cit., pp. 206–215.

the changes. 'Elder' is used throughout for 'priest'; the form of absolution uses 'us' for 'you', and becomes a petition rather than declaration; the phrase 'the burden of them is intolerable' is omitted from the prayer of confession, probably on the grounds that they hardly suited the mood of a congregation who had gained the joy of 'assurance'. The one change which seems totally unwarranted is the omission of the Nicene Creed —probably in the interests of brevity, for the Apostles' Creed was not omitted from the Daily Offices. There are other minor omissions and additions, but the most significant of these is the inclusion of this rubric after the Gloria in Excelsis:

'Then the elder, if he see it expedient, may put up a prayer extempore; and afterwards shall let the people depart with this blessing. . . .'

Extemporary prayers, alongside the hymn-singing which we have already noted were incorporated into the service, was the great innovation made by Wesley. This indicates a change of mind from the pre-conversion years; and we know from several references that it became customary to include this type of prayer in addition to those of the Prayer Book. Wesley was not, however, over-enamoured of them; he knew from experience that they could often be just as rigid as written prayers; in a letter of 18 October 1778[50] he wrote: 'I find more life in the Church prayers than in the formal extemporary prayers of the Dissenters.'

Once again, as with his Eucharistic doctrine and practices, we find that in his liturgical principles Wesley was both Catholic and Protestant, sacramental and evangelical. Bowmer puts this thought in one succinct sentence:[51]

'The fact that he made and insisted upon the use of a revision reveals him the Churchman; the manner of the revision on the whole, reveals him the evangelical.'

V. WESLEY'S ORDINATIONS

It may be reasonably asked why, in view of Wesley's manifest High Churchmanship, and his often expressed determination to remain a loyal son of the Anglican Church ('Whenever the

50. Ibid., p. 91.   51. Ibid., p. 215.

Methodists leave the Church, God will leave them', he once declared) he took such a drastic and irrevocable step as actually to ordain men himself, knowing as he must have done that this would set the Anglican Church finally against him and the Methodists generally, with the inevitable consequence of justifying some of the criticisms of his fiercest opponents in the minds of many who had previously withheld judgement.

The facts can be briefly outlined. Although requests by Methodist lay preachers to administer the sacrament had been made as early as 1755, both the brothers (especially Charles, who opposed the idea with exceptional vigour) refused. It was not until 1784 that any compromise in this antagonism was made: and then only in America, where shortage of ordained clergy was resulting in thousands of Methodists being deprived of the sacrament. Three men were therefore ordained by Wesley to meet this need: Richard Whatcoat, Thomas Vasey, and Dr. Coke as superintendent. The following year he ordained three men to serve in Scotland, with the proviso that they should not be permitted to administer when in England. Then, in 1789 (significantly, only after his brother's death) Wesley, after prolonged hesitation, ordained three men to serve in England: Alexander Mather, Thomas Rankin, and Henry Moore.

It is easy to condemn Wesley for committing an act of gross egotism. But before condemning, it is necessary to consider the dilemma Wesley was in—a dilemma arising out of conflicting principles. First, there was the principle we have already noted: that all members of Christ's body should be at His Table every week, or at least as often as possible. The developing situation, with more and more Anglican churches refusing communion to Methodists, made this increasingly impossible to fulfil. The second principle was his view of the priesthood as having a unique authority, the main outward expression of this being the right to administer the sacraments. In one of his letters he answered the criticism that to be logical he should not only allow laymen to preach (and lay preachers were one of the outstanding features of the Methodist system, as they have always remained) but also to administer sacraments, by stating that while there was abundant New Testament evidence of non-ordained men preaching, there was no evidence of such men administering, with the sole exception—in extreme circumstances—of Philip's baptizing. He did not belittle preaching, but did not include this in the priestly function. To have allowed lay celebration would have meant laying aside his belief in the supreme authority of Scripture, as well as opposing the teaching and practice of the Church he loved, and to which he always belonged.

Because of his stand on these two principles, there was only one alternative left: to ordain. But was this not doing what he refused to do on the second principle—acting against both New Testament teaching and that of his Church? Wesley believed not; against his Church's practice, certainly: but not against New Testament beliefs and practices. This had not always been his view; until 1746 he held the traditional view of the Apostolic Succession. But in that year he read two books which brought a radical change in his thinking: Peter King's *Account of the Primitive Church*, and Bishop Stillingfleet's *Irenicon*. These two books caused him to change his mind in three ways: first, they convinced him that the idea of episcopacy as a kind of monarchy had no Scriptural foundation—but that every congregation in the early Church was independent of others. Secondly, while an episcopal form of Church government is clearly described in the New Testament, 'it is not prescribed.'[52] Thirdly, and most important, the conviction was reached that bishops and presbyters were the same order; consequently whatever a bishop had the right to do, so had Wesley; and that included ordaining. In a letter of 1780 he wrote: 'I verily believe I have as good a right to ordain as to administer the Lord's Supper. But I see abundance of reasons why I should not use that right, unless I was turned out of the Church.'

The rights or wrongs of the case are not at issue here; we are simply trying to understand Wesley's position. Because the assumption of the right to ordain, and acting upon this assumption, were totally contrary to the view of his Church as it saw the question, Wesley hesitated for as long as possible. But in the end, it seemed to him that the third way offered least offence to his principles, revolutionary though this way still was. If any-

52. Ibid., p. 157.

body stands in the place of judgement for what happened it is not Wesley, but the Anglican bishops and clergy who by their coldness of heart and blindness of understanding forced Wesley into this cruel dilemma. (The Methodists were to do it themselves eighty years later in their treatment of William Booth.)

It is a final sign of Wesley's heart-searchings and continued hesitancy on the whole matter that, having taken the step of ordaining men for work in England, he did not leave plans and arrangements for a continuance of this as a permanent feature of Methodism. Perhaps he hoped that there would still be a change of heart on the part of the Anglicans; more likely, he was too ill during his final months of life to set about the major task of organization and liturgiology which such an arrangement would have necessitated. The fact remains that after his death there were no further ordinations for forty-five years; and that it was in this period that Methodism's swing to the side of nonconformity generally occurred, with several branches (in the divisions which took place) opting for the second alternative which Wesley had vigorously refused to allow: lay administration. And when, in 1836, further ordinations did at last take place in Methodism, the sole surviving ordinand at Wesley's own hands, Henry Moore, was not even invited to take part. The Wesleyan succession, if such a pretentious title can be given to something so short-lived, ended with Wesley's death.

(b) After Wesley

Nineteenth-century Methodism is not noted for its liturgiology. One simple test of this can be made by comparing the size of John Bowmer's two books: *The Sacrament of the Lord's Supper in Early Methodism* has 237 (large) pages; the sequel to this, *The Lord's Supper in Methodism, 1791–1960* has fifty (small) pages—and Dr. Bowmer has privately confessed to the writer that he had difficulty in filling even this small number.

Why was it that a tradition so obviously stamped into Methodism throughout Wesley's long life should so quickly disintegrate? The answer lies largely in the sort of people who constituted 'the Methodists'. They can be divided into three main groups. First, there were those who, while seeing in

Wesley's ideas certain elements which they recognized to be sadly lacking in their Mother Church, remained fundamentally Anglicans. The majority of these were back in the Anglican fold within a few years of Wesley's death. The remainder were composed of two groups: those who were fundamentally opposed to the Church, primarily because of its manifest class distinction (for instance, by the system of pew rents, so that there were simply no seats left over for the poorer classes) and were dissenters through and through; and those who, while antipathetic to the Church of England, desired to see Methodism established as a Church in its own right, an alternative to the Anglican Church on the one hand, and to the other nonconformist Churches on the other. Only a person of Wesley's strength of character could have kept such a varied company together; with his death the one great barrier to the blatant expression of their differing points of view was removed.

The first step away from Anglicanism came in 1795, with the Plan of Pacification. This laid down two points:

'The Lord's Supper shall not be administered in any chapel except the majority of the trustees of the chapel on the one hand and the majority of the stewards and leaders belonging to that chapel . . . on the other hand, allow it. . . . The Lord's Supper shall be administered by the superintendent, or such of his helpers as are in full connexion, as he shall appoint; provided no preacher be required to give it against his approbation; and should it be granted to any place, where the preachers on the circuit are all unwilling to give it, the superintendent shall in that case invite a neighbouring preacher, who is properly qualified, to administer it.'

This would not necessarily have offended Wesley; there are indications (and his ordinations are one of them) that he realized the inevitability of Methodism's becoming a denomination quite separate from Anglicanism, rather than remaining a 'ginger' group within it. There was certainly no hesitancy on the part of the Methodist people to seek communion outside the Church of England, and very few Methodist preachers refused to administer it.

For some, the Plan was too conservative; they wanted lay preachers, as well as ordained, to administer, and in 1797 this led to the first division within Methodism, with the formation of the Methodist New Connexion. This emphasis on lay ad-

ministration, and other radical ecclesiastical ideas, were typical
of most of the bodies who during the next thirty or so years
broke away from the main body of Methodists, the Wesleyans.
These include: the Primitive Methodists (1811), The Bible
Christians (1819), and the United Methodist Free Churches
(1857) who were actually a union of three independent groups
—the Protestant Methodists (1827), the Wesleyan Methodist
Association (1835) and the Wesleyan Reformers (1849); in
1907 the Methodist New Connexion, the Bible Christians, and
the United Methodist Free Churches united to form the United
Methodist Church. In all these Churches, worship was 'free';
there were service books, but these contained, or were used for,
only such services as marriage, burial, and the Covenant service. (The Methodist New Connexion 'handbook' did not
contain an order of service for communion.) Lay administration was a regular part of their church life—here the dissenting
note is sounded most strongly; and the communion itself was
held at most monthly, often quarterly. Their emphasis is seen
in the chapels they erected throughout the century—often
leading to a village having three Methodist chapels, all of
different branches. In them the dominant feature was the pulpit, with the communion table subordinated.

The branch of Methodism which remained most loyal to
Wesley's principles and practices was the Wesleyan Methodist
Church, but even there compromises were made. The weekly
communion became monthly; the glorious morning communion services of Wesley's day were replaced with evening
celebrations; and frequently these were truncated versions of
the liturgy, held at the close of the normal preaching service.
Wesley's Service Book went through a number of revisions,
but the indications are that it was not used in many areas;
some admittedly used the Book of Common Prayer but it is
probable that a large number followed the other Methodist
Churches in having a free service. Although lay celebration
was discouraged, Conference allowed for it where it could be
shown that without it congregations would be deprived of a
monthly sacrament.

If we ask, what happened to the enthusiasm of the first
Methodists, the answer is that it was redirected into other

channels, social and political. In the formation of the earliest Trade Unions,[53] in various acts of social reform,[54] and later in the foundation of the Labour Party,[55] Methodists were intensely active. For many of them their Sunday worship became primarily a means of gaining 'fuel' for the following week.[56] In recent times questions have been asked within Methodism as to whether the social work of the nineteenth century was as effective as was once believed;[57] but that it was an honest attempt to translate piety into practical living there can be no doubt. Gibson Winter comments:[58]

'When one considers the social concerns and practical charity that issued from the movements of Spener, Franke, and the Methodist Revival, it is quite evident that pietistic concern with the experiences of faith need not degenerate into the private preoccupations of pietism. The Methodist movement in England is perhaps the most decisive example of the social significance of a piety which was appropriate to a particular form of the Church in a specific social situation. The working classes had entered English cities in search of work as they were closed off the land. . . . The labouring poor were simply excluded from the common worship of the English people. Moreover, the conditions of the working classes during these centuries following the Reformation were worse than anything experienced in the horrors of nineteenth-century America. The ministry of reconciliation exercised through the Methodist revival remains a landmark of mission and social concern in the history of the Christian Church.'

Winter here does not do justice to the sacramental and catholic note in the Methodist revival, but his point seems nonetheless valid. The fact that the spokesmen of the Anglican Church during this century were almost exclusively unsympathetic to

53. Six of the seven Tolpuddle martyrs were Methodists, and the leader, George Loveless, was a local preacher.

54. E.g. The National Children's Home and Orphanage, founded by Dr. Stephenson, a Methodist minister.

55. 'The Labour Party owes more to Methodism than to Marx'—Morgan Phillips, Secretary of the Party in 1959.

56. And often, political guidance: many members of Parliament used to attend regularly at the Kingsway Hall to hear Hugh Price Hughes preach; a few of their successors still occasionally hear the present incumbent, Dr. (now Lord) Soper.

57. This theory is strongly held by a student of the nineteenth century, the Rev. Colin Morris, at present President of the United Church of Zambia.

58. Winter, op. cit., p. 22.

the working classes was one reason for the growing alienation; the other, as we have noted, was the anti-liturgical aspect of nineteenth-century Methodism. The Oxford Movement, which in many respects would have appealed to Wesley (as it was in part inspired by Wesley) was incomprehensible, if not positively frightening, to the majority of methodists.

In 1932 the remaining separated branches of Methodism— The Wesleyans, the Primitive, and United Methodists—came together to form the Methodist Church. It was a remarkable combination, bringing into one Church people of widely differing ecclesiastical and liturgical views. These differences continue, though not in such extreme form, to the present day. One of the unifying factors has been the Methodist service book, 'The Book of Offices', which besides having the usual occasional services, contains the Order of Morning Prayer and two orders of service for the communion. The former is used in a small, but increasing number of churches as the normal Sunday morning service; one of the latter is almost invariably used in celebrating the sacrament.

These two services greatly differ; the first is a modified (though now only slightly) form of Cranmer; the second is an abbreviated service, intended to be used at the close of the preaching service by congregations unused to any kind of service book. Two elements of this truncated service are interesting. It places the Prayer of Oblation *before* communion, where it rightly belongs; one can only feel that this was an accident on the part of those who prepared it; and it includes two verses of one of Wesley's Easter hymns as a regular part of the post-communion—an admirable move on the part of the committee.

Communion in modern Methodism has a more important place than it had a century ago, though most churches will not celebrate it more frequently than monthly; but it is becoming a little less frequent that the sacrament is held as an after-service. Much credit for this must go to the Methodist Sacramental Fellowship which was founded in 1935 with three aims: to reintroduce basic dogma into Methodist church life; to work for the union of all Churches; and to recover the centrality of the Eucharist in Methodism. Alongside this may be mentioned the Order of Christian Witness, which on the surface seems 'Billy Graham-ish' in its evangelical aims, but in fact is far removed from this, both by the honesty of its approach to people, its social concern and, most significantly, its emphasis on communion: all local 'campaigns' organized by this Order have the final communion service as their keynote.

There are indications of increasing concern in contemporary Methodism about some of the issues raised by the Liturgical Movement. The Conference Report on Worship (1961) was an indication of a renewed interest in the structure of worship, and we shall refer to it in the next section. In 1963 the first Methodist Liturgical Conference was held in Bristol, and members present have agreed to make a study of various aspects of liturgy. The Book of Offices is in the process of revision by sub-committees of the Methodist Faith and Order Committee: the Baptismal service was completed first. The Notting Hill group ministry have been allowed to go ahead with remarkable experiments both in worship and social witness. In 1961 the Renewal Group was formed, and now has upwards of a hundred members, mostly in their thirties. The Group has seven aims: to study the nature of the Church, to find patterns of ministry and worship relevant to the age; to discover the real function of the layman; to find ways of Christian action in social and political life; to find new methods of evangelism; and to work for Christian unity. At the Methodist Conference of 1965 there were indications of fairly widespread approval among representatives for some of these aims. Finally, and most remarkably, is the current move to unite with the Church of England. Seventy-eight per cent of the representatives at the 1965 Conference voted to keep moving in the direction suggested by the 1963 Report on the Conversations between Anglicans and Methodists.

All these are promising signs; but one feels that they are not enough. Amid all the new ideas which are abroad there remains a strong core of indifference. Methodists at circuit and local church level seem generally unable or unwilling to think along the lines suggested by the Liturgical Movement. We must now turn to a detailed consideration of the insights of the movement as they might be applied to the current Methodist situation. We shall therefore take each of the six points in turn, and see what they imply; then we shall, in the light of these implications, look to the future, and attempt to foretell what the next steps and changes will be.

B: THE IMPLICATIONS OF THE LITURGICAL MOVEMENT FOR METHODISM

In this section we propose to take each of the 'insights' of the Liturgical Movement in turn and relate them, where possible and necessary, to contemporary Methodism. This procedure is somewhat artificial, inasmuch as practical applications of one issue may well overlap another; but this seems the most straightforward way of treating the problem. The three areas where there is most to say are those of worship generally, the Eucharist, and the link between worship and witness. What little there is to say about the implications of the return to basic dogma will be included under the section on the Eucharist. The section on the rediscovery of the Church as the body can have little amplification; in itself this is a theoretical point, which becomes practical only when applied to the questions of worship and witness. On symbolism and architecture there can be little to add to what has already been said, as Methodism has no *unique* needs in this sphere.

It must be added that in any consideration of the situation in contemporary Methodism, one is aware of the great changes which appear likely to occur during the next ten or twenty years. The Anglican-Methodist Conversations on the one hand, and the hope expressed at the Nottingham Faith and Order Conference that there will be unity between all the major English non-Roman Catholic Churches by 1980 on the other, both suggest that there can be nothing static in current Methodism, with the consequence that at least some of the suggestions here made will soon be superfluous. One wishes that this were likely to be the case; but experience warns the modern reformer that changes in ecclesiastical structures will not take place overnight. Even if the proposed service of reconciliation between Anglicans and Methodists does eventually take place, it is envisaged that there will be a period of 'growing together' before any form of organic union can be finalized; and this period could be anything from ten to thirty years.

It is in this context that the proposals contained in this thesis are put forward: in the belief that the pattern of church life herein envisaged is the one most likely to enable Methodism to make her approach to Anglicanism, and to the other denominations, so that she may become best equipped to play her part in the 'coming great Church'.

(a) The Church as the Body of Christ

The great requirement here is for more study on the nature of the Church—which for Methodists means, in the main, more reading of works by non-Methodists. The belief dies hard that being a Christian is essentially to have a personal faith, preferably resulting from a definite personal experience leading to an act of self-commitment to Christ; with the consequence that all church activities are viewed as a means of encouraging one's faith. The aim of worship becomes inspirational; midweek meetings become escapist, in the sense that they aim at the deepening of the spiritual life without reference to the world situation in which the members are placed. The mission of the Church becomes geared to the determination and enthusiasm of the individual members in persuading non-members to 'come to church'. The result is rather like a religious club, excellent for those who are temperamentally inclined that way, but far removed from the sense of being the leaven in the lump, the salt of the earth. Instead of being the manifestation of Christ's presence in the world which God made and loves, the Church becomes a movement directed *against* the world, a fellowship of believers, the depth of whose Christian conviction is judged by the number of regular appearances they make at the church meetings.

This attitude will ultimately only be overcome by a developed sense of what it is to be in the body of Christ. In worship there must be the greatest possible discouragement to the individual who views the whole procedure as a kind of mystical entertainment, prepared for his benefit; there must be more teaching on what it means to be part of 'the sacramental society'; the thinking of members must be so directed that they begin to think of the Church and the world in incarnational terms—and of themselves as a partial expression of this. The age-old distinction between 'sacred' and 'secular' must be abandoned on the grounds that, because we inhabit a world created by Almighty God, and because He is omnipresent, there can be no *places* inherently secular—or sacred: there can be only sacred or secular *people*; and whether what they do is sacred or secular depends on their motives and intentions.

To discuss any of these propositions in detail here would be to encroach on a later section. At this point we shall discuss one issue only: the question of baptism. A right understanding of this sacrament can be a major aid to a right understanding of the body. Present procedure hardly encourages this understanding. The service, lasting about ten minutes, is generally held at the close of the main morning act of worship, attended by those members of the congregation who feel inclined to remain (most do stay). It is not rare for baptisms to be held in the afternoon, with only the minister present as a representative of the local church. Occasionally the service is conducted within the context of the main act of worship; more rarely, the whole service is conducted as a baptismal service. A record is kept of the babies baptized, and in most churches a member is given the job of keeping in touch with the homes of baptized infants. While the Methodist Youth Department is becoming increasingly insistent on the importance of this task, in many churches it is little more than a formality.

Concerning the theology of the sacrament, ideas are somewhat vague. For the majority of the parents—being nonchurchgoers—it is difficult to avoid the conclusion that superstition is the main motive behind their presenting their offspring. Most church members would concede that the sacrament has some kind of Scriptural authority, but would reject any theory of regeneration. Only a minority of them, along with a larger proportion of the ministers, would view the sacrament as primarily an act of Christian initiation, the first step into the family of God, in which the process of regeneration will, it is hoped, continue all through the child's life.

Manifestly, a strong emphasis on baptism as the rite of

initiation into the body, with the appropriate form of liturgy to express this, could be an outstanding means of bringing back a sense of the body to the Church as a whole. There are hopeful signs in this direction. The service approved by the Methodist Faith and Order committee has as its main title, 'Entry into the Church', with 'Baptism' as its sub-title. The intention is that this service shall be more closely linked with confirmation, or entry into full Church membership, than hitherto. The preamble states explicitly that the service must, if at all possible, be held in church during the main act of worship; and it is stressed that the local church must maintain 'regular oversight' of those who have been baptized. The proposed service could, with a little adaptation, be made into the entire service for the occasion: it is a weakness that the service does not stand entire in its own right, but some account, it seems, must be taken of reactions throughout the Methodist Church generally.

The Renewal Group are not so concerned about such reaction, and have produced a draft order of baptism which is an entire service in itself. It has been used very effectively in Notting Hill, where the responsibilities of the church in maintaining a link with the homes of the baptized are firmly undertaken. The concluding prayers of both these services affirm the sacrament as initiation into God's family. The Renewal Group order has a prayer of thanksgiving which begins:

'Holy and merciful God, we thank Thee that Thou hast called us to be Thy people, and dost also call our children unto Thee, marking them with this Sacrament, as a sign and a seal of Thy love. . . .'

The Faith and Order committee's service reads:

'We thank Thee, most merciful Father, that it has pleased thee to receive *these children* for thine own *children* by adoption within thy family the Church.

'We humbly ask thee, therefore, that *they* may learn to show forth by *their* living what *they* now *are* by thy calling, and may come at the last to thy eternal kingdom. . . .'

It is the hope of many who are concerned about the doctrine of the Church in the minds of the Methodist people that the new baptismal service approved by Conference when used throughout the Connexion, through its liturgy a greater sense of the privileges and responsibilities of being part of a corporate community, rather than a group of like-minded individuals, will begin to develop. This will depend to some extent on the form of the Covenant Service after it has been revised (fortunately, the same group who prepared the draft baptismal service are to work on this too). As it stands, this service is so intensely personal ('I am no longer my own, but Thine; put me to what Thou wilt, rank me with whom Thou wilt . . .' etc.) that it has become one of the weapons in the armoury of those who react against the 'body' concept. On these grounds alone there is enough justification to be rid of the service altogether; yet by one of the greatest ironies in current church relationships one constantly hears Anglicans declaring that they envy Methodists their Covenant service! Not a few Methodists would be happy to hand it over in its entirety; but this would be a gift with a sting in its tail, hardly appropriate to the current cordial mood between the two Churches. If, as seems sadly probable, the service is to be retained, it is to be hoped that it will be revised to become a corporate renewal of the Covenant, a rededication of the whole Church to its responsibility of being the expression of Christ in the world. But as the liturgy of the Eucharist makes this point week by week, there seems little reason for preparing a special service in which to say it.

One further way whereby this sense of community could be inculcated in Methodism is the encouragement of members to take a daily office as the framework of their private prayers. It would be a bold Methodist who would attempt to assess the current depth, or extent, of the devotional life of the Methodist people; it must be accepted that in many it is non-existent, or else extremely shallow; and Methodists are not alone in this. One of the main reasons for this must be the paucity of teaching on the best way to use the few minutes a day which are put aside for prayers. Many have ceased praying because their 'quiet time' was becoming repetitive or aimless. A daily office has long been overdue—not least for the ministers. (The proposed revisions of Morning Prayer and Evensong made by the Joint Liturgical Group, the main change being that of abbreviation, make this a greater possibility, at least for the ministers.) If church members had a given framework, into which they could introduce their own private prayers at a certain point, they would lose nothing from their present practice and gain much: a sense of shape and direction, a staff to rely on when they did not 'feel like' praying; and above all, a link with others who were using the same office (this is, of course, assuming that the office were used at home).

In brief, one can only express the hope that any procedure in Methodist church life which can help to inculcate a sense that the individual is an integral part of the local Christian community, so that at no point, not even in his prayer life, is he 'on his own', will be introduced and encouraged. A great onus of responsibility for this falls on the shoulders of the ministers; but there are increasing signs that (at least among the younger men) they are aware of this, and prepared to act as necessary. The fact that this awareness exists at all must be seen as a sign of the increasing understanding of the Liturgical Movement, under the guidance of the Holy Spirit.

(b) The Nature of Worship

Of the various aspects of worship which we discussed in connexion with the Liturgical Movement in chapter 2, the two which emerge as most applicable to Methodist worship today are its corporate aspect, with which may be linked its objectivity, and its need for relevance.

I. CORPORATE WORSHIP

The best way of treating this theme in the context of contemporary Methodism appears to be that of presenting the main arguments frequently presented by Methodists, either in defence of their present procedure, or in opposition to what is happening in manifestations of the Liturgical Movement in other denominations. These arguments resolve themselves into three.

1. *Our Worship is already Corporate*

This argument is based primarily on a comparison between Methodist worship and Roman Catholic worship as it has been traditionally conducted in this country. As we have described it[59] this appears to most Free Churchmen what Roman Catholic leaders are now beginning to condemn it for being—a spectacle, where only the priest is active, and the congregations are passive observers. Against this background, Methodist worship emerges as a genuinely congregational activity, with all present both knowing and understanding what takes place, and making their contribution to the proceedings.

If this were true, one of the main contentions of this thesis would be inapplicable; but is it true? Any visitor to a typical Methodist service must deny this. There are exceptions (and they are fortunately becoming more widespread) but generally speaking there are only two places in our worship where the congregation actively (that is, verbally) participate: in reciting the Lord's Prayer, and in the hymns. For the rest of the service —the lessons, prayers, notices, and sermon—the congregation sits back and listens to the voice of one single person: the minister or layman planned to conduct the service. The choice of hymns and lessons, the theme of the prayers and the sermon—all these are left entirely to him. He even decides the order of service (though, as we shall see, this has become almost as invariable as the services of the Book of Common Prayer). In short, if we are justified in criticizing a Roman Catholic congregation for being no more than observers of an act of worship, an equally justifiable criticism of Methodist worship is that the worshippers are little more than listeners-in. It is a moot point whether sight or sound demands the most active concentration: experience of television versus sound radio suggests the former.

The real tragedy in this is that this situation need never have arisen had the point about congregational participation been fully grasped generations ago. At every point in the worship there is the opportunity for corporate activity. The lessons could be read by members of the congregation. The Creed could be said by all (it is one of our gravest weaknesses that, outside the communion service—and it is often omitted there— the Creed is seldom spoken by the gathered body of Christians). The prayers could become the expression of the congregation

59. pp. 53f.

if they could *see* them, and join in saying them: even extemporary prayer, which must not be ruled out (as we shall discuss in the next sub-section) could, if carefully prepared, begin with a short statement of the themes to be covered. The notices could be read by a church official (this usually means more time is taken over them, but this disadvantage is offset by the change in voice); in the West Indies it is frequently the custom for members of the congregation to rise spontaneously to make announcements, and provided these be at the end of the service one sees no objection to this custom; after all, the notices are basically the concerns of the church in its life as a community during the week. Even the sermon need not be a monologue; at the very least, it could emerge from a discussion between preacher and congregation during the previous week, so that those members who attended the preliminary meeting would have made a contribution to the thought; but there seems little reason why the sermon should continue to be a monologue in any case. If, as is generally admitted, the main need today is teaching, then the twenty or twenty-five minutes' address is not the most efficient method of doing this. There is the need for the congregation to have the opportunity of raising issues which the speaker arouses in their minds; it would not necessarily be inapposite to have a different point of view from the preacher's presented by a member of the congregation. This kind of dialogue sermon faces the risk that members of the church will be too shy, in a church building, to speak up at first; but experience suggests that after a time this does not constitute a difficulty. This is especially true if the seats are movable, so that they can be rearranged in a rectangular or circular formation. It is a great psychological drawback to any kind of corporate activity in worship if those who attend can see, apart from the preacher, only the backs of their fellow-worshippers' heads.

The question of hymns in Methodism demands a separate discussion. In terms of time (there are usually five of them, lasting on an average four minutes each) they take up a considerable part of the services, so that on the surface it would seem that the contention that Methodist worship is corporate to quite a considerable extent is correct. It is indeed often argued that our hymns are our liturgy: in the hymn-book are hymns for all occasions and moods, and for every element of worship. There are hymns of praise and adoration, hymns of confession and thankfulness for the forgiveness which follows, hymns of intercession and petition, and of dedication and oblation. Admittedly, a haphazard choice of hymns will not allow these varied elements to emerge; but most Methodists know their hymn-books better than their Bibles, and Methodist preachers, both ministerial and lay, usually spend more time over their choice of hymns than over any other part of the worship except the sermon. (There is now a 'hymnary' published annually, with a selection of hymns for every Sunday in the year.)

One's hesitation at this point arises not from any denial of the corporate nature of hymn-singing, but from the nature of the hymns themselves. In the first place, it is too easy for a congregation to be diverted from the words they are singing by the tune. The implications of Wesley's great hymn of thanksgiving for forgiveness, 'And can it be that I should gain An interest in my Saviour's blood?' are lost on large numbers of the singers because of the hilarious tune to which it is usually sung (there is an alternative tune, 'Lansdown', which suits the words better, but this is unknown to most Methodist congregations). Even worse than this is the way preachers choose, and congregations sing, hymns with totally unworthy words, simply because the tune is known and liked. They will sing anything from the verbal catalogue of 'Lord! it is good for us to be High on the mountain here with Thee' or the utter doggerel, if not positive heresy, of 'Once to every man and nation Comes the moment to decide', with its reference to 'Some great cause, God's new Messiah', to the world-hating masochism of 'Come Saviour Jesus from above! . . . Empty my heart of earthly love . . . Nor will I hear, nor will I speak, Of any other love but Thine'—a hymn written by a woman who had just been jilted by her lover (significantly, translated from the French by John Wesley, whose relationships with the opposite sex were not entirely fortunate).

There would be less need for concern on this point if it were true that in Methodist worship only the best hymns were being sung. Unfortunately, this is not so, as several recent surveys suggest.[60] About half of the hymns in the much-vaunted Methodist Hymn Book were written in the nineteenth century, a singularly dire period for hymnology. There is a trivial and even boring quality about them which is not to be found in the hymns of the three great periods of hymnology: the first three or four centuries, when the great Latin and Greek hymns were composed; the Reformation; and the seventeenth and eighteenth century, when the hymns of Wesley and Watts were written. But it appears that the nineteenth century effusions are generally preferred.

A further objection to the policy of making hymns into a liturgy arises from the fact that they were not written with this in mind. A hymn is, or should be, what the name suggests: an expression of praise to God, a shout of joy, an offering by the hymn-writer to the God to whom it is addressed. The majority of hymns do not express this, and thus the objectivity of worship is lost. In too many of the hymns the worshipper is encouraged to think of himself. One of the most popular hymns in Methodism (top of the poll in a recent nation-wide survey) is, 'In heavenly love abiding' which ends with the words:

> My hope I cannot measure,
> My path to life is free;
> My Saviour has my treasure,
> And He will walk with me.

It is no wonder, with this kind of hymn being sung in abundance and the attitude of mind to which it inevitably leads, that one Roman Catholic, after attending Methodist worship on many occasions, could declare, 'You act as though you had God in your pockets.' The fact is that, generally speaking, hymns lack the objective note contained in such canticles as the Te Deum or the Venite, or in many of the Psalms. Even Wesley's hymns are often too introspective to be of great value in genuine corporate and objective worship; and the hymns in which he is most objective—the hymns on the Lord's Supper—are ironic-

60. The *Methodist Recorder* conducted such a survey some years ago. The result was revealing. In the 'top twenty' the Victorian hymns almost completely ousted everyone else—including Wesley.

ally enough the very hymns which find least representation in the current hymn book.

A third objection to hymns—their vocabulary—will be dealt with in a later section. Meanwhile, one concludes that if hymns are to play the role in Methodist worship which our present structure offers to them, there must be a much greater degree of care in choosing them. At least half of the present 984 could be confined to oblivion without any great loss; of the remainder (together with others more recently written) it would be wisest to make two sections: one for use in public worship, the other for private devotions (into which most of the hymns of Wesley in the present hymn book would be put). If it be objected that this will leave a very small range from which to choose, the answer is that Methodists must be encouraged to sing other parts of their services. We have already mentioned the Psalms and Canticles (which are found at the back of the hymn book, are quite often spoken by the congregation, but—paradoxically, because they are all set to music—seldom sung); the Creed could be sung; and, particularly in the Eucharist, many of the great prayers of the Church offer themselves for congregational singing (nobody who has sung the Gloria in Excelsis at Taizé could ever again condemn this as a boring prayer). With these added opportunities for singing, the choir might then rediscover its true function: to lead the congregation in the musical part of the worship. At present, Methodist choirs are generally reduced to justifying themselves by singing an anthem, almost as a set piece; frequently these anthems not only lack the spirit of worship but are positively sub-Christian. This kind of choir activity is a further example of the lack of truly corporate worship in Methodism.

We have spent what is perhaps a disproportionate amount of time on the question of hymns, but this has been dictated by the hold they have on Methodist worship. Congregations generally will allow even the most shoddily-prepared worship, including a poor sermon, if they are given a 'good sing'. This attitude can only be changed by demonstrating that such 'enjoyment' can be found in the worship itself, through the liturgy. There is much to rejoice over in the kerygma, without relying on artificial aids. If the basic worship is cold, stiff, and dead, such singing will appear to be little more than 'whistling to keep one's spirits up'. The answer lies in the worship generally; one's conviction is that if the insights of the Liturgical Movement are allowed to operate in the structures of it, a sense of joy will be an inevitable corollary.

2. *Extemporary Prayer can be Liturgical; and Written Orders Militate against the New Testament (and Methodist) Emphasis on Spiritual Worship*

The argument contained in the second part of this objection is not a frivolous one; it is sincerely held by a large number of Methodists. They point out that to enshrine our prayers exclusively in a written form is to oppose the free operation of the Holy Spirit who 'bloweth where he listeth', and thus to remove the inspirational note from worship. Most Methodists who argue in this way will affirm that the Anglican way of worship is a perfect example of what they are most afraid of: liturgically excellent, aesthetically satisfying, but spiritually dead.

Not a few Anglicans would, it appears, sympathize with this judgement. There is a good deal of Anglican self-criticism abroad, and the Book of Common Prayer is not being treated as sacrosanct. Indeed, Anglicans are considerably more critical of their worship than Methodists are of theirs. In the process it is being realized that some form of extemporary, or free prayer can be beneficial in an act of worship. A rubric in the 1928 Prayer Book said:

'Note, that subject to any direction which the Bishop may give, the Minister may, at his discretion, after the conclusion of Morning or Evening Prayer or of any service contained in this book, offer prayer in his own words.'

Despite the rejection of this book, the practice of some form of free prayer is now a regular procedure in many Anglican churches. There is nothing which has emerged through the insights of the Liturgical Movement which suggests that extemporary prayer has no value: what is emerging is that the two types of prayer are not alternatives, but are self-complementary. Each has its strong and weak points. Written prayers have dignity and brevity, but lack the immediacy of extemporary prayers: but is 'the Spirit' likely to be any more manifest in the latter?

The answer to this is by no means as clear-cut as many Methodists assume. Anyone who has had regular experience of praying extemporarily, or hearing others do so, knows how easy it is to fall into certain patterns of phraseology and theme. This is inevitable, because both are limited to the vocabulary and thought-forms of any individual. In many ways, therefore, written prayers, because there is an almost infinite number of themes to choose, and because the vocabulary is gleaned from the liturgical writings of countless Christians through the centuries, are wider in their scope than are extemporary prayers. These can certainly on occasion be inspired, so that the whole congregation is caught up in a mood of fervour; more frequently they are as uninspired as the dullest forms of written prayers.

There are numerous reasons why these written orders are preferable for congregational (that is, corporate) worship. The first has already been indicated: when a congregation can see and read prayers, they are more likely to be able to understand them and participate properly. Extemporary prayer can do this also—provided it is extremely carefully prepared, and that the congregation is told beforehand what themes are to be prayed about, and possibly allowed to make some kind of response to each section, or clause. The traditional extemporary prayer, where the preacher begins without any clear idea of what exactly he is going to say, will usually leave a modern congregation unmoved, and incapable of following his flights of thought. One's own experience is that, among young people in particular, there is a deeper sense of worship when the service is set before them, and they can say the prayers themselves.

A second factor in favour of written forms arises out of the different moods of worship. The very fact that most Methodists would not understand this point indicates how feeble is our understanding of liturgy. There is movement in worship, as there is in a symphony; there are tranquil moods and exultant moods; moments of preparation and moments of crisis; occasions when the movement is speedy towards its goal, and occasions of slower, more peaceful meditation. When the service is taken just as the preacher announces it, it is almost impossible to be aware of these differences of mood. With written orders it is possible to be aware (even if not all members of Anglican churches are) of the 'shape of the liturgy'. Furthermore, repetition of certain prayers at certain points in the worship can be a means of impressing this on the minds of the worshippers. To desire different phraseology, different themes, week after week is almost like desiring changes in 'The Messiah' for variety's sake. As Dr. Rattenbury points out[61] any parent who reads stories to his children knows how fatal it is to change the words or omit a section, for children are natural ritualists, as they reveal in their request, 'Tell me it again'. Similarly, most adults know the joy of hearing again the well-known speeches of a Shakespearean play. The same is true in worship. To say the same prayers week after week need not be vain repetition, but can give the worshipper the opportunity of finding new significance in the phrases uttered. The collect for purity, the General Confession, and the General Thanksgiving, are prayers which can be described as spiritual simply because they speak to varying circumstances of worshippers at different times, even though the actual wording of them remains the same.

Furthermore, the phrase 'spiritual worship' begs several questions. The spirit of whom we speak is the Spirit of Christ, not just an atmosphere of enthusiasm, Christian or otherwise. Worship which is of the spirit must be subject to theological constraint; even the freest forms of worship are constrained by the teaching of Scripture; if this did not happen, some extremely odd concepts might easily emerge. Again, because the Spirit is the Spirit of truth, 'spiritual' worship will have links with the worship of Christians through the centuries—worship which is enshrined in the various church liturgies. Raymond Abba, a Congregationalist, writes:[62]

'In so far as liturgy is shaped by the Christian revelation and embodies the spirit-prompted worship of former days, it may well be the channel of the same Holy Spirit's activity in the Church today.'

61. Rattenbury, *Vital Elements of Public Worship*, Epworth, 1936, p. 122.
62. R. Abba, *Principles of Christian Worship*, O.U.P., 1957, p. 9.

The fact is that ordered worship implies restraint on individual contributions. Even the prophet needs a disciplined organization, as the early Church soon discovered: otherwise the worship would tend to become a mixture of confusion and chaos, as I Corinthians 14 reveals. Both discipline and freedom are needed in worship; the former needs to be stressed in those Churches which have emphasized the latter, and vice versa.

'When ordered service eliminates spontaneous worship, too great a price may be paid for order. At the same time, the fact that too great individualism can destroy common worship, and break up communities, as it often has, must not be ignored. . . . The Church which follows exclusively the one or the other will lose in power. The Church which somehow combines both in one body, will approach most nearly to the early Christian ideal.'[63]

3. *These suggestions embodied in the Liturgical Movement are not Methodist emphases*

This argument leaves several issues unresolved, not least what the 'Methodist emphases' are. (John Vincent has suggested[64] that, whatever they may have been in the past, the only definite emphasis which gives Methodism a contribution in the world Church today is her pragmatism. If this is so, perhaps she will be not unwilling to view what is happening through the Liturgical Movement and act upon it.) Normally when our 'emphases' are being discussed, it is those which are typical of nineteenth-century Methodism, rather than the classical Methodism of the eighteenth century. If Wesley's approach is taken as a guide, the desire for corporate, objective worship will not seem alien to our traditions.

Even if we grant the truth of the assertion, it still does not follow that this is a relevant argument. Methodism may have distinctive features, but she is still part of the body of Christ, sharing basic truths and practices with all other denominations. Rattenbury writes:

'The features . . . are of course vital to the *distinctive* character of Methodism. If Methodism loses them . . . it would have a name but no spiritual substance. . . . [But] Methodism cannot stand upon its

63. Rattenbury, op. cit., p. 40f.
64. J. J. Vincent, *Christ and Methodism*, Epworth, 1965.

features, it must stand upon its feet. What is always to be feared in any society with special features is the error of over-valuing the features and under-valuing the body.'[65]

It is not our purpose to consider here whether in fact the traditional Methodist emphases—justification by faith, assurance, Christian holiness etc.—remain: one's impression is that they do not, and that it is time this were said clearly and often. Even if this be too pessimistic a judgement, it appears obvious that Methodism can no longer subsist on these alone; she is not so independent that she can afford to spurn a gift of the Spirit—the Liturgical Movement—which has manifestly been bringing a breath of new life to other denominations.

Hidden behind this argument, however, are two other ideas. One is, that what the Liturgical Movement has to offer is the call for us, very simply, to 'imitate the Anglicans'. This is not necessarily a bad thing, of course, but if it could be proved true, it would naturally rid the Liturgical Movement of any wide-reaching claim on Methodism, and give it an extremely narrow image. It must be admitted that a large number of liturgical innovations in our time have appeared to be reflecting certain elements in the Church of England: the 8 a.m. communion service; the Holy Table pushed back against the wall; Mattins as the 11 a.m. service. The basic answer to this charge is, as we have seen, that the effect of the Liturgical Movement in the Anglican Church is precisely the opposite of these trends. There, altars are being drawn forward and the Basilican position adopted; 8 a.m. communion and 11 a.m. Mattins are being dropped in favour of the Parish Communion. It would be difficult to see the Spirit at work in the movement if its effects in different denominations were so widely different. It is necessary, therefore, to emphasize that those elements in Methodism which desire greater similarity between Methodist and Anglican worship may well have reason on their side, but are acting, in the main, independently of any influence from the Liturgical Movement. This Movement is calling for nobody to imitate anyone else, except possibly the Primitive Church, and this is a call to every denomination. It offers certain guiding principles which each denomination must itself

65. Rattenbury, op. cit., p. 83f.

apply to its own situation. We have already seen how the movement, in calling all Churches to go back to their common ancestry before their separate traditions started with their disputes with other Churches, is thereby taking them back to their common source, and is furthering the aims of the ecumenical movement. There are many other written orders of worship which Methodism could well use, besides the Book of Common Prayer, including South India, Taizé, and the American Lutheran service; but one hopes that Methodism will herself experiment in this field, using the best of the liturgical services which are available, but also bringing her own insights into the developing situation. We shall discuss in the next section the question of the Eucharist, but can suggest here that for our non-eucharistic worship (if there can be such a thing!) we need a new edition of the book of services published in 1935, 'Divine Worship'. One would hope that any new book will not be so verbose, so repetitive or so dull as this book is; but the purpose for which it was intended remains relevant to contemporary Methodism.

The other, usually unspoken, thought behind the argument which heads this section, is that 'we like things the way they have always been': in other words, change of any kind is to be resisted. To put this instinct into words is to condemn it. It is an attitude encouraged, strangely enough, by the itinerant system for ministers. This has its advantages, but a big disadvantage is the opportunity it gives strong-willed local leaders to become entrenched in their traditional ideas and to resist all change. The consequence of this attitude is to be far removed from the idea of worship as a God-given thing; instead it is unconsciously accepted as 'what we like doing' and one believes that this attitude is stronger in Methodism than in any other major denomination. It is an attitude which must be ruthlessly opposed. To run local churches as though they were clubs, with their elected officials who determine the rules, is to miss the vision of the wider Church, to be blind to any movements beyond the four walls of the building, and eventually to lose one's way in the great turmoil which is now descending on all the Churches. It cannot be over-emphasized that the Church is not ours, but God's; and that there is a certain

THE LITURGICAL MOVEMENT AND METHODISM

'given-ness' about worship which means that it is there for acceptance, not debate. What those who resist change seem incapable of appreciating is that what they have to offer is being increasingly rejected by contemporary England. There is the need for decisive action, before our rut becomes a grave.

One practical problem which, more than any other denomination, Methodism has to face in considering her worship, is that of her local preachers. Seven out of every ten services on an average Sunday are conducted by this body of laymen. Inevitably a good deal of variation occurs, both in the ability to lead worship, and in the general approach to the question. Hitherto, while examinations in Old and New Testament and in Christian Doctrine have been compulsory, the exam in Worship and Preaching has been an optional extra (though, before being finally 'recognized', local preachers on trial have always had to conduct a service in the presence of representatives of the local ministers and laymen, and theoretically could be refused recognition if their capability in this sphere were questioned). A further weakness concerning their practical training has been that their text-book on worship and preaching has been overweighted on preaching—three-quarters of it dealt with this half of the theme.

Strong attempts have been made by the Local Preachers' Department to rectify the situation, and a new, more evenly balanced text-book prepared. Previously, a supplement to the text-book by the writer had been approved, and was used for two years. After that, the examination in the subject became compulsory.

It is clear that if congregations are to be encouraged to 'think liturgically', there must be a greater degree of consistency than at present obtains. The situation therefore calls for considerably more constraint on local preachers' freedom to construct services as they wish. Admittedly, most of them (and most ministers too) accept a set pattern, which varies little throughout Methodism. But within this pattern—which can always be varied at will—it is possible for essential elements of worship, such as the assurance of forgiveness, to be overlooked. It must be concluded that Methodism needs certain 'given' structures for her non-eucharistic services—perhaps six to ten of these—within which there is scope for the personal contribution of the preacher, but to the basic structure of which he must adhere. This will demand a greater degree of Conference authority over our worship than the Church has hitherto been willing to assume; but one feels this is essential if the different anomalies in Methodist worship as at present conducted are to be removed.

II. RELEVANT WORSHIP

At this stage we are concerned solely with the 'initiated'—the regular churchgoer, to whom the recital of, for instance, the Creed has a certain amount of meaning. The question of worship for the non-initiated, and the whole attitude of the Church generally to those 'outside', will be considered separately in our final section.

Even to the initiated there are several ways in which modern worship must appear 'irrelevant': to their own thought-processes, to the worship conducted in other denominations, and to the world in which they are placed. We shall consider each of these in turn.

1. *Relevant to the Congregation concerned*

The point at issue here may be presented by two quotations, one by a Lutheran, Vilmos Vajta,[66] the other by Louis Bouyer[67]:

'What at one time was decisive in the history of the liturgy is not an indisputable necessity for the present-day congregation. The liturgical creativity of the spirit in the contemporary congregation dare not be disregarded. It is, therefore, always dangerous to enforce forms upon a congregation which were produced in another era. A liturgical revival dare not take as its ultimate goal the mere renaissance of discarded liturgical forms.'

'We must not try to provide an artificial congregation to take part in an antiquarian liturgy, but rather to prepare the actual congregation of the Church today to take part in the truly traditional rightly understood.'

66. V. Vajta, 'The Theological Basis and Nature of Liturgy', in *The Lutheran World*, Vol. VI, No. 3, p. 239f—quoted by E. S. Brown, 'The Worship of the Church and the Modern Man' in *Studia Liturgica*, Vol. II, No. 1, p. 55.
67. Bouyer, op. cit., p. 15.

We can apply this idea in two ways to Methodist worship: the themes and the vocabulary.

The themes express themselves in every part of worship; over some of these there can be little control: the lessons, (particularly if the set lessons be adopted) the Creed, and the traditional prayers of the Church. Over the hymns there can be a greater control by careful choice, as we have seen; over the subjects for prayer there can be more control still, and over the sermon themes most of all. The prayers should be so chosen or formulated as to express the genuine spiritual needs and outlook of the worshippers. Too many prayers are dominated by a sense of world-hatred; they ask the Almighty to save the people out of the world, instead of in its midst, and do not reflect the mood of this age, with its deepening awareness of the sacredness of all parts of life. Moreover, many prayers, and even more sermons, are centred on the theme of redemption, salvation from sin, conversion. There is of course a valid experience behind these concepts, but the old-fashioned evangelical way of expressing these means little to a modern congregation. The need is for a greater sense of the abundant life of which our Lord spoke: the sense of victorious living in the power of the Risen Lord. The great problems on the minds of congregations today are not those resulting from a sense of personal guilt—or, at least, this is no longer confined to a two-way relationship between themselves and God only; the problems they face are those of how to make the love of God real in the difficult situations they often face in daily living; how to be a gracious neighbour; how to find a sense of purpose in the humdrum and often repetitive activities they are engaged in. It is these themes which must become central in our worship, if we are not to fall into the error which Bouyer warns us of; of preaching and praying very fluently about matters which congregations manage to persuade themselves they ought to be concerned about, but know that they are not. In effect, what is required is to bring the theme of the Resurrection with all its implications back into the heart of Christian worship.

The second problem is vocabulary. In every part of current worship, words are used which are either totally meaningless to modern congregations, or else have changed their meaning.

The latter is a relatively easy thing to rectify, and it is to be regretted that most experimental liturgies make little attempt to do so. But basically this is a problem of the highest magnitude, demanding revision of every part of every type of worship, if the end product is not to seem absurd because of inconsistency. (When the Renewal Group produced a new order of Holy Communion, for instance, they addressed the Almighty as 'You'—except in the several traditional prayers like the collect for purity, which still retained the 'Thou' form: the result is not quite so strange as it sounds, but odd enough to bar the service from general acceptance.) The easiest part of the service to change is the Scripture lessons, and there seems no overwhelming reason why the R.S.V. should not be accepted as the New Authorised Version for the Church in England, leaving the A.V. to take its honoured place in history. A bigger problem is the hymns, which, by the discipline of the metre, do not easily lend themselves to revision. It is manifestly absurd that modern congregations should be asked to sing,[68] 'Here I raise my Ebenezer', when not one, and possibly not even the preacher, is likely to have the slightest idea what he is singing about. A more well-known hymn, but just as esoteric, is:[69] 'There is a book, *who runs may read . . .*' The only way out of the problem of hymnody is for encouragement to be given to modern writers to compose hymns more representative of the ideas of our times—the best encouragement being that of learning and using the hymns. Sydney Carter is an outstanding example of this: his 'Lord of the Dance', by its boldness and relevance, must have the inevitable result of bringing any congregation to life. There is no reason why congregations should not encourage their own members to write hymns to express their outlook; their products are hardly likely to be less inspired than those of the Victorians.

What lay critics of the language used in worship do not always appreciate is the incredible difficulty of expressing many of the concepts of the Christian faith in everyday language: specialized, or technical vocabulary is almost inevitable, and to any one brought up on the old vocabulary (and which liturgical revisionist does not fall into this category?) it

68. Methodist Hymn Book, 417, 2.   69. Ibid., 43, 1.

is abundantly easy to slip back into the familiar constructions. The ideal would be to introduce a total outsider to the Christian faith, and let him make the revision! Difficult though the problem is, one feels that one of the supreme tests of the Church today is of its courage, patience, and ability in doing this. Sermons must be expressed in words which the people can understand; prayers and other parts of worship must be relevant to their thought-processes, and expressed in a way to which they can fully commit themselves. Congregations must know what they mean in their worship; and mean what they say. Anything less than this will be inadequate.

2. *Relevant to the Worship of Other Denominations*

There can be few Methodist churches which do not have in their vicinity a number of churches of other denominations, quite possibly worshipping at the same time as the Methodists do. We have not yet reached the stage of Church negotiations when a greater amount of uniformity in worship can be insisted on; but there seems no reason why Churches should not accept a degree of voluntary uniformity. The chief people to gain in such an arrangement would naturally be in the Free Churches, the Anglicans already having a large amount of uniformity through their common use of the Book of Common Prayer. There are two areas in particular where Methodists could benefit greatly.

The first is by a more disciplined acceptance of set lessons, and possibly a companion collect. There would then be more uniformity at least in the Ministry of the Word. From personal experience of marking local preachers' examination papers in 'Worship and Preaching' (as well as from hearing them conduct services) one has reached the firm conviction that many of the deficiencies in Methodist worship—the varieties of presentation, the idiosyncratic ideas, the treatment of everything before the sermon as 'preliminaries'—spring from a lack of constraint in choosing the scripture readings. The Conference does publish an annual Lectionary; but its use is optional, and few local preachers use it, if they even know of it. The result can easily be divined: favourite passages are read *ad nauseum*, the themes of the sermons consequently become limited, and new ideas get little chance of being expressed; the minds of both preachers and worshippers become sterile. If local Councils of Churches could prepare lectionaries for use in non-Eucharistic services in their area, this would not only draw them closer together, but also give more opportunity for all the basic Christian doctrines to be expressed, with the inevitable widened understanding in the minds of the worshippers of what it is to be a Christian in this modern age. There might also be periods of agreed texts for sermons, made possible by a little imagination and goodwill.

The second sphere is in a stricter observance of the Church Year. This is not suggesting that all is well with this. There are many changes which need to be made (and fortunately the Joint Liturgical Commission is in the process of making some of them) to make it less artificial. The period of Lent has lost most of its significance to modern congregations; if a penitential season is needed, the fortnight of Passiontide should suffice. The placing of Ascension Day on a weekday means that most Church members miss one of the major festivals of the Church; the Sundays after Trinity ought—as at Taizé, South India, and in the Roman Catholic Church—to be renamed after Pentecost; the six months after Trinity should include definite dates for the major non-ecclesiastical Sundays, such as Education Day, Industrial and Hospital Sunday, all of which have great relevance to the lives of the worshippers. It is too sophisticated a theological point to begin the Year with the theme of Judgement: this should be near the end of the year. It would be more logical and therefore to be preferred, if the Year began on what we now call Septuagesima—with the Creation and Fall; then the Year will take worshippers through the entire theme of God's plan for mankind in Christ, concluding with judgement and the Epiphany—the revelation of Christ, in the period beyond judgement, to all flesh. The date of Christ's birth is of course totally arbitrary, and has no genuine place in the present structure of the Year.

However, even the present inadequate structure would improve the situation in Methodism, where only the three or four major festivals—Christmas, Good Friday, Easter and

Whitsunday can be sure of observance—though even on the last two of these it is not unusual to find such independent festivals as Sunday School Anniversaries and Chapel Anniversaries replacing them. Methodism has a peculiar aptitude for holding festivals in honour of separate organizations or sections of their churches: so we find Men's Weekend, Women's Anniversary, Trust Anniversary, Choir Festival, Guild Sunday, and Local Preachers' Mutual Aid Day. The emphasis laid on these is a further indication of the introspective nature of Methodist worship, for one cannot imagine any of them having much significance for a visitor.

Besides the link with other denominations, a disciplined observance of the Church Year would offer two further benefits to Methodism: it would, as mentioned in a previous chapter, take the Church through the entire gamut of Christian teaching, helping to ensure that no major doctrine is ignored; and it would be an added discipline to the one who conducts worship. His theme, and with it probably his lessons and hymns, would be chosen for him. He would become less the organizer of the service than a part, albeit a major part, of the liturgical act of the whole congregation; he would be a *servant* of the Word, offering himself, with the other worshippers, in obedience to God. Dr. Rupp[70] summarized the value of observance of the Church Year in these words:

'If we are going to treat (the Church Year) seriously we should see that we have the whole coherent story of redemption pegged down in scripture, hymn and preaching. We shall not lightly set aside the joyful mystery of the Epiphany for Men's Sunday, the painful mystery of Passion Sunday for Young People's Day, the glorious mystery of the Ascension for Women's Weekend. It is as the Church lives closest to God's mighty acts that it becomes most adventurously human.'

3. *Relevant to the World*

The point to bear in mind here is that when a congregation meets for worship, they do not come to escape *from* the world, but to discover new meaning *in* it. Therefore there must be the expression in their worship of the world's needs; they must

70. In an article in the *Guardian* some years ago. The exact date I have not kept a record of.

learn to understand one of the functions of being priests: that they represent their fellows before Almighty God; they bring the world symbolically before Him by their own presence. This symbolism is seen most clearly at a Harvest Festival—especially, for a city congregation, an industrial Harvest, for the normal type of festival in these places has become mainly a nostalgic memory of England's rural past. It is seen on a smaller scale in the weekly offertory procession in those churches which practise this in the Eucharist.

There are three places in our worship where this relevance to the world can be expressed. The first is in the intercessions. These can easily become vague and general ('Lord, bless the Africans'), without giving the congregation any sense that they are particularly involved in the issues mentioned. More imaginative preparation of these prayers, more knowledge of the local situation than is often evinced, perhaps the use of the daily newspaper, could all make these prayers more direct and urgent. It should also be possible for members of the congregation to suggest themes for these prayers (at Taizé a book is left near the door for them to write these in); there is no reason why, occasionally, members of the congregation should not be invited to make their own verbal contribution at this period of the service.

These prayers often call for greater concentration on the part of the worshippers, if they cover themes previously considered in the sermon. This introduces the second area where this relevance can be clearer than it often is. So many sermons preached are too imprecise; they deal in generalities without bringing matters firmly to the particular: how does it apply to the congregation? It is of little use to suggest that 'certain programmes' on television have dubious value, without specifically naming them. It is a mere waste of words to declare that Christians must be peacemakers if the preacher cannot point out ways of being this which are within the scope of the worshippers' activities. Sermons demand teaching; but the teaching must not be left 'in the air'; there must be the attempt to apply this in a way which makes sense to a company of people who will all return the next day to a world of problems and conflicts from which they cannot escape.

It is worth mentioning, though not strictly relevant to our theme, that one of the major reasons for the decline in interest in the Church generally today is the failure of prophecy within it. It appears that too many preachers are too scared of giving offence—hence their limiting of what they say to generalities.

The third area whereby the world may be brought more actively into worship is in the music, and the instruments which produce it. In a sense this could be the most prophetic aspect of the worship, for nothing penetrates the consciousness of people like music. It is this which is surely the motive behind most of the current experiments in 'beat' hymn tunes, rather than the attempt to be 'gimmicky'. A gimmick is motivated by the desire to call attention to oneself, to draw people for the sake of the new-fangled activity; but the need for modern-style music is in the congregation proper: that they can realize that yet another sphere of the world's life is being used to the glory of God, and so sanctified. The phrase 'church music' ought to be recognized as a misnomer; there is music which is used in church worship, but this may well be the current popular music of the day—as Charles Wesley showed by taking song-tunes to put to his hymns, and William Booth a century later.

If the right instruments were introduced the effect on the congregation could be even more penetrating. The idea that an organ (or, even worse, a harmonium) is a 'holy' instrument, and therefore specially suitable for worship is a sad misconception. It helps to give a sense of being cordonned off from the world; and worship is already in danger of this for other reasons. As a simple statement of fact, congregational singing is better when accompanied by a piano; but other instruments have a contribution to make: the most exuberant of all instruments is the trumpet, and this could well be used to accompany hymns of triumph such as the great Easter hymns: the clarinet is perfect for accompanying the quieter, more meditative hymns; and the more cheerful hymns are aided with guitar accompaniment. With such instruments as these the worship must inevitably assume a more dynamic note; it becomes more joyful, more real. We should surely encourage any move which aims to remove the sense of being withdrawn in worship from the world of reality to an artificial world of the Church's making.

(c) The Centrality of the Eucharist

In what has been said about worship so far, we have had in mind the non-eucharistic worship which is still the main type of worship conducted in Methodist churches. One must be realistic and accept that this will remain for the foreseeable future a, if not the, major type of worship in Methodism. Nevertheless, in this section we shall ask the question whether the Eucharist as the main act of worship of the day could not be introduced more widely, and in not a few churches as a regular procedure. The main objections to this are practical, but we shall first consider briefly some theoretical objections.

I. OBJECTIONS ARISING FROM THE METHODIST ATTITUDE TO THE EUCHARIST

1. *Methodism arose from the Evangelical Revival: more emphasis on the Eucharist would mark a departure from our heritage*

The answer to this is contained in what we have already said about Wesley. The fact that this comment is still made at all indicates how far removed is modern Methodism from her founder. Ecclesiastically and liturgically, the spirit of nineteenth-century Methodism still affects us more than that of the eighteenth. This argument would have a greater degree of justification if modern Methodism were still continuing, even if in a different form, the other methods which Wesley found so potent in building up the societies: class meetings, with conscientious and well-trained class leaders, acting in a pastoral capacity to about a dozen of the congregation. Anglicans often mention it in envy; most Methodist churches might well envy their forbears both this and other aspects of early Methodism.

2. *The Kerygma is proclaimed in our worship in the Ministry of the Word; weekly communion is not, therefore, needed.*

It is not likely that this argument would be presented if more Methodists had such an understanding of the Eucharist as is

167

contained in, for instance, Brilioth's *Eucharistic Faith and Practice*. In fact, most of the discussion in this section is necessitated primarily by ignorance: Methodists have rarely (many of them never) had the opportunity to take part in a great celebration; consequently they cannot know what it is to 'let the liturgy be splendid'. In the ministry of the word referred to above there is the need for considerably more teaching about the Eucharist; and congregations should be encouraged to experiment.

Three replies suggest themselves if the argument is to be treated on its merits, all of them already hinted at. First, while the importance of preaching must not be overlooked, it is clearly impossible to do more than consider one facet of the Christian faith in the course of a sermon. In the Eucharist, the entire kerygma is revealed: Creation (the elements used); Incarnation (the divine known through the material); Atonement (Christ's Body broken and Blood shed for mankind); Resurrection (communion with the Living Lord); Exaltation (the whole service an act of praise and oblation); and the eternal love of God, the essence of life, manifested throughout the Meal. The whole great drama is unfurled at every celebration. With regular communion these truths must become more firmly entrenched in the worshippers' minds and personalities.

Secondly, with preaching, unless discipline is instilled in the preacher (either by himself or by higher authorities) there is the danger that even in a course of sermons not all these truths will be declared. In the Eucharist they are revealed whether the celebrant, or preacher, think them important or not—whether they believe them or not. The Eucharist lifts the kerygma above human weaknesses and preferences: it stands out as an objective fact, which can be avoided only by refusing to join with the other worshippers.

Thirdly, even if neither of the first two points were true; if every act of worship without communion were so planned that every great dogma were introduced at some point, there would still be grounds for regular celebrations: for in this service what has previously been made audible to the congregation is given visible manifestation. Many Churches in Christendom appreciate the worth of this: the fact that, by appealing to a second sense—sight, as well as hearing—the kerygma can make a deeper impression. The word of promise is delivered in the Liturgy of the Word; the reception of that promise as a living reality in the lives of God's people is made in the Liturgy of the Upper Room. (It may be that Methodist objections to incense would also disappear if it was appreciated that its purpose is to reach yet another of the human senses; and there is no sense so charged with subconscious memories like that of smell.)

3. *While Holy Communion means much to some people, this is not true of all*

We seem here to be facing the same arguments that Wesley had to deal with two centuries ago. His answers are still valid: that the argument is often an excuse, the person making it never really giving himself the chance to enter into the celebration, and experience its real significance. The testimony of many people—the writer included—is that *at first* before full realization dawns, there may well seem nothing rewarding in the service (with the writer this was primarily because of the way it was conducted). But persistence will bring enlightenment. This communion service has grown from the direct words of our Lord, 'Do this'; it would be strange if the Church through the centuries had been supported and nourished on a service with limited appeal. The fact that, though in various forms, this Meal has survived to the present is a sign that God has blessed it; one wonders how the Church would have fared if the invitation had been, 'Come if you feel like it; but we understand it if you don't, and stay away.'

This argument has its converse: that frequent communion leads to a lack of appreciation of the service. Since this could be said about any of the Methodist services, it does not merit serious discussion.

4. *We can be sacramental in our worship without having an actual celebration of the Eucharist*

This cannot be denied; indeed, where services are conducted by local preachers no celebration is possible, and this fact becomes of crucial importance. It is highly desirable that in their training they shall learn to understand the two parts of worship: God's initiative, expressed in the reading and preaching of the Word, and in some of the hymns; and man's response, expressed in the offertory and in prayers and hymns of oblation and dedication (this is a further reason for conducting these prayers *after* the sermon, instead of earlier in the service which is normally the case).

However, since it is easier for the congregation to grasp the dual nature of their worship if they are actually taking part in a celebration of the Eucharist, it surely follows that where possible—that is, when an ordained minister is conducting the service—this should be the Eucharist. There is a place in Methodism for the 'sacramental service without a celebration'; but the suggestion we are making is that this type of service is too frequently held, and the Eucharist too infrequently. It is a redressing of the balance which is required; and this process involves certain practical problems which must now be discussed.

II. PRACTICAL PROBLEMS

1. *The Circuit System*

At first sight the exigencies of the circuit plan which appoints a minister to conduct services at several places during a quarter, seem a barrier to more frequent celebrations. In fact, the problem in the majority of circuits is not so great as it appears, provided there is imaginative planning.

Although he will have a certain number of commitments in other sections of the circuit, the majority of a minister's appointments will be in his own section. What his own section consists of varies from circuit to circuit, but falls into three main categories. He may have just one church in his charge; this is particularly the case in the larger city churches, and of course in the central halls. There is nothing to prevent a weekly celebration in this situation, perhaps alternating it between morning and evening, as a number of members could attend the one but not the other.

The second, and probably the most usual, type of appointment is one with a single central church, and several smaller outlying or country churches. In such a circuit he will normally be planned at his main church on an average once per Sunday.

It should be possible to arrange at least a fortnightly celebration, either in the morning or the evening, and invite members from the smaller churches to attend what would thus become the main act of worship for all the churches in his section. The majority of members of the smaller churches would not hesitate to make the journey thus involved for other purposes, and the age of the motor-car makes for independence of bus time-tables.

The third type is that of having two, or possibly three, fairly strong churches, with about equal membership in them all. The probability is that the minister will be planned at each of these at least fortnightly, and so could make this the frequency of their celebrations. It seems clear that in the vast majority of circuits—in all but the widely scattered rural circuits when a man may have as many as fifteen or twenty small churches to look after—there is really no barrier to a fortnightly celebration, and in many of these it could easily be weekly. The system is far less a barrier than is the attitude of mind of the people for whom it is worked.

2. *Local Preachers*

The objection here is that if the main act of worship week by week in the larger churches became the Eucharist, local preachers would never have the opportunity to minister to these larger congregations. The inevitable result of this, it is argued, would mean that their status in relation to the ordained man would seem grossly inferior.

This argument seems to miss the point that already, by the very fact that he is not allowed to celebrate, the local preacher's status is seen to be different from that of a minister: the changes envisaged alter this only in degree, not in kind. Again, imagination seems to be a prime commodity: while he may not actually celebrate, there are several other parts of the liturgy in which the local preacher could take a part. He could preach, provided he were capable of disciplining himself to preach from the set lessons; he could read the lessons; and in the Methodist system there is nothing to prevent his acting in the capacity of deacon; it would be an excellent thing (and incidentally save much time) if he could be allowed to administer the wine; it is one of the strange anomalies of Methodism that on this point she has been stricter than the Anglicans, though there are signs of a change and the 1968 Methodist experimental service makes provision for laymen and women to help in the distribution.

It appears that the time is ripe for a complete reappraisal of a local preacher's functions. To give him the sole task of flitting around the circuit Sunday by Sunday is surely limiting his scope. In many country areas a local preacher with pastoral gifts might well take one of the churches as his special pastoral charge: the membership is not likely to be more than the average class meeting of old, and regular appointments at this particular church would give the opportunity to the right kind of person to exercise a concentrated ministry—more so than the ordained man, with several other churches to care for, could possibly exercise. If house churches are to be developed these offer the local preacher further opportunities for concentrated activity; and if the evening (or alternative) service is to become experimental, as we shall suggest shortly, his gifts might well be employed there. In short, it would seem preferable that Methodism began to view her local preachers as people with a distinctive task, different from the priestly functions of the ministers. At the moment, there is too much emphasis on their rights to be like the ministers, having the same opportunities. For their own sakes it would seem best that this attitude of mind be resisted.

3. *Children in Worship*

Whatever recommendations had been made in these pages, this would have been one of the problems! At the moment the custom is growing rapidly of having morning Sunday Schools; children and teachers attend for the opening few minutes of a service, then leave for their own lesson, sometimes (and preferably) returning for the close of the main service. The difficulty here is that if that morning service were normally the Eucharist, teachers would be deprived of attending.

The answer surely lies in holding the Sunday School either before or, preferably after, the main service. (If it were the latter this service would probably have to be held somewhat earlier than the statutory 11 a.m., but this would be no drawback; habit alone has prevented a 10 a.m., or even earlier service, for a number of years. In the summertime a 9 a.m. service would be greatly preferable, so that those who wished to get away would not lose the morning by staying until after the service.) The criticism will then be made that a communion service is too difficult for children to follow. The answer to that is that it is no more difficult to follow than any adult act of worship; the sermon is usually shorter, and there is more to see. (The writer's eight-year-old son certainly prefers sung Eucharist to Sunday School, and shows it by the regularity of his attendance.) The children could, as in the Parish Communion, come forward with their parents at the time of communion and receive a blessing. It is hard to gauge what transpires in a child's mind, but it is difficult not to believe that the dignity and beauty of the Eucharist are making a more lasting and worthwhile impression on it than the more informal and often casual worship of the 'preaching service'. Some will suggest that there is nothing in the Eucharist specifically for children, whereas in the preaching service it is possible for the preacher to give a special 'children's address'. Experience suggests that the end of these will be no great loss; it is significant that the policy of the Methodist Youth Department is to abolish them.

It would appear that the practical difficulties, which are usually suggested as insurmountable when the proposition of more frequent celebrations is made, are not so great after all. The main enemy is tradition—and perhaps laziness.

We may add here, though strictly it relates to the previous section, that in those circuits which cannot adopt more frequent celebrations, and even in those which can, the time has come to make considerable changes between the two services held on a Sunday. At the moment the diet is the same both morning and evening; the only change is likely to be in the one conducting it. It seems no cause for wonder, therefore, that only a small minority (mostly church officials) appear for both morning and evening services. The rest might be more willing to do so if there were a change in the pattern of the evening service from the morning's. There is, for instance, the opportunity for questions and discussion, or some other form of teaching. There are modern methods such as films, tape-recorders, and record players which could be used intelligently in the service of the congregation. The time spent in evening worship might well be allocated for house churches (requiring previous training for the leaders). It would seem reasonably certain that if the day of the weekly Eucharist in Methodism is not yet with us, the day of the two preaching services has gone; boldness and imagination—and courage in facing the diehards—again seem to be the qualities needed in making the best use of the day.

There are two obstacles, one arising from the other, which we have met constantly in the foregoing discussion, without specifically naming them. The first is the nature of the present communion service. The only full-scale service known to Methodists is the slightly altered order of the Book of Common Prayer. It must be stated that this service does not attract Methodist congregations so that they clamour for it week after week. They will normally accept it if asked to do so, but there is no joy manifested in their doing so. It is surely obvious that we shall not find any surging enthusiasm for the Eucharist until we have a liturgy in constant use in which such enthusiasm could be shown. Those who have taken part in the Renewal Group's experimental service have almost invariably been astonished at the extent to which they felt drawn into the worship, in a way not previously experienced. One believes that a service like that of Taizé would have the same effect. But all this demands training in the liturgy, and in its music. Few people in Methodism can give this training—and most of those have learned it at the hands of other denominations.

This leads to a second comment: Methodism desperately needs a chair in liturgy in her theological colleges. Until training in this is made a part of every theological student's general preparation for the ministry, the present haphazard process must inevitably continue. We cannot continue the present system whereby the study of liturgy is looked on as the hobby of a few idiosyncratic enthusiasts; study of this kind would have considerably more practical application after students have left college than have some of their compulsory subjects of study at present. A good test of the seriousness with which Methodism views the Liturgical Movement might be to see how seriously she would be willing to pursue this suggestion.

All that we might have said under the fourth heading in chapter 2—the Liturgical Movement and the rediscovery of basic dogma—has been amply covered in these last two sub-sections: that for Methodists this rediscovery will come most fittingly through a rediscovery of the liturgy. We shall therefore proceed to consider what was point five in the previous chapter.

4. *Methodist Architecture and Symbolism*

We have seen that the two supreme requirements of church buildings are to express the glory of God, and to suit the needs of worshippers; and that these two tend to militate against each other. In the nineteenth century the majority of Methodist chapels fitted the second requirement, but not the first; it is difficult, in these buildings with their large central pulpits overshadowing the tiny communion tables (probably covered with vases of flowers and/or hymn books and various papers), to have a sense of the numinous. Over the past seven years the Methodist Church has spent £9 million on new churches, and it is clear from a report recently published by the Methodist Chapel Affairs Department that the wheel has come full circle. These new churches are all, in different ways, imitation medieval churches, none of them centrally planned, all rectangular, all with the Table against the wall. It appears that the department has never heard of the Liturgical Movement; without exception these buildings were out-of-date from the day they were opened. They are a manifestation of a strange kind of snobbery abroad in contemporary Methodism, motivated apparently by the desire to demonstrate that we can be just as 'churchy' as the Anglicans. Douglas Wollen makes a suitably caustic comment:[71]

'Every modern or rebuilt Parish Church was put up in a style suggesting that the Church was not in the mainstream of life; all have an antiquarian and escapist flavour. Let Trustees responsible for new churches avoid architects who specialise in churches and atmosphere, and get in touch with a man who has designed factories

71. D. Wollen, 'What Kind of Church Building?', in *The Bulletin* of the Fellowship of the Kingdom (an association for Methodist Ministers), December 1960.

and schools and flats, and ask him to tackle their projected church.
. . . And they may well get a building a working man could enter
without getting the impression that religion involves a double life,
ancient on Sunday, modern on Monday. Let the church take hold
of the latest building methods, pouring concrete and steel and glass
and prefabrication, and claim them for Christ. The exciting thing
is that the modern church does look like a church after all, despite,
or because of, the encouraging fact that critics insist that at first
sight it looks like a factory. Who can see buildings like Saarinen's
Evangelical Church at Minneapolis, or the Johanneskirche in Basle
without being helped to lift up his heart to God? Is this the case with
our new churches at Mitcham or Bournemouth?'

We have already indicated that the great requirement in
modern buildings is that those present in them shall feel that
they are part of the gathered community, meeting in koinonia
for the worship of God. This means that the symbols of the two
pillars of the Church's life—Word and Sacraments—shall be
prominent, and balanced. So the real problem for architects
is to achieve a right harmony between pulpit, Holy Table, and
font; and to have all these so centrally placed that the congregation can feel that they come to gather around them, not to
gaze at them from afar. Chancels and choir stalls must go:
let choirs be at the back, where they can be heard but not seen;
let the Communion Tables be uncluttered with the different
paraphernalia which tend to proliferate; let the font be large
and permanently placed (the new Baptismal service states that
this should happen wherever possible); let the tiny basin-style
fonts be removed; let the Holy Table be bare rather than allow
mass-produced Crosses to be stood thereon; let the pulpit
be small and low enough as not to overwhelm a congregation
should the preacher decide to make his sermon 'teach-in' in
style; and let great care be taken over the notice boards and
posters outside the church, for these more than anything else
impress the passer-by: an out-of-date poster indicates an out-
of-date church; a gimmicky poster ('We help to put the sun
in Sunday') indicates a church bereft of a basic sense of
purpose.

Having had the opportunity to see a large number of the
modern German Churches—in Frankfurt, Munich, Cologne,
and Hamburg—one begins to despair that architects in

England will ever awake to the insights of the Liturgical Movement. Gilbert Cope makes this comment, which expresses exactly the writer's own feelings:[72]

'It must be said that if this booklet ("New Methodist Churches") is set alongside two similar German publications, "Hamburgs Neue Kirchen 1951–61" (Lutheran) and "Neue Kölner Kirchen" (Roman Catholic), it is at once obvious that church building in England is sadly lacking in architectural adventurousness and liturgical insight. It is to be hoped that English church builders of every denomination will anticipate our formal entry into the Common Market and grasp the fact that architecture, like Christianity, is international.'

(e) The Relationship between Worship and Witness

We have already discussed the implications of this fact for Methodist worship: that it must be relevant. In this section we consider the implications for our witness.

The basic requirement in understanding the relationship between the two is the realization that to live liturgically involves the whole of life, not just a brief period each week. We have seen, in discussing relevant worship, that the congregation performing the liturgy do not and cannot escape from the world; rather, as God's priests they represent the world before Him. So in their witness they express the second function of priests: to represent God to men. The particular insight of the Liturgical Movement on this function is that it is not a matter for the individual to be a keen 'personal evangelist', making it his aim to persuade colleagues and associates to 'come to church', but that it is primarily the function of the church community to act communally in 'being Christ'—that is, expressing *agape*—in the world.

This requires a much 'higher' view of the Church than has usually been found in Methodism. At the same time, to many Methodists it will appear to be a more 'secular' interpretation of their Christian duty. They have been reared to the view that their fundamental task is to tell others of what Christ means to them; but our view of the liturgical life makes far greater demands on God's people. It is comparatively easy to make a personal statement of faith; the real test lies in the

72. G. Cope, 'In Which to Preach'—in the *Guardian*, 25 September 1964.

extent to which this expresses itself day by day—and year by year.

The current popular word to express this is involvement; this is quite adequate for our purposes. It implies that the real duty of Christians in their working lives is to be fully integrated in the various activities which take place: on works councils, study groups, Trade Unions, social activities, and so on. Through these activities the love of God can be expressed: to try and divorce this love from the day-to-day matters of life is to attempt to create an artificial world whose nature it is impossible to conceive.

The local church community must also see itself involved in the life of the area. This does not exclude social work on church premises—youth activities, old-age pensioners' clubs—but more important than this is the extent to which the church makes an impact on local life generally. There is the need to penetrate the secular structures: for church members to be active in social activities run by the local council, and in whatever other local activities offer the opportunity for Christian service. We have seen how various experiments along these lines have resulted in the formation of 'house churches' whereby a local member assumes a certain pastoral responsibility for the people in his street. A house church properly run will include not only church members but others who share many of their concerns, but do not wish to get involved in church life generally. They meet for various purposes in the home chosen, to study some local problem which affects people in the area, and to make some attempt to understand what light the teachings of the Christian faith have to shed on these issues. The members will know where there is any special need in the area—a father out of work, an old person unable to do her shopping, a teenager facing moral problems—and will try, without imposing themselves, to act according to the need. They may give a lead to the whole community if they are convinced that this is demanded in the face of some local problem.

These house meetings demand training in leadership, and this would seem to be the main function of the minister. He should encourage the keen members of his church to meet regularly: and this may well include an occasional weekend conference away from the area, so that problems raised can be pursued at length. (There is no reason why occasionally the church services should not be cancelled, and the whole Christian community go away for such a weekend conference. Trade Unions and political parties find these one of their most effective training methods. More progress can often be made on such a weekend than in a whole series of weekly meetings.)

In all this the role of the theological colleges comes increasingly under question. The traditional forms of training in these colleges—in Greek and Hebrew, Old and New Testament etcetera—need not be laid aside; but they must be extended so that men emerge with a reasonable knowledge of the structures of contemporary society. Too often their specialized training equips them for little else except the caring for the church members in the narrowest sense. Thus they are being trained for a situation which, generally speaking, no longer exists. The Church's walls are being broken down through the advent of a secular, technological society; in this society the traditional minister with his 'churchy' interests and appearance has no longer any part to play. Indeed, one questions how much longer the majority of the clergy will continue to be financially maintained exclusively by the Church. With the present decline in membership and income, it appears that economic necessity will force more and more men to at least supplement their incomes in other work. It would be preferable to put this practice on a sound theological basis by accepting that the worker-priest has a place in the contemporary Church.

There seems, therefore, no reason why the insights of the Liturgical Movement should not have impact upon Methodism. Our system and theology are not inherently alien to a great deal of what the movement suggests; the only real obstacle is the ostrich-like attitude which is too often manifested. However, there are signs that an increasing number of Methodists are beginning to realize that they cannot continue along traditional lines, and it is hoped that in the suggestions made in this section there may be indications of the way forward in various fields. There are no doubt others which have not been included; but there are surely enough here to indicate the principles which must increasingly govern Methodist practice in worship and witness—that is, in her liturgical life. It may well be that God has still a purpose, however different this may be from the one traditionally received, for the 'people called Methodists'.

EPILOGUE
THE FUTURE

WE live in an era of rapid change, and the Church is not exempt from this. Traditional concepts are being challenged, both from inside and beyond. Practices which previous generations accepted without question are being replaced by those which seem more suited to the present age. Nothing is sacrosanct, nothing untouchable: this is indeed an age of reformation.

Even the Liturgical Movement, which has been described in these pages as though it were a concrete entity, is altering in its spheres of application, as its influence spreads to different parts of Christendom, with different customs and different needs. In our application of the insights of the movement to the current Methodist situation we have as it were stopped the film in order to concentrate on the 'still' of the movement; but the film cannot be stopped, and the movement has already progressed beyond the stage described.

In what direction will it influence the Church during the next quarter-century? Can we make so bold as to prophesy what is not yet revealed? It is surely possible to read the signs of the times; and these all point in one direction. If the nineteenth century in this country was an age of rediscovery of the nature of the *ministry*, and the first half of the twentieth century a time of rediscovery of the nature of the *Church*, then it appears that we are now in the process of rediscovering the nature of the *Kingdom*—which is a good deal more prominent in our Lord's teaching than was either of the first two. The themes of some of the most impressive and thought-provoking writings of our time, several of them quoted in our second chapter, indicate that this is the direction which is being taken by the twentieth-century prophets. Titles of other contemporary books indicate the same: *The Church Reclaims the City*, *The Church in Metropolis*, *The Secular Relevance of the Church*—and so on.

To state the aim expressed, in varying degrees, in all these books is to indicate the supreme problem of the Church in our time: it is for the Church so to penetrate the secular structures that the kerygma becomes real and meaningful in every part of life. The problem then is this: with such an aim, and in such a situation, what is the function of the Christian liturgy? Does worship, which inevitably means withdrawal from the world to a certain extent, still have any place in the fulfilment of this aim? How can there be a connexion between the gathered community of Christians, meeting to take part in a liturgical act which would be almost totally meaningless to the majority of their fellow-men, and the expression of love in social, industrial, local, and national life? Does not the history of the Church teach us that Christians fall into one of two categories: they are either 'world-haters' who take every opportunity to cultivate the spiritual life by retreating into some religious building; or they are primarily men with a practical outlook, anxious to express goodwill and kindness in daily life, who attend worship only out of a sense of duty, and then as seldom as possible?

Summarily expressed the question facing the Church today is: should we treat all men as though they need to worship like the Christian community, or do we accept that worship is only for the few, which they do on behalf of the rest of their fellows? If we accept the first alternative then we immediately land ourselves at the heart of an impossible situation: even if we were able to persuade men to 'come and worship' they would on arrival find very little which they could understand. The prayers of the Eucharist—indeed, its whole procedure—would be almost entirely meaningless to them. One has known people to be deterred for life from ever returning to church after casually appearing on an isolated occasion. If the answer is that they must have training in worship before they can participate, where, with the majority of men expressing general lack of interest, is this training to be done? A sense of realism compels us to admit that nothing would induce most people today to step foot inside a church building; industrial workers in particular have 'written off' the Church, as a meaningless anachronism in twentieth-century society.

Do we then fall back on the doctrine of the Church as a coterie—a specialized group of initiates who, it is hoped, will be so inspired by their worship that they will go out to change the world in the cause of the Kingdom? But is not part of this cause the conversion of all men to commitment to Christ? And does not such commitment automatically make them part of His body—and therefore part of the worshipping community? There can be no finally satisfying answer to this problem; the tension involved in the two thoughts and policies must be the Cross to be borne by the Western twentieth-century Church. It certainly seems no exaggeration to describe in this way the agony of mind in any Christian who is alive to the conflict.

The best solution we can accept at the present stage of Christian thought has two aspects. First, worship must be seen as a piece of prophetic symbolism: a dramatic expression in one place, and for a short period, of what is ideally true everywhere always. Christ is to be glorified throughout the world; men are everywhere to be committed to Him; and worship is maintained by those who accept Him, as though His univeral Lordship were already an accepted fact. In this sense the worship becomes a foretaste of the Kingdom; it expresses the life of the Age to Come—and its validity or worth must be judged by the extent to which Christ becomes *real* for the worshippers, so that they can, to a limited extent, reflect this reality in daily life.

As a converse to this, the aim of Christians in their daily contacts must *not* be to persuade people to come to church: rather it must be the attempt to make real in the work or leisure situation the glorification of God which has been made in worship. This will not necessarily involve talking 'religiously' at all: rather it will mean making the whole of life an expression of love. This is a more nebulous procedure, without any quick returns, but it is paralleled in the ministry of our Lord. The hope is—and this must never be lost sight of—that eventually the process will lead to a gathering of people around the representative of the body; that discussions about the meaning of the faith will ensue, possibly within the context of dealing with local problems. It is impossible to state absolutely how matters might develop from there. A group might become so interested as to meet periodically during the lunch break; or after work in the home of the member; or in a public house. Discussions in depth have occurred as a result of this approach; and in Mainz-Kastel, Horst Symanowski reports that one of the results of two years' work on the shop floor of a local factory was that a small group of men began to share a simple meal with him, in the course of which they suggested what he should preach about the following Sunday. The fact that they did not attend church to hear the sermon did not worry Symanowski: the fact was that in two years half a dozen men had begun to think seriously about the faith, and their meal together was developing as an extremely simple Eucharist.

It seems that the Church must accept a long period in which the most that can be expected is that such a group should emerge. For fifty years the Church in this country has been basically out of touch with society as a whole; it will take a long period of listening and learning, of sympathizing and understanding before any change is likely to be manifested. It is not likely to happen in this generation, and it may not in the next. But the Church must live, and worship, and witness, as though it could happen at any time. Its worship must be offered with the world in mind; its witness pursued in the light of its worship; and the ultimate aim which must not be forgotten is so to make the kingdoms of this world into the Kingdom of God, that all of life becomes an expression of His glory, and there is no longer any need for special, localized expressions of this.

How can the structures of the Church best ensure that Christ is exalted everywhere, so that men can be most easily led to commit themselves to Him? It is impossible to deny that many aspects of the present structures often make this difficult; and sometimes one feels that they are the biggest single drawback to the manifestation of the Kingdom. (In *The Noise of Solemn Assemblies* Berger goes so far as to express the belief that the Church as at present constructed cannot bring about commitment: its divisions, its 'established' status, its other-worldliness and the indifference in many of its members to any sense of sacrifice in daily living are effectively masking its real purpose.) It seems necessary if the theme of this thesis is not to appear purely an academic matter, of interest only to specialists within a minority group, to indicate what seem to be the main lines of development for any relevant Church of the future.

It will be a united Church; and with union will come considerably fewer buildings. The buildings will be multi-purpose, and will include 'secular' work—among, for instance, youth and aged—in their activities. The worship will be accepted as basically for the initiated, and will centre around the Eucharist in a liturgy which will be relevant and alive (if these qualities are not found, there will be few left to worship at all). Even 'preaching' services will have the two pillars of Word and Upper Room clearly adumbrated. The main extra-worship activity will be training sessions to equip the laity to apply their faith in daily life. There will be a staff, or team, attached to the centre, comprising all those who are willing to commit themselves to certain disciplines in connexion with the church (these would include weekly worship of course, but in addition a weekly staff meeting, daily prayers, and occasional retreats.) The team will have at least one full-time parochial priest, with traditional functions to fulfil; in addition there will be part-time priests/ministers, part of whose income will be earned from secular sources; there may well be a number of worker-priests, working locally during the week, but with a minimum of duties within the church structure. Members of other professions will also be attached to this team, provided they accept its disciplines: teachers and sociologists, for example, who serve (as the clergy are usually asked to serve) where the need is greatest, rather than in the most comfortable or affluent areas. Being ecumenical, this staff will naturally comprise members of all denominations so that the insights of them all will be brought to bear on the issues that are faced.

This will be a Church genuinely trying to express the body of Christ: in a word, it will be a community, living liturgically, its service of God in the world driving it back for the service of worship, and this in its turn inspiring and motivating the week's activities. E. S. Brown, in a prophetic article[1] makes this point:

1. E. S. Brown, op. cit., p. 65.

'The compelling promulgation of its doctrines and the loving service of its patterns of ethics may restore to the church the greater sphere of influence it desires for the Gospel. Yet always there must be that other activity of Christian obedience which nurtures the believer in his intimate relation with God. Thinking, knowing, and teaching, together with unselfish service of one's fellows can only draw their inspiration at the wellsprings of corporate devotion. In no other area of its activity does the church touch the lives of men with quite the same potential for impulsion to love that it does in its worship. The investigations into the meaning and practice of the cultus, and the accompanying experiments born of imagination, portend a hopeful sign. If these will but bear fruit in parish churches throughout the world—among the family of God—the future looms bright for the Gospel.'

We have come a long way from Dom Guéranger and the Gregorian Chants; but through all the changes and emphases one can see the guiding hand of the Holy Spirit, renewing and revitalizing the people of God everywhere. If Methodism will but recognize this and take its message to heart, she will find that she still has a part to play in the Church as a whole; for the Movement's insights will be expressed in the context of her particular ethos, and must therefore be a *new* contribution to the present search for truth. If the Church throughout the world shows an equal readiness to respond to the Spirit's lead, it may well be that it will experience as never since the earliest centuries of the faith what it is to be, in worship and in witness, the Body of Christ.

APPENDIX A

Some suggested orders of service where there is no celebration

WE HAVE acknowledged in the text that although a weekly celebration in Methodism is highly desirable, realism compels us to admit that, until Church unity has taken place throughout the country, this cannot yet happen in a large number of Methodist churches. The overwhelming need in these churches, therefore, is to ensure that the shape of the liturgy be as sacramental as possible: that the dual structure of Ministry of the Word, and Ministry of the Upper Room, clearly emerges. We append several examples of services where this happens. Two of the services are almost entirely translations of parts of the 'Office de Taizé'; two more are translations of the Lutheran 'Buch der Gottesdienste', adapted from the Old Prussian Agende of 1894 (Christlicher Zeitschriftenverlag Berlin, 1952). This has an order of service for every Sunday in the Church Year, together with special festivals; its strength is that in the services there is combined repetition and variety, and it is the writer's conviction that any future Book of Common Prayer in this country must combine both of these, and thus (one hopes) avoid the extremes of both the present Book of Common Prayer and the completely haphazard nature of present Free Church worship at its worst. The same applies to the Taizé Offices: they have an invariable format, and certain invariable prayers; but there are different offices for all the seasons; and even the weeks after Pentecost have variety, for the book has morning and evening offices for a fortnight. Some slight adaptation of the Taizé material has had to be made to fit them for a full act of Christian worship, and this has been indicated in the text.

To the professional translator these efforts of the writer will no doubt appear amateurish. One hopes that a new English translation of Taizé will be commissioned, that its language will at least reflect R.S.V. rather than A.V., and that somebody will be induced to undertake the translation of the German book, which seems to be strangely unknown in this country.

1. SERVICE FOR CHRISTIAN UNITY, BASED ON THE TAIZÉ OFFICE FOR THE UNITY OF CHRISTIANS (*Office de Taizé*, pp. 392–8)

(The only additions to the Taizé text are: O.T. lesson instead of Epistle after the Psalm; N.T. lesson, Creed, and Sermon before the Meditation; and a hymn before the blessing.) *Italics* (here and in the other services) indicate words spoken by the congregation.

MINISTRY OF THE WORD

INTRODUCTION

O Lord, open Thou our lips
And our mouths shall show forth Thy praise
O Lord, make speed to save us
O Lord, make haste to help us
Give thanks to the Lord for He is good
For His mercy endures for ever
Who will tell of the wonders of the Lord
And make His name resound?
Happy the man who acts uprightly
Who practises justice at all times
Remember us, O Lord,
Remember us through love of Thy people
Save us, O Lord our God,
Gather us from amongst the nations
That we may give thanks to Thy holy name
And bow down in Thy praise
Blessed be the Lord God of Israel
For ever and ever

THE WORD OF GOD

Psalm (Gelineau)
Old Testament Lesson
Response (sung)
For the love of my brothers and my friends I will say, Peace be with you
For the love of my brothers and my friends I will say, Peace be with you

188

For the love of the house of the Lord I pray for your wellbeing
I will say, Peace be with you.
Glory be to the Father, and to the Son, and to the Holy Spirit
For the love of my brothers and my friends I will say, Peace be with you
New Testament Lesson
Creed (Apostles' or Nicene)
Sermon
Meditation
Hymn

MINISTRY OF THE UPPER ROOM

He who relies on the Lord shall be like Mount Sion
Nothing shall shake him, he shall stand fast for ever
Let us pray.

PRAISE

Let us thank God, that He has united us in Him and in one another.

For our unity in Thyself, and for Thy eternal presence in Thy
Church
We give Thee thanks, O Lord
For the action of Thy Holy Spirit, who throughout the whole world
is renewing the life of the Church, and her mission to the world
We give thee thanks, O Lord
For the fruits of the sufferings of Thy Church, completing that
which is lacking in the sufferings of the whole body, and con-
firming her union with Thyself
We give Thee thanks, O Lord
For all the gifts received from Thee despite our divisions, and for
having learned to share them in the ecumenical movement
We give Thee thanks, O Lord

PENITENCE

In the presence of our Lord Jesus Christ let us repent and humbly
confess our sins.

For our lack of emphasis on Thy prayer, on the eve of Thy passion,
for the unity of Thy followers, and for the suffering Thou hast
endured because of our divisions
Lord, grant us Thy forgiveness
For our indifference and complacency, our ignorance and prejudi-
ces, our lack of humility and of steps towards mutual enrichment
Lord, grant us Thy forgiveness
For the bitterness of our controversies, for our irony and narrow-
ness of mind towards our fellow Christians, and for our hostility and
impetuosity towards them
Lord, grant us Thy forgiveness

For the sin of establishing among Thy children boundaries of race and nationality, and of raising social and cultural barriers
Lord, grant us Thy forgiveness
For the half-heartedness of our love, and the inadequacy of our intercessions for our brother Christians
Lord, grant us Thy forgiveness
For our lack of enthusiasm, and for the obstacles to the spreading of the Gospel, created by our divisions
Lord, Grant us Thy forgiveness

INTERCESSION

Let us ask the Holy Spirit to kindle in us the fire of His love, that everything in His Church which is contrary to His will may die, and that the gifts of the Spirit may live and grow in her
Lord, hear our prayer
Let us ask the Holy Spirit to inspire those who work and pray for Christian unity, and to guide them into all truth
Lord, hear our prayer
Let us ask the Holy Spirit so to open our hearts that Christ Jesus may offer through us His prayer for the unity of His people, and so make us grow together in union with Him
Lord, hear our prayer
Let us ask the Holy Spirit that we may share in the sufferings caused to our Lord by our disunity and unfaithfulness, so that we may also share in the power of His resurrection
Lord, hear our prayer
Let us ask the Holy Spirit that the Church on earth may be ready to be broken, as the Saviour giving His life for mankind, to give herself for the needs of the world, that the Kingdom of God may come
Lord, hear our prayer
The Lord be with you
And with thy spirit
Let us pray to the Lord in silence . . .
Almighty Lord God, who didst send Thy Son Jesus Christ that He might gather Thy people into one flock, under one Shepherd: we join our prayers with the universal prayer of Thy Church on earth and in heaven; we beseech Thee to hasten the day when, with one heart and one spirit, we may serve and adore Thee in the peace and love of the Body of Christ, through Jesus Christ Thy Son our Lord, who lives and reigns with Thee in the unity of the Holy Spirit, one God, world without end.
Amen
The Lord's Prayer
O Christ, remember us when Thou comest in Thy Kingdom
Teach us Thyself to pray: Our Father . . .
Hymn

The Blessing
Let us bless the Lord
Thanks be to God
May the God of patience and of consolation grant us to live with one
another in the true wisdom of Jesus Christ, that we may with one
heart and one mouth give glory to God, the Father of our Lord
Jesus Christ.
Amen

(The meditation is of course a regular feature at Taizé, both
in the daily offices and in the Eucharist. One feels that it is a
vital aspect of worship which we need to discover—cf. Benoit,
op. cit. pp. 80–82: 'The need and desire for silence for individual prayer which is making its appearance in the very
heart of the solemnities of the liturgy is a development particularly to be noted' (p. 82). It would be good if all church members could have a weekly subject for meditation not only in
public worship but also in private devotions.

Many Methodists would argue that this service does not
contain enough hymn-singing. Further hymns could, of course,
be imported *ad lib.*; but the answer is that the Introduction,
Psalm and Response could all be sung, so that only the Lessons
and the Sermon in the Ministry of the Word, and the main
prayers in that of the Upper Room, are spoken. At Taizé these
prayers are beautifully intoned, and congregations could be
taught this—if they and the ministers were willing to set their
hearts to it. Throughout the whole service it will be noted that
every part which can possibly lend itself to this, is corporate.

2. SERVICE FOR WHITSUNTIDE

(Compiled from the Taizé morning and evening offices for the
Octave of Whitsuntide, *Office de Taizé*, pp. 258–66.)

INTRODUCTION

Send, O Lord, Thy Spirit
And renew the face of the earth
Come, Creator Spirit
Rekindle the hearts of believers
The Spirit of the Lord fills the universe
He embraces all things
Let us glorify the Father Almighty
And His Son Jesus Christ the Lord

And the Spirit who dwells in our hearts
As it was in the beginning, is now, and ever shall be
Glory to God, who is, and was, and is to come
For ever and ever. Amen.

Psalm
Old Testament Lesson
Response
The Spirit of the Lord fills the universe, alleluia, alleluia!
The spirit of the Lord fills the universe, alleluia, alleluia!
He who controls all things embraces all truth
Alleluia, alleluia!
Glory be to the Father, and to the Son, and to the Holy Spirit
The spirit of the Lord fills the universe, alleluia, alleluia!

New Testament Lesson
Creed
Sermon
Meditation
Hymn

MINISTRY OF THE UPPER ROOM

PRAYER

The Apostles spoke in different tongues, Alleluia!
Of the marvellous works of God, Alleluia!
O living God, come and make our souls temples of Thy Spirit
Lord, sanctify us
Baptize Thy whole Church with fire, that her divisions may soon be ended, and she may stand before the world as a pillar and bulwark of Thy truth
Lord, sanctify us
Grant to each of us the fruits of Thy Holy Spirit: love, joy, peace, patience, kindness, faithfulness
Lord, sanctify us
May Thy Holy Spirit speak through the lips of Thy servants who preach Thy Word, here and everywhere
Lord, sanctify us
Send Thy Holy Spirit to all who are in distress, or are victims of human wickedness
Lord, sanctify us
Preserve all nations and their leaders from hatred and war, and by the power of Thy Spirit create a true community of nations
Lord, sanctify us
Holy Spirit, Lord and source of life, imparter of the sevenfold gifts
Sanctify us, Comforter
Spirit of wisdom and understanding, Spirit of counsel and might
Sanctify us, Comforter

Spirit of knowledge and godliness, Spirit of obedience to the Lord
Sanctify us, Comforter
The Lord be with you
And with thy spirit
Let us pray to the Lord in silence . . .

INTERCESSIONS

(Names of people and events, as suggested beforehand by members
of the congregation)

COMMON PRAYER

Lord, grant that Christians may recover visible unity
That they may all be one, that the world may believe
Lord, may the Holy Spirit kindle us with that fire which our Lord
Jesus Christ brought upon earth, and longed to see burning: He who
lives and reigns with Thee in the unity of the Holy Spirit, one God,
for ever and ever. *Amen.*
Hymn
The Blessing
Come, Creator Spirit
Visit the souls of the faithful
Shower with grace from on high
The hearts which Thou hast created
Let us bless the Lord
Thanks be to God
May we be blessed by the grace of the Holy Spirit, go forth in peace,
and may the Lord be with us all. *Amen.*

(In both these services, the notices could be given immediately
before the final hymn, and the offertory taken and/or brought
forward during the singing of it. This second service does not
include the Lord's Prayer, which could be added either at the
close of the Introduction, or (preferably) after the silent prayer.)

3. EVENING SERVICE FOR PENTECOST

(This service includes a small portion from Taizé as used in the
previous outline; it also includes a section from another part of
the Taizé offices for Pentecost. It has a portion of Compline
at the end. The collect was written by the writer; this may
appear somewhat presumptuous, but the traditional collect for
Pentecost, apart from being ugly and old-fashioned in its
wording, does not—or so it appears to us—mention the crucial
aspects of the Pentecost message, as in the present collect. Is

there not a strong case for rewriting a considerable number of the collects? The outline here is exactly as it was for the congregation at St. Mary's, Woolwich, Whitsunday 1965. The congregation is a union of Anglicans and Presbyterians; and the service was conducted by a Methodist!)

MINISTRY OF THE WORD

Processional Hymn: Creator Spirit! by whose aid
Call to Worship
O send out Thy light and Thy truth; let them lead me
Let them bring me unto Thy holy hill, and to Thy tabernacles
Then will I go unto the altar of God
Unto God my exceeding joy
The hour cometh, and now is, when the true worshippers shall worship the Father in spirit and truth
For such doth the Father seek to be His worshippers
God is a Spirit
And they that worship Him must worship in spirit and truth
Let us confess our sins before Almighty God
Our Heavenly Father, who by Thy love hast made us, and through Thy love hast kept us, and in Thy love wouldst make us perfect: we humbly confess that we have not loved Thee with all our heart and soul and mind and strength, and that we have not loved one another as Christ has loved us. Forgive us for what we have been; help us to amend what we are; and through Thy Holy Spirit direct what we shall be; that Thou mayest come into the full glory of Thy creation, in us, and in all men, through Jesus Christ our Lord. Amen
Absolution
May the Almighty God have mercy upon you, forgive you your sins, and bring you to everlasting life. *Amen*
Collect for the Day
Lord God Almighty, who didst pour Thy Holy Spirit on the disciples at Pentecost, and didst thereby give them the power both to preach Thy Word with boldness and to serve Thee with love: grant that Thy Holy Spirit may so descend upon us and upon Thy whole Church that we may truly worship Thee and show forth Christ in simplicity, compassion, and joy; through Jesus Christ our Lord, to whom, with Thee and the Holy Spirit, be all honour and glory, now and for ever. *Amen*
Psalm 139 (Gelineau)
Old Testament Lesson: Ezekiel 37:1–14 (Knox's translation)
Te Deum
New Testament Lesson: Acts 1:6–8; 2:1–4
The Apostles' Creed
Hymn: Come, Holy Ghost, our hearts inspire (Wesley)

Sermon: 'Can these bones live?'
Silence

MINISTRY OF THE UPPER ROOM

Hymn: Come down, O Love Divine
Prayers
Come, Creator Spirit, visit the souls of Thy faithful people; re-
plenish the hearts Thou hast created with grace from on high
Come, Creator Spirit
Thou art the Comforter, the gift of the most high God, the fount
of life; Thou art fire, Thou art love, Thou art the unction of grace
Come, Creator Spirit
Thou dost shower upon us all Thy gifts; Thou art the power of God,
the authentic promise of the Father
Come, Creator Spirit
Illuminate our senses with Thy light; fill our hearts with Thy love;
strengthen our bodies with Thy might
Come, Creator Spirit
Help us to know the Father through Thee, and reveal the Son to us;
and grant that we may believe in Thee always, O Holy Spirit of the
Father and the Son
Come, Creator Spirit
Let us pray in silence for all who are in distress, or the victims of
human wickedness
Lord, hear our prayer
And let our cry come unto Thee
Let us pray for the unity of the Church . . .
O living God, baptize Thy whole Church with fire, that her divisions
may soon be ended, and she may stand before the world as a pillar
and bulwark of Thy truth
May we all be one, that the world may believe
The Lord's Prayer
By the spirit of adoption we are bold to say
Our Father . . .
Holy Spirit, Lord and source of life, imparter of the sevenfold gifts
Sanctify us, Comforter
Spirit of wisdom and understanding, Spirit of counsel and might
Sanctify us, Comforter
Spirit of knowledge and godliness, Spirit of obedience to the Lord
Sanctify us, Comforter
Memorial for the Evening Hour
Into Thy hands, O Lord, we commend our spirits
For Thou hast redeemed us, O Lord, Thou God of Truth
Keep us, O Lord, as the apple of an eye
Hide us under the shadow of Thy wings
We will lay us down in peace and take our rest

For it is Thou, O Lord, only that makest us to dwell in safety
Look down, O Lord, from Thy heavenly throne, illuminate the
darkness of this night with Thy celestial brightness, and from the
sons of light banish the deeds of darkness; through Jesus Christ our
Lord. *Amen*
*Preserve us, O Lord, while waking, and guard us while sleeping, that awake
we may watch with Christ, and asleep we may rest in peace*
The Lord be with you
And with thy spirit
Let us bless the Lord
Thanks be to God. Amen
The Concerns of the Church (Notices)
Hymn: Come, Holy Ghost, our souls inspire. (Offertory brought
forward during this hymn)
The Blessing, after which the last two verses of the previous hymn
are sung as the choir is leaving.

4. HARVEST FESTIVAL SERVICE

(This is translated verbatim from the *Buch der Gottesdienste*,
pp. 300–304. All that have been added—for these are left for
free choice of place—are hymns, sermon, notices, and offertory.
The writer has used this service many times in Methodist
churches, having a number of duplicated copies to distribute
to the congregation. One believes that this service catches the
spirit and message of harvest-tide more than any other encountered.)

Theme text: Thou openest Thy hand, O Lord, and satisfiest the
desires of every living thing (Psalm 145:16)
In the Name of the Father, and of the Son, and of the Holy Spirit.
Amen. Our help rests in the name of the Lord, who has made
heaven and earth.
The Lord our God is our Sun and Shield; the Lord cares for us
and blesses us; God is in heaven, He can create what He will.
Thanks be to God, for He is good, and His mercy endures for ever.
Hymn
Let us pray.
*Glory be to the Father, and to the Son, and to the Holy Ghost. As it was in the
beginning, is now, and ever shall be: world without end. Amen*
Almighty God, our Heavenly Father, whose mercy is without end,
who art patient, gracious, and of great goodness, and dost forgive
our rebellions, transgressions, and sins: we confess that we have
done evil in Thy sight, and have often provoked Thee. Have mercy
upon us and help us, Thou God of our salvation; deliver us, and

forgive us our sins, for the sake of Jesus Christ, Thy Son, our Lord.
Amen

Lord, have mercy upon us
Lord have mercy upon us, Christ have mercy upon us, Lord have mercy upon us

For the mountains shall depart, and the hills be removed, but my kindness shall not depart from thee, neither shall my covenant be removed, saith the Lord who has mercy on thee.

Glory be to God in the highest
And on earth peace, goodwill towards men

The Lord be with you
And with thy spirit

Let us pray
We come before Thy face, O eternal and merciful God, to thank Thee, on behalf of all our people, that once more Thou hast given us the bread we need, and the industry of the farmer has not gone unrewarded. Accept the offering of our thanksgiving, and may the adoration of our hearts be a means whereby Thy promised salvation is revealed to us. *Amen*

Psalm

Hymn

New Testament Lesson: Luke 12:15–21

Praise be to Thee, O Christ
Glory be to Thee, O Lord

Let us praise God with the confession of our faith

Apostles' Creed

Sermon

Hymn

Notices; Offertory

Lift up your hearts!
We lift them up unto the Lord

Let us give thanks unto our Lord God
It is meet and right so to do

It is very meet, right, and our bounden duty to give thanks to Thee, Almighty God, who dost crown the year with Thy goodness, and dost help Thy people and satisfy all who trust in Thee. Therefore with angels and archangels, and all the host of heaven, we sing unto Thee and Thine eternal majesty a song of praise
Holy, Holy, Holy, Lord God of hosts. Heaven and earth are full of Thy glory. Hosanna in the highest. Blessed is He who cometh in the name of the Lord. Hosanna in the highest.

Let us pray
Almighty and merciful God, we come in thanksgiving before Thee. Once more Thou hast not left Thyself without witnesses, and hast been very good to us. Thou hast protected the seeds, and blessed the fruit of our fields. Therefore we rejoice in Thy help, and magnify Thy name with cheerful voice.

Intercessions and Petitions

We pray, O Lord, that amid these tokens of Thy goodness Thou wilt also give unto us Thy Holy Spirit, that we may use the gifts of Thy hands according to Thy will. Implant in us believing hearts and discerning minds, that we may rest content with what we have, and faithfully and confidently trust in Thee alone

Lord, hear our prayer

And let our cry come unto Thee

By Thy grace remove all danger and need far from us. In Thy mercy remember the poor and the distressed. Awaken the hearts of those who have reaped richly, that they may not forget to do good, and to share. Watch over the fields that they may continue to bring forth their fruit in their season, and we lack nothing

Lord, hear our prayer

And let our cry come unto Thee

We pray for our people, and our country. Guide all in authority, that their endeavours may be according to Thy Word. Restrain all unrighteousness, and make us willing to bear another's burdens as our own

Lord, hear our prayer

And let our cry come unto Thee

We pray for Thy Church. May she witness with joy unto Thee, and seek only what Thou dost command. Make room for Thy Word in our homes and in our hearts; be with those throughout the world who suffer for Thy name's sake, and keep their hearts joyful, and confident in Thy truth

Lord, hear our prayer

And let our cry come unto Thee

Open Thine ear, O Lord, to all the cares and needs which each one of us brings in silence before Thee. . . . Help Thou those who cannot help themselves. Remember in Thy mercy the sick and the dying; and preserve us all from a sinful and unrepentant end

Lord, hear our prayer

And let our cry come unto Thee

And when the day of the Great Harvest comes, then let us once more joyfully bring our sheaves unto Thee, and receive from Thy hands the crown of honour which fadeth not away. Grant this and all our prayers for the sake of Jesus Christ our Lord.

Amen

Our Father . . .

Hymn
Aaronic Blessing

(The dividing up of the main body of prayers, in the Ministry of the Upper Room, with the versicles and responses, is the sole alteration made.)

5. SERVICE FOR THE FIRST SUNDAY IN ADVENT

(*Buch der Gottesdienste*, pp. 7–11; changes exactly as for previous service.)

Key Text: Behold, your king cometh unto you; triumphant and victorious is he. Zechariah 9:9

In the Name of the Father, and of the Son, and of the Holy Spirit. *Amen.* Our help rests in the name of the Lord, who has made heaven and earth.

Lift up your heads, O ye gates, and be ye lift up, ye everlasting doors, that the King of Glory may come in

Thus saith the Lord: my salvation cometh nigh unto you, and my judgement shall be revealed

Hymn

Let us pray.

Glory be to the Father and to the Son and to the Holy Ghost. As it was in the beginning, is now, and ever shall be: world without end. Amen.

Almighty and eternal God, we bring before Thy holy countenance our disobedience, our unbelief, and our guilt. Thou hast called us to Thy light, but we have strayed in the darkness; Thou hast shown us Thy way of love, but we have preferred our own selfish path. Forgive us, we pray Thee, for all our sin, and renew a right spirit within us. *Amen*

Lord, have mercy upon us

Lord have mercy, Christ have mercy, Lord have mercy

In His goodness, the Lord will not forsake us. His mercy is without end, but is renewed every morning; great is His faithfulness towards us. Glory be to God in the highest

And on earth peace, goodwill towards men

The Lord be with you

And with thy spirit

Lord God, heavenly Father, Thou hast called us to the glory of Thy heavenly Kingdom. We ask that during the Church year which we begin today together Thy holy Word may perfect, strengthen, and establish us, and may unite us in one fellowship well pleasing in Thy sight. Lord, we await Thy salvation. *Amen*

(The congregation can here, if desired, use as a prayer the verse 'Komm', o mein Heiland Jesu Christ'; the first verse of 'Come down, O Love Divine', or the first and last verses of 'Come, Thou long expected Jesus . . . By Thine own eternal Spirit', would be a suitable substitute.)

New Testament Lesson: Romans 13:11–14
Let us rejoice: the promised Saviour is near. Halleluja!
Halleluja, Halleluja, Halleluja!
New Testament Gospel: Matthew 21:1–9
Praise be to Thee, O Christ
Glory be to Thee, O God
Apostles' Creed
Sermon
Hymn
Lift up your hearts
We lift them up unto the Lord
Let us give thanks unto the Lord our God
It is meet and right so to do
It is very meet, right, and our bounden duty, that we should at all times and in all places give thanks to Thee, Almighty God, through Jesus Christ our Lord. Behold, we prepare ourselves to welcome the arrival of Thy Son, whom Thou hast sent to redeem us from all our sins. Therefore with angels and archangels, and with all the company of heaven, we sing unto Thee and Thy eternal majesty a song of praise
Holy, holy, holy, is the Lord of hosts. All the earth is full of Thy glory. Hosanna in the highest. Blessed is He who comes in the name of the Lord. Hosanna in the highest
Almighty God, Father of our Lord Jesus Christ, we praise Thy holy name that Thou dost this day permit us to begin a new Church year. We thank Thee that Thy holy Word is still proclaimed and heard amongst us, and that through the holy sacraments we are privileged to partake of Thy grace and Thy life. We pray that Thou wilt seek out those who are still in the far country. Awaken those who sleep. Restrain those who strive against Thy truth; overcome those who rise up against Thy Gospel
Lord, hear our prayer
And let our cry come unto Thee
We pray for Thy Church throughout the world: give her strength and endurance, through Thy word, against scorn and derision, against doubt and despair. Give unto her servants who will joyfully proclaim the glad tidings of the coming of Thy dear Son, through the power of Thy Spirit
Lord, hear our prayer
And let our cry come unto Thee
We pray for our country: rid her of the error and godlessness of pride and greed. Subdue all injustice; uphold truth and mercy
Lord, hear our prayer
And let our cry come unto Thee
We pray for our congregation: stir us up with Thy Holy Spirit, that we may be ready to receive Thy dear Son, the Saviour of mankind, in our homes, our schools, and wherever we work and meet together

Lord, hear our prayer
And let our cry come unto Thee
Take into Thy gracious care all those who mourn, the sick, the
anxious, the despairing
Lord, hear our prayer
And let our cry come unto Thee
Prepare for a blessed end those who in Thy wisdom (Ratschluss) will
not see the end of this year. Yea, come, Lord Jesus, and bring in the
day of Thy salvation, when Thou shalt reign for ever and ever.
Amen.
Our Father . . .
Hymn
Aaronic Blessing

(The Lutheran emphasis on the Word is frequently found
throughout the prayers in this book; it is of course one of the
Lutherans' special 'emphases', and will be part of their contribution to any future united Church liturgy.)

Many Methodist local preachers would argue that while
some of the above may be practical in the larger churches, this
is certainly not the case in village chapels, with congregations
of perhaps under a dozen. Here, a little imagination needs to be
used, but even with adaptation the two aspects of the liturgy—
Word and Upper Room—can be quite clearly brought out.

The opening prayers could be taken from the back of the
hymn-book, which includes such ancient prayers as the
Salvator Mundi, and the Gloria in Excelsis—ideal for congregational participation. A third of the psalms are also printed,
and one of these could be read antiphonally. An informal
discussion around the lessons could well replace a sermon; then
the ministry of the Upper Room would begin with the offertory
being brought forward: the prayers at this point could be
extemporary, drawing together any issues which have emerged
during the discussion, and concluding with the oblation of the
worshippers and the dedication of the offertory. This focalizing
of the whole service in an act of sacrifice would be a simple
expression of the prayer of oblation in the Eucharist.

APPENDIX B

The Development of the Roman Rite

To HAVE involved ourselves in a detailed consideration of the various phases of this development would have meant being diverted from the main theme of this thesis. The subject is given definitive treatment in Josef Jungmann's two volumes, *The Mass of the Roman Rite* (Bezinger Bros., New York, 1956). Nevertheless, because of certain aspects of the rite which occur in the text in connexion with both the Reformation and the Liturgical Movement generally, a brief account of its development can profitably be given.

From the fluid state of worship in the primitive Church the Eastern and Western liturgies developed separately, though both retained the dual structure, the liturgy of the Word, and of the Upper Room. The Western rites were distinguished from the Eastern by their brevity and sobriety; in the East the liturgy became more diffuse and flowery; to this day High Mass in the Orthodox Churches lasts anything up to three hours. Moreover, while in the East the liturgy was almost completely 'fixed', in the West there were a reasonable number of variables —the 'propers'.

From about 500–900 A.D. there were two forms of the rite in the West; the Gallican and Roman. While the latter began as primarily the rite used in Rome itself, the Gallican rite, of which there were a large number of local variants, was used in Europe generally until condemned by Pepin III (714–68) and his son Charlemagne (742–814), after which they became virtually extinct, although they had certain influences on the Roman rite. Latin became the language for this from at least the beginning of the fourth century; and with the conversion of Constantine at that time, the Eucharist could be celebrated publicly, which tended to encourage greater solemnity and splendour of ceremonial. Maxwell, in *An Outline of Christian Worship*, pp. 56–57, outlines the Roman Mass as it was observed during the century before Gregory the Great (540–604):

LITURGY OF THE WORD

Introit by two choirs as clergy enter
Kyries
Celebrant's salutation
Collect(s)
Prophecy or Old Testament lection
Antiphonal chant
Epistle
Gradual (Psalm sung originally by one voice)
Alleluia
Gospel, with lights, incense, responses
Dismissal of those not communicating

LITURGY OF THE UPPER ROOM

Offertory: Collection of elements, spreading of corporal (linen cloth)
on altar, preparation of elements for communion, offering of
gifts, admixture, psalm sung meanwhile
Salutation and Sursum Corda
Prayer of concecration:

> Preface
> Proper Preface
> Sanctus
> Canon

Kiss of Peace
Fraction
Lord's Prayer with protocol and embolism
Communion, celebrant first, then people (psalm sung meanwhile)
Post-communion collect (Thanksgiving)
Dismissal by deacon

For a description of the rite at this time, Maxwell (op. cit., p. 59) quotes Bishop, *Liturgica Historica* (Oxford, 1918):

'Those very things which in the popular mind are considered distinctive of Romanism, and which go to make up in the main what people call the sensuousness of the Roman rite, form precisely the element in it which is not originally Roman at all, but has been gradually borrowed, adopted in the course of the ages. The genius of the native Roman rite is marked by simplicity, practicality, a great sobriety and self-control, gravity and dignity. But there it stops. Rome had a receptive, but not a creative imagination. The two chief characteristics of the Roman rite, then, are these: sober-ness and sense.'

The Canon which is mentioned in this rite came under dis-cussion in connexion with the Lutheran and other rites of the Reformation. Originally it was probably connected with the Sanctus which precedes it, but as over the years the Sanctus was said by the people and the Canon was not, it began to be looked upon as a separate item. It is a succession of short prayers, each named after the opening words: Te Igitur, Memento, Communicantes (intercession), Hanc Igitur, Quam Oblationem, Qui Pridie (the actual words of consecration), Unde et Memores (equivalent of the Greek anamnesis), Supra Quae, Supplices Te Rogamus (possibly the remains of an early Epiclesis), Memento, Nobis Quoque Peccatoribus, and a concluding doxology, Per Quem Haec Omnia.

It was the Canon which, more than any other part of the Mass, encouraged the idea of transubstantiation. Maxwell (op. cit., p. 63) remarks:

'It is evident how hospitable the Roman Canon is to a particular idea of sacrifice peculiar to later Roman theology. The intention is to reenact validly what Christ did by anticipation at the Last Supper. The method followed is to use, as nearly as possible, our Lord's own words and actions. Thus the theology of a later period, based upon current philosophical conceptions of "substance" and "accident", came to describe the bread and wine as being "transub-stantiated" into the Body and Blood.'

The Middle Ages saw the emergence of the Low Mass; the High Mass was conducted by a Bishop, assisted by several clergy, and having a trained choir. These were not always available, therefore the Low Mass emerged with one celebrant, assisted by servers; there was less ceremonial in this, and it was said, rather than sung—and a large part of it was said inaudibly by the priest, only the choral parts from the High Mass being audible. After the ninth century the practice of receiving communion at High Mass became rare; and Gallican influence tended to destroy the austerity of the earlier rite. The whole liturgy became a spectacle for the congregation, culminating in the moment of consecration in the Canon, and the habit of attending only for this part of the service (as described in the text) began to creep in. By 1215 even the three prescribed occasions for communicating—Christmas, Easter, and Pentecost were reduced to Easter only. In the eleventh century the Nicene Creed was added, and also a number of private prayers of the celebrant. A mystical element emerged, in which the whole Mass was given a symbolic meaning. This is described by Brilioth (op. cit., p. 83):

'The typical and the most influential of these expositions was that of Amalarius of Metz, the disciple of Alcuin. The main idea was that the liturgy itself should be used so as to bring to remembrance the passion of Christ; the first part of the mass, however, deals with the history of Christ before his entry into Jerusalem. Some confusion of the order of events is inevitable. While the Introit symbolises generally the coming of Christ and his ministry, the Gloria shows the joy in heaven after his Resurrection; and when the Bishop sits down in his throne, there is symbolised the session of Christ at the Father's right hand. The Epistle, Gradual and Gospel, signify the proclaiming of the Old and the New Covenants, and Christ's own preaching. The salutation before the Offertory is the greeting of the crown at the Triumphal Entry. When the priest offers the oblation, Amalarius sees the entry of Christ into the temple to offer himself to the Father. In the Sanctus he is greeted with the people's praise; the first part of the canon recalls the beginning of the Passion, and the disciples' flight. The remainder of the service symbolises the death of the Lord, the centurion's confession, the taking-down of the body, the burial, the resurrection, the appearance at Emmaus, and lastly the Ascension.'

During the Middle Ages another development was in the number of private masses, and masses with special 'intent', by means of which merit could be earned. This custom was the object of much of Luther's (and other reformers') denunciations.

In 1570, at the Council of Trent, the service was given a final fixed form; we take the outline from Maxwell (op. cit., pp. 69–71):

THE LITURGY OF THE WORD
Introit and Kyrie eleison (ninefold)—sung by choir
Entry of ministers
Private preparation of ministers at altar steps (said secretly)
   Invocation, In nomine Patris . . .
   Psalm 93 with v. 4 as antiphon, and Gloria

Psalm 124:8
Confiteor and Misereatur of celebrant to ministers
Confiteor and Misereatur of ministers to celebrant
Versicles and responses from psalms
Collects Aufer a nobis and Oremus te
Blessing of incense, and censing of altar and ministers
Gloria in Excelsis said secretly by celebrant, sung by choir
Salutation and collects of the day, then the celebrant says Epistle
  and gradual silently
Epistle, sung by subdeacon; response, Deo gratias
Gradual sung by choir
Tract or Sequence (if any) sung by choir, while are said
  Prayers and Preparation for the Gospel: Munde cor meum,
  Jube Domine benedicere, Dominus sit in corde tuo, Salutation,
  announcement of Gospel, and ministers' response, Gloria tibi
  Domine, Gospel recited in low tone, Response by ministers:
  Laus tibi Christe—all these by the celebrant
Gospel, with lights and incense, sung by deacon, responses sung by
  ministers
Preacher goes to pulpit: gives notices, Bidding Prayers,
  Epistle and Gospel read in vernacular, Sermon
Nicene Creed sung as Gloria in Excelsis
Salutation and bidding to prayer, but no prayer

LITURGY OF THE UPPER ROOM

Offertory: Psalm verses sung while celebrant proceeds secretly:
  Offering of bread: collect, Suscipe sancte Pater; Admixture of
  water to wine: collect, Deus qui humanae; Offering of chalice:
  collect, Offerimus tibi; Prayers, In spiritu humilitatis and Veni
  sanctificator; Blessing of incense: Per intercessionem; Censing
  of elements: Incensum istud; Censing of altar, saying Psalm
  141:2-4; Censing of ministers; Washing of celebrant's hands,
  as he recites the Lavabo, Psalm 25:6-12, with Gloria; Oblation,
  Suscipe sancta Trinitas, Orate fratres (said audibly), and
  Suscipiat Dominus; Secrets (collects)
Salutation and Sursum Corda (sung)
Prayer of Consecration: Preface and Proper Preface, sung by celebrant (then Sanctus and Benedictus said audibly); Sanctus
  sung by choir while celebrant proceeds with the Canon said
  quietly (except voice raised at Nobis quoque), bell rung to
  announce beginning; Elevation, with bells and incense at
  Words of Institution and Benedictus qui venit sung; Canon
  concludes with ecphonesis.
Lord's Prayer sung by celebrant, with protocol and embolism
Pax, Fraction, and Commixture
Agnus Dei said by celebrant, then sung by choir

Celebrant's Communion (while Agnus Dei sung): Collect, Domine Jesu Christe; Kiss of Peace to clergy; Collects (two) and Centurion's words, Domine non sum dignus (said audibly); he receives Bread, saying Words of Delivery; Thanksgiving, Psalm 116:12f; receives Cup, saying words of delivery

(Communion of the people rare at High Mass)

Communion Psalm sung by choir: Cleansing of chalice; Collects (2) Covering of Chalice

Salutation and Post-communion collects

Deacon's salutation and dismissal of people

Collect, Placeat tibi

Blessing of People, Benedicat vos

Last Gospel, John 1:1–14 and response, Deo gratias.

The early Basilican position of the celebrant had, as indicated earlier, now been replaced by the 'Western' position.

BIBLIOGRAPHY

1. On Liturgy Generally

R. Abba, *Principles of Christian Worship*, Oxford University Press
G. Aulén, *Eucharist and Sacrifice*, Oliver and Boyd
J-D. Benoit, *Liturgical Renewal*, S.C.M.
L. Bouyer, *Life and Liturgy*, Sheed and Ward
Y. Brilioth, *Eucharistic Faith and Practice, Evangelical and Catholic*, S.P.C.K.
G. Cope, *Symbolism in the Bible and the Church*, S.C.M.
O. Cullmann, ed. Leenhardt, *Essays on the Lord's Supper*, Lutterworth
J. G. Davies, *The Architectural Setting of Baptism*, Barrie and Rockliff
C. Davis, *Liturgy and Doctrine*, Sheed and Ward
G. Dix, *The Shape of the Liturgy*, Dacre
R. Guardini, *The Spirit of the Liturgy*, Sheed and Ward
A. G. Hebert, *Liturgy and Society*, Faber
A. G. Hebert, *The Parish Communion*, S.P.C.K.
F. Heiler, *The Spirit of Worship*, Hodder and Stoughton
J. Jeremias, *The Eucharistic Words of Jesus*, Blackwell
E. Koenker, *The Liturgical Renaissance of the Roman Catholic Church*, University of Chicago Press
E. L. Mascall, *Corpus Christi*, Longmans
W. D. Maxwell, *An Outline of Christian Worship*, Oxford University Press
W. D. Maxwell, *Concerning Worship*, Oxford University Press
N. Micklem (ed.), *Christian Worship*, Oxford University Press
G. F. D. Moule, *Worship in the New Testament*, Lutterworth
W. Nicholls, *Jacob's Ladder*, Lutterworth
E. Rattenbury, *Vital Elements in Public Worship*, Epworth
J. Robinson, *Liturgy Coming to Life*, Mowbray
C. Ryder Smith, *The Sacramental Society*, Epworth
A. R. Shands, *The Liturgical Movement and the Local Church*, S.C.M.
M. H. Shepherd (ed.), *The Liturgical Renewal of the Church*, Oxford University Press (New York)
M. Thurian, *The Eucharistic Memorial* (2 vols), Lutterworth
E. Underhill, *Worship*, Nisbet
Ways of Worship (World Council of Churches), S.C.M.

2. On Reform Generally

T. Allen, *The Face of My Parish*, S.C.M.
P. Berger, *The Noise of Solemn Assemblies*, Doubleday, N.Y.
H. Cox, *The Secular City*, S.C.M.

J. de Blank, *The Parish in Action*, Mowbray
C. Driver, *A Future for the Free Churches?*, S.C.M.
B. Kenrick, *Come out the Wilderness*, Collins
Abbé Michonneau, *Revolution in a City Parish*, Blackfriars
J. Robinson, *The New Reformation?*, S.C.M.
J. Robinson, *On Being the Church in the World*, S.C.M.
E. Southcott, *The Parish Comes Alive*, Mowbray
P. Van Buren, *The Secular Meaning of the Gospel*, S.C.M.
J. J. Vincent, *Christ and Methodism*, Epworth
C. Williams, *Where in the World?*, Epworth
C. Williams, *What in the World?*, Epworth
G. Winter, *The Suburban Captivity of the Churches*, Doubleday, N.Y.
G. Winter, *The New Creation as Metropolis*, Macmillan, N.Y.

3. On Wesley

H. Bett, *The Spirit of Methodism*, Epworth
J. C. Bowmer, *The Sacrament of the Lord's Supper in Early Methodism*, Dacre
J. C. Bowmer, *The Lord's Supper in Methodism, 1791–1960*, Epworth
W. H. Holden, *An Old Methodist—John Wesley in the Company with High Churchmen*, London
J. Parris, *John Wesley's Doctrine of the Sacraments*, Epworth
M. Piette, *John Wesley in the Evolution of Protestantism*, London
J. E. Rattenbury, *The Eucharistic Hymns of John and Charles Wesley*, Epworth
J. E. Rattenbury, *The Conversion of the Wesleys*, Epworth
J. H. Rigg, *The Churchmanship of John Wesley*, London
W. J. Sparrow-Simpson, *John Wesley and the Church of England*, London
Tyerman, *The Oxford Methodists*, London
J. Wesley, *The Journal of John Wesley* (4 vols), Everyman, Dent

4. Liturgies and Devotional

W. D. Maxwell, *John Knox's Genevan Service Book 1556*, Edinburgh
A Book of Public Worship, Oxford University Press
Book of Common Order, Oxford University Press
Eucharist Liturgy of Taizé, Faith Press
Buch der Gottesdienste, Christlicher Zeitschriftenverlag, Berlin
Office de Taizé, Les Presses de Taizé

5. Various

F. L. Cross (ed.), *The Oxford Dictionary of the Christian Church*, Oxford University Press
J. G. Frazer, *The Golden Bough*, Macmillan
C. Gore, *The Body of Christ*, Murray
H. M. Gwatkin, *Selections from Early Church Writings*, Macmillan
J. Robinson, *The Body*, S.C.M.

R. Schutz, *This Day Belongs to God*, Faith Press

6. Magazines, Periodicals, and Pamphlets

All in Each Place, British Council of Churches pamphlet
La Maison-Dieu, Editions du Cerf, Paris
Over the Bridge, Magazine of the South London Industrial Mission
Studia Liturgica, published in Rotterdam; circulation office: Postbus
    2, Nieuwendam, Holland

7. Additional Books, not mentioned in text

H. de Candole, *The Church's Offering*, Mowbray
N. Clark, *Call to Worship*, S.C.M.
G. Cope (ed.), *Making the Building Serve the Liturgy*, Mowbray
Cope, Davies, Tytler, *An Experimental Liturgy*, Lutterworth
J. G. Davies, *Worship and Mission*, S.C.M.
Horton Davies, *The Worship of the English Puritans*, Dacre
P. Hammond, *Liturgy and Architecture*, Barrie and Rockliff
J. Jungman, *The Mass of the Roman Rite* (2 vols), Benzinger Bros,
    N.Y.
J. H. Srawley, *The Liturgical Movement*, Mowbray

INDEX OF SUBJECTS

INDEX OF PERSONS

BIBLICAL REFERENCES

LIBRARY.